BEING HEALTHY

B E I N G
HEALTHY

Larry K. Olsen
Professor of Health Education
The Pennsylvania State University
University Park, Pennsylvania

Richard W. St. Pierre
Professor and Head
Department of Health Education
The Pennsylvania State University
University Park, Pennsylvania

Jan M. Ozias, Ph.D., R.N.
Coordinator of Health Services
Austin Independent School District
Austin, Texas

SENIOR EDITORIAL ADVISORS

Ernest D. Buck, M.D.
Pediatrician
Corpus Christi, Texas

Barbara A. Galpin
Teacher of Health and Physical Education
Islip Public Schools
Islip, New York

Howard L. Taras, M.D., F.R.C.P.C.
Assistant Professor of Pediatrics
University of California, San Diego
  and District Medical Consultant
San Diego Unified School District
San Diego, California

HARCOURT BRACE & COMPANY
Orlando   Atlanta   Austin   Boston   San Francisco   Chicago   Dallas   New York
Toronto   London

ACKNOWLEDGMENTS

CONTENT ADVISORY BOARD

MENTAL HEALTH

Sharon Smith Brady, Ph.D.
Licensed Psychologist
Lawton, Oklahoma

Charlotte P. Ross
President and Executive Director
Youth Suicide National Center
Burlingame, California

HUMAN GROWTH AND DEVELOPMENT, DISEASES AND DISORDERS, AND PUBLIC HEALTH

Thomas Blevins, M.D.
American Diabetes Association,
Texas Affiliate, Inc.
Austin, Texas

Ernest D. Buck, M.D.
Pediatrician
Corpus Christi, Texas

Linda A. Fisher, M.D.
Chief Medical Officer
St. Louis County Department
of Health
St. Louis, Missouri

Howard L. Taras, M.D., F.R.C.P.C.
Assistant Professor of Pediatrics
University of California, San Diego
and District Medical Consultant
San Diego Unified School District
San Diego, California

CONSUMER HEALTH PRACTICES

Robert C. Arffa, M.D.
Adjunct Professor of
Ophthalmology
Medical College of Pennsylvania
Allegheny General Hospital
Pittsburgh, Pennsylvania

Bertram V. Dannheisser, Jr., D.D.S.
Florida Dental Association
Pensacola, Florida

John D. Durrant, Ph.D.
Professor of Otolaryngology and
Communication and Director
of Audiology
University of Pittsburgh
Medical Center
Pittsburgh, Pennsylvania

NUTRITION

**Janet L. Durrwachter,
M.N.S., R.D.**
Nutrition Consultant
Cogan Station, Pennsylvania

**Maryfrances L. Marecic,
M.S., R.D.**
Consultant
Montville, New Jersey
(Former Instructor in Nutrition,
The Pennsylvania State
University)

**Linda Fox Simmons,
M.S.H.P., R.D./L.D.**
Registered Dietician
Austin, Texas

EXERCISE AND FITNESS

Steven N. Blair, P.E.D.
Director, Epidemiology
Cooper Institute for Aerobics
Research
Dallas, Texas

Deborah Waters, M.D.
Colorado Springs, Colorado
(Former Team Physician,
The Pennsylvania State
University)

MEDICINE

**Donna Hubbard McCree,
M.P.H., R.Ph.**
Assistant Professor
Pharmacy Administration
Howard University
College of Pharmacy
Washington, D.C.

Judith Ann Shinogle, R.Ph.
M.S. Candidate
Harvard School of Public Health
Boston, Massachusetts

SUBSTANCE ABUSE

Robert N. Holsaple
Supervisor of Prevention Programs
The School Board of Broward
County
Fort Lauderdale, Florida

SAFETY AND FIRST AID

American Red Cross
Washington, D.C.

CONTRIBUTORS AND REVIEWERS

Danny J. Ballard, Ed.D., C.H.E.S.
Associate Professor of Health
Health and Kinesiology
  Department
Texas A&M University
College Station, Texas

Linda Barnes
Teacher
Wahl-Coates School
Greenville, North Carolina

Robert C. Barnes, Ed.D., M.P.H.
Associate Professor and
  Coordinator
Health Education
East Carolina University
Greenville, North Carolina

David L. Bever, Ph.D.
Coordinator of Health
  Education
Department of Human Services
George Mason University
Fairfax, Virginia

James M. Eddy, D.Ed.
Professor and Chair
Health Studies
The University of Alabama
Tuscaloosa, Alabama

Sue Ann Eddy
Teacher
Stillman Heights Elementary
Tuscaloosa, Alabama

Ruth C. Engs, Ed.D., R.N.
Professor
Applied Health Science
Indiana University
Bloomington, Indiana

Tina Fields, Ph.D.
Associate Professor
Health Education
Texas Tech University
Lubbock, Texas

Patricia Barthalow Koch, Ph.D.
Associate Professor
Health Education
College of Health and Human
  Development
The Pennsylvania State University
University Park, Pennsylvania

Patricia Langner, P.H.N., B.S.N., M.P.H.
Health Educator and Nurse
San Ramon Valley Unified
  School District
Danville, California

Samuel W. Monismith, D.Ed.
Assistant Professor
Health Education
The Pennsylvania State University
Capital College
Middletown, Pennsylvania

Marcia Newey, P.H.N., M.P.H.
Health Educator
San Ramon Valley Unified
  School District
San Ramon, California

Brenda North
Chair of Health and Physical
  Education
Lanier Middle School
Houston, Texas

Florence R. Oaks, Ph.D.
Psychologist
San Ramon Valley Unified
  School District
Danville, California

Bea Orr
Past President of the
  American Alliance for
  Health, Physical Education,
  Recreation and Dance
Health and Physical Education
  Supervisor
Logan County Schools
Logan, West Virginia

Nancy Piña
Teacher
Braeburn Elementary School
Houston, Texas

Kerry John Redican, Ph.D., M.P.H.
Associate Professor
Health Education
Virginia Polytechnic Institute
  and State University
Blacksburg, Virginia

David Sommerfeld
Instructional Supervisor
Ysleta Independent
  School District
El Paso, Texas

William J. Stone, Ed.D.
Professor
Exercise and Wellness
Arizona State University
Tempe, Arizona

Patrick Tow, Ph.D.
Associate Professor
Department of Health,
  Physical Education,
  and Recreation
Old Dominion University
Norfolk, Virginia

Donna Videto, Ph.D., C.H.E.S.
Adjunct Professor
Health Department
SUNY College at Cortland
Cortland, New York

Molly S. Wantz, M.S., Ed.S.
Associate Professor
Department of Physiology
  and Health Science
Ball State University
Muncie, Indiana

Shirley Ward
Curriculum Specialist
Broward County Schools
Fort Lauderdale, Florida

READING/LANGUAGE ADVISOR

Patricia S. Bowers, Ph.D.
Associate Director
Center for Mathematics and
  Science Education
University of North Carolina
  at Chapel Hill
Chapel Hill, North Carolina

Contents

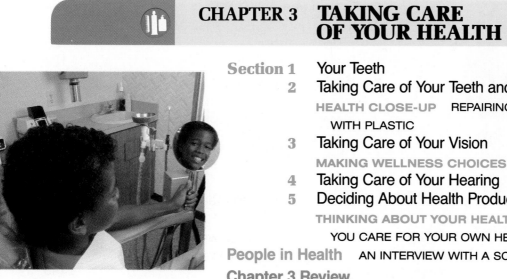

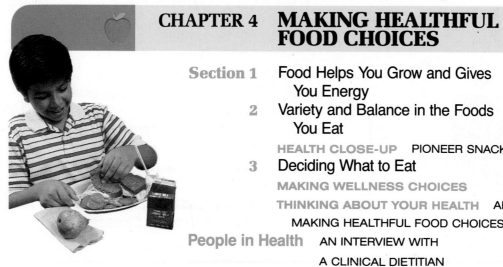

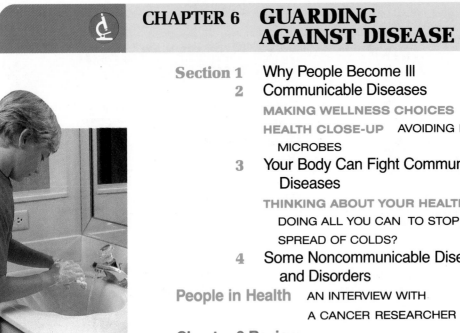

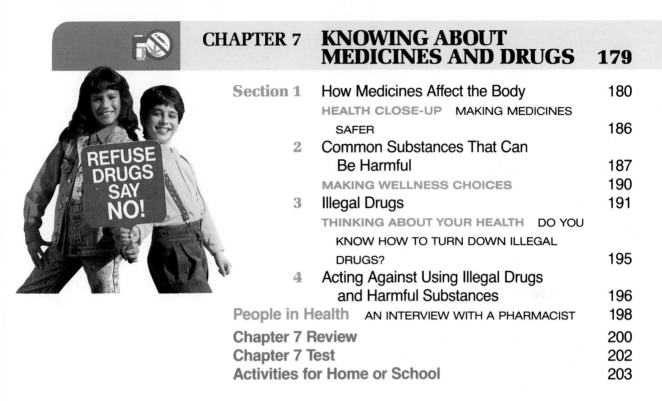

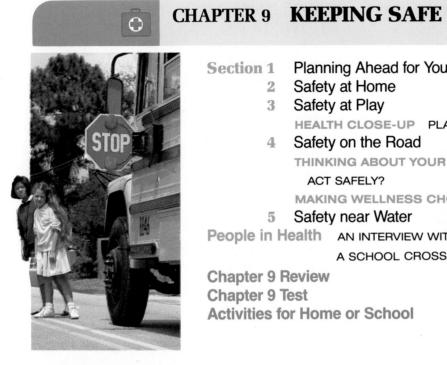

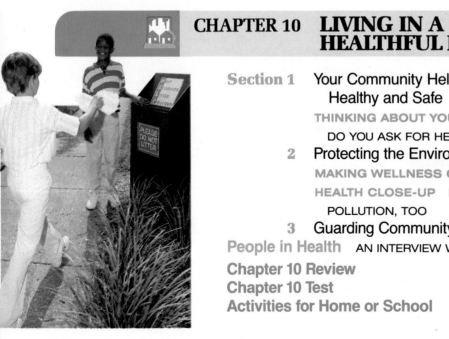

FOR YOUR REFERENCE 291

THINKING ABOUT YOUR HEALTH

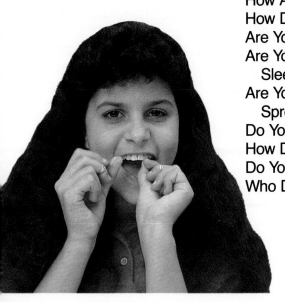

REAL-LIFE SKILLS

HEALTH CLOSE-UPS

PEOPLE IN HEALTH

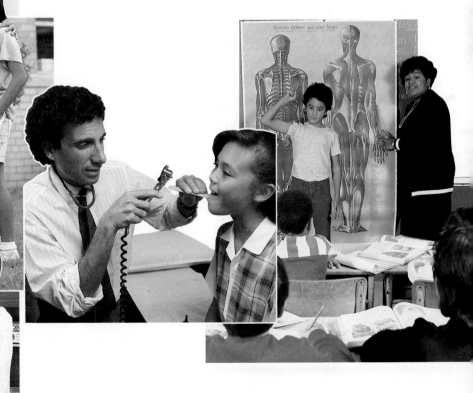

Being Healthy Is About You

You are at your best when you are healthy. When you feel good, you are able to enjoy life to its fullest. However, staying healthy can be a challenge. To handle this challenge, you will need knowledge—not only about health issues, but about yourself and your environment. With the right information and thoughtful preparation, you will find the challenge of being healthy both exciting and enjoyable.

As you read *Being Healthy,* you will learn about many health habits that can help keep you feeling your best. Some of these habits require special knowledge. With up-to-date health information and good health habits, you can meet the challenge of being healthy. By taking responsibility for your health now, you are preparing for a healthy future.

You probably think that good health requires exercise and a healthful diet. You are right; it does. However, these are not the only things that contribute to good health. To be healthy, you must also satisfy mental, emotional, and social needs. In other words, your mind, feelings, family, friends, and community are also important to your health. Just about everything you do during a day can affect your health.

Practicing good health habits can help you avoid many kinds of diseases. Also, the healthier you become, the better you will feel about yourself. You will increase your self-esteem. When you refuse to use dangerous drugs, you will increase your self-esteem even more. In refusing harmful substances, you are protecting not only your own health, but also the health of others in your community.

Being healthy does not just happen. You must choose to live in a healthful way. You must take responsibility for your well-being and develop habits that will help keep you healthy. This responsibility will require you to make some important and sometimes difficult decisions. By reading *Being Healthy* you will help yourself prepare for these decisions. You will then be ready to make the wise choices for being safe and being healthy.

THINKING ABOUT YOURSELF

Have you ever wondered what makes you different from other people? Nobody else looks, thinks, acts, or feels exactly the way you do.

You are like other people in some ways, too. All people need the same basic things in order to be healthy and happy. Like all people, you can help yourself meet your needs by learning to make good choices. Your choices tell a lot about you.

You have the same needs as other people. You make your own choices to meet your needs. Your choices help make you different and tell a lot about you.

GETTING READY TO LEARN

Key Questions

- Why is it important to learn about yourself?
- Why is it important to know the way you feel about yourself?
- How can you learn to make choices to help yourself be healthy?
- What can you do to feel good about yourself?
- What can you do to help keep yourself healthy?

Main Chapter Sections

1 Traits Make You Special
2 Your Traits Make Up Your Personality
3 You Have Needs
4 Choosing Ways to Meet Needs

1

1 Traits Make You Special

special (SPEHSH uhl),
different from everyone
else.

Today was Kim's first day at a new school. Her teacher, Mr. Diaz, asked Kim to tell the class a little about herself.

"My name is Kim. I am nine years old. My family just moved to this state. I have an older brother and a younger sister. I like soccer, and I like to play the piano."

Kim told many facts about herself. She told her name and age. She told about her family and about what she likes to do. All these things, along with how she feels and thinks, make her **special**—different from everyone else.

■ On her first day of school, Kim tells her classmates about herself. Part of what makes Kim special is playing soccer.

Kim shows some of her traits by the things she does. A **trait** is something about you that shows what you are like. The ways you look, think, act, and feel are all traits. Taking care of yourself is also a trait. Staying healthy is another.

When your traits are at their best, you have wellness. **Wellness** is a high level of health. Wellness means that your whole body feels good to you. When you are well, you are able to get the most out of your work, your play, and the time you spend with your family and other people.

How Do Physical Traits Make You Special?

Your physical traits tell about your body. You can see many of your physical traits when you look into a mirror. You can see the color of your eyes and hair. You can see how tall you are. You can see how you look.

The way you look tells about more than just your body. The way you dress and if you are neat are part of the way you look. How often you smile or frown is also part of the way you look. These traits tell something about the way you think about yourself. The way you think about yourself is your **self-concept.**

trait (TRAYT), something about you that shows what you are like.

wellness, a high level of health.

self-concept (sehlf KAHN sehpt), the way you think about yourself.

■ *Feeling good about yourself and what you can do helps your self-concept.*

Some of your physical traits are not easy to see. The size of your heart is a physical trait. How well you see and hear are physical traits, too.

Good daily health habits, such as brushing your teeth and playing actively, help keep your body as healthy as it can be. Some of your friends may use things like hearing aids and wheelchairs to help them be as healthy and active as they can be.

How Do Mental Traits Make You Special?

Julie wants to learn about animals. She reads books about them. She likes to go to the zoo with her parents. Julie asks her parents many questions about animals. Wanting to learn is one of Julie's mental traits. It is part of the way she thinks and learns.

The ways you think and learn make up your mental traits. Perhaps you remember facts better when you read them rather than when you hear them. You may learn some kinds of skills more easily than others. Maybe you learned to read more easily than you learned to skate. Some people are able to learn new skills just by watching others. They learn best by figuring out the steps for themselves. Other people learn by saying the steps out loud before they try something new. These are all examples of mental traits.

■ Bill is learning to repair a bicycle by watching his father. Next time, Bill may be able to repair it himself.

4

What Are Social Traits?

No one acts exactly as you do. The way you act is
one of your traits. The way you act also depends partly
on what is happening to you at the time. Robert is
friendly most of the time with classmates, friends,
members of his family, and other people he knows
well. He acts shy when he is with older students and
people he does not know.

Some social traits make other people feel uneasy.
Bullying and always trying to get attention make people
feel uneasy. Being helpful and friendly makes people
enjoy being with you. Social traits like helping others
make you feel good about yourself, too.

What Are Emotional Traits?

David and Ruth are both new at school this year.
David is excited to be at his new school. He is ready to
start making friends. Ruth feels a little afraid. She acts
shy with classmates she does not know. The same
situation can cause people to have different feelings.

■ *Janet feels good about
herself because she is
helping a classmate with
his homework. Because
Janet is helpful and
friendly, others feel good
about being with her.*

Being excited is one way David feels. Being afraid is one way Ruth feels. They have different feelings in the same situation. In other situations, their feelings, or **emotions,** may be different again. All people feel the emotions of love, fear, anger, and happiness at one time or another.

emotions (ih MOH shuhnz), feelings.

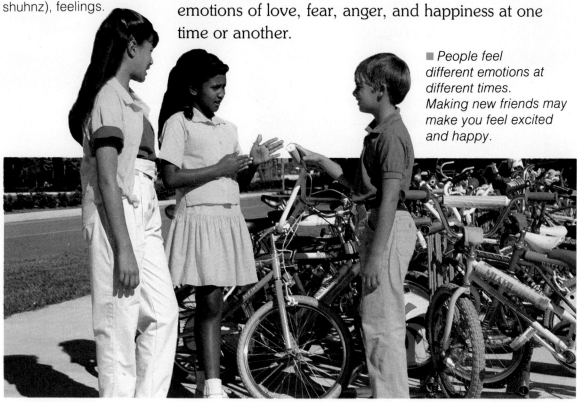

■ People feel different emotions at different times. Making new friends may make you feel excited and happy.

STOP **REVIEW**
SECTION 1

REMEMBER?

1. Name two physical traits you can see. Name two physical traits you *cannot* see.
2. How are mental traits different from emotional traits?
3. What are social traits?

THINK!

4. Suppose you were asked to tell the class about yourself. What traits would you describe?
5. Why is being friendly a social trait?

2 Your Traits Make Up Your Personality

The combination of the ways you think, act, and feel makes up your **personality.** Your personality makes you the special person you are. No one has a personality that is just like yours.

Your personality depends partly on traits with which you were born. It also depends on things that have happened to you. Your personality depends on the choices you make to help yourself reach wellness.

How Can You Know Your Strengths and Weaknesses?

Some special traits are called strengths. A **strength** is something you do well. You may read very well. Friends may also tell you that you are a good listener.

Your strengths might be talents with which you were born. A good singing voice is a natural talent. Your strengths might be skills you have learned. For example, skateboarding is a learned skill.

Other parts of your personality may not be strong. A **weakness** is something you do not do well. When a task is difficult, you may act stubborn and not get help.

KEY WORDS

personality
strength
weakness
self-esteem

personality (puhrs uhn AL uht ee), the combination of ways you think, act, and feel.

strength (STREHNGTH), something you do well.

weakness (WEEK nuhs), something you do not do well.

■ *Getting help can turn a weakness into a strength.*

It may be hard for you to accept that you cannot do a task alone. It is all right if you are not good at everything.

Sometimes your parents, friends, and teachers can help point out your weaknesses. They can tell you things about your personality that are not easy for you to see. They can help you try to understand your weaknesses.

What Is Self-Esteem?

Knowing your weaknesses and working to change some of them into strengths can help you feel good about yourself. The good feeling you have about yourself is called **self-esteem.** Self-esteem is self-respect. High self-esteem is part of having a positive or good self-concept. Self-esteem is built on enjoying your strengths and understanding weaknesses you cannot change. It also comes from working to change any weaknesses you can.

Your self-esteem is always changing. Family members, friends, and things that happen to you help shape your self-esteem. As you learn more about your traits and your personality, you will have a better chance of having high self-esteem. Feeling good about your traits and your personality helps raise your self-esteem.

self-esteem (sehl fuh STEEM), a good feeling you have about yourself.

■ *Learning a new game or learning to play a musical instrument can raise self-esteem.*

You can help other people raise their self-esteem. You can tell others what you like about them. Being friendly to someone you do not know well can help, too.

STOP REVIEW
SECTION 2

REMEMBER?

1. What is personality?
2. On what is self-esteem built?

THINK!

3. What are some daily habits that can help you raise your self-esteem?
4. Why might it be easier for other people to see your weaknesses than for you to see them?

Thinking About Your Health

How Do You See Yourself?

On a sheet of paper, draw a hand mirror like the one shown here. Divide the mirror into four equal parts. Number each part. Below are four questions about the way you see yourself. Write each answer in the part of the mirror that matches the question.

1. What do you like most about yourself?
2. What do you like least about yourself?
3. What do you do well?
4. How would other people describe you?

Think about why it is important to know how you see yourself.

3 You Have Needs

All people have their own traits, personalities, and levels of self-esteem. These differences are what make each person special. In some ways, however, you are just like other people. One way you are like other people is that you share certain needs with them. A **need** is something that a person must meet or satisfy to be healthy. People of all ages have basic needs.

need, something that a person must meet or satisfy to be healthy.

■ *These students have different physical traits. However, they have the same basic needs, such as the need for food.*

What Physical Needs Do All People Have?

Your physical needs have to do with your body. Mr. Chavez asked the class to make a list of the things that everyone needs to stay healthy. Andy said that everyone needs water. Angelo added that everyone needs healthful food. **Healthful** means "good for your health." Elena said that people need to breathe clean air. Lee said that people also need shelter, or a place to live.

healthful (HEHLTH fuhl), good for your health.

10

The class made this list of things that people of all ages all over the world must have to stay alive. To help themselves remember these things, the students made up the word *WAFS*.

Physical Needs:
W – water
A – air
F – food
S – shelter

Everyone also has physical-care needs that are important for good health. Some of these needs are healthful rest, enough sleep, and regular exercise.

What Are Your Mental Needs?

Your mental needs are a second kind of need. These needs have to do with thinking, learning, and using your mind. Agnes wants to be a teacher. To become a good teacher takes many years of school and practice. Agnes will need to learn how to gather and use a lot of information. She will also need to learn how to teach skills to others. These are Agnes's mental needs.

You may not wish to become a teacher, but you still have mental needs. You need to know mathematics to use money wisely. You need to be able to read so you can shop wisely. You need to know how to use facts so you can make wise choices.

■ *A computer can help Agnes and her friends meet a mental need by helping them gather and use important information.*

What Are Your Social and Emotional Needs?

A third kind of need is your social needs. Your social needs have to do with other people. Getting along with family members and others is one example of meeting a social need. Making new friends and keeping old friends is another. The need to share feelings with family and friends is also a social need.

Finally, your emotional needs are needs that have to do with your feelings. You need to have someone to talk to about feelings, such as fear or anger. You need to feel loved. You need to trust people and feel trusted. You need to feel proud of yourself for doing things well. In what ways can a parent or friend help you meet your emotional needs?

■ Being part of a team can help a person meet his or her social need to share feelings.

 **REVIEW SECTION 3**

REMEMBER?

1. Name three physical needs that are important for living.
2. How are mental needs different from emotional needs?
3. Describe a social need.

THINK!

4. What are some daily health habits that meet one of your physical needs?
5. What are the mental needs of adults like your parents or teachers?
6. What can children do to help grandparents or older neighbors with their social and emotional needs?

Health Close-up

Taking Charge of Anger

How do you feel after a bad day at school? How do you feel during an argument with a friend? How do you feel when someone teases you?

At times like those, you might feel anger. Everyone feels anger at some time. Like happiness and sadness, anger is an emotion.

Feeling anger is not wrong. In fact, anger is a normal feeling sometimes. The way you express your anger is what can cause problems. Some people yell and scream when they feel anger. Some people get quiet when they feel anger. Many people become ill over their anger. They may get headaches or upset stomachs.

Holding anger inside you can cause anger to grow stronger. So you need to express anger in a healthful way. For some people, sports are outlets to work off anger. Sometimes talking about your anger with a parent, a teacher, or a friend is helpful.

Knowing how to talk about feelings like anger takes practice. The next time you feel angry, try to say exactly what angers you. Put it into words. Start by using phrases like "It bothers me when . . ." or "I get upset when. . . ." Talk about your anger calmly, and give the other person a chance to talk with you. The other person might be able to help you point out the cause of your anger. You also need to find a way to solve the problem without causing yourself more anger.

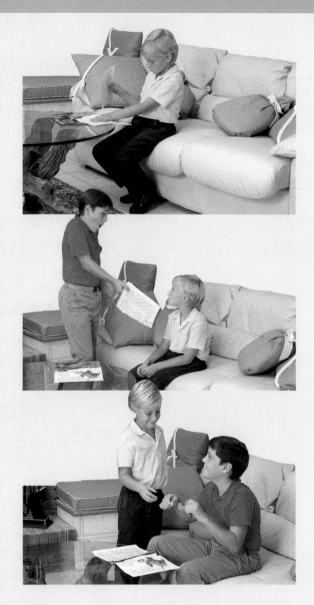

■ *Solving a problem without anger helps everyone feel good.*

Thinking Beyond

1. What are four ways people handle anger?
2. How might anger cause a person problems if it is kept inside?

13

4 Choosing Ways to Meet Needs

What can you do if your needs are not being met? Sometimes you can change the way you think or feel. Sometimes you can meet your needs by changing your actions. You can do something that makes you feel good about yourself. When you feel good about yourself, you can be proud of yourself. When you feel good about yourself, you are happier and more friendly. There are many ways you can choose to meet your needs.

How Can You Change a Trait to Meet a Need?

Amy liked to watch television. But choosing to watch television kept her from doing her homework well. Sometimes her work was messy or late. Then she could not feel proud of herself. She felt angry with herself.

■ Writing down what you want to change about yourself can be helpful when you are trying to meet certain needs.

WHAT I LIKE ABOUT MYSELF
1. I keep my room neat.
2. I am honest with everyone.
3. I do not give up easily.

WHAT I WOULD LIKE TO CHANGE
1. Get homework done earlier.
2. Practice the guitar more often.
3. Make more friends.
4. Take better care of my fishbowl.

Amy decided to do something to change the way she felt. She thought about herself for a while. Then she made two lists. One list showed things about herself that she liked and did not want to change. The other list showed things about herself that she wanted to change.

Amy started watching less television. Now she has more time for homework, so her work is always neat and done on time. She also has more time to practice the guitar. And she has made some new friends.

Amy has changed the way she acts. Her new actions have changed the way she feels about herself. Now she is not angry with herself all the time. By changing some of her actions, Amy has helped satisfy her need to feel proud of herself. She has helped raise her self-esteem.

■ Amy wanted to change the way she felt about herself. By doing her homework instead of watching television, she has met her need to be proud of herself.

FOR THE
CURIOUS

By choosing to be cheerful, you can be happy with the things you can do and feel good about yourself.

What Happens If You Cannot Change a Trait?

You can change your actions in some ways. Sometimes you can change the way you look, feel, or think. But you have some traits that cannot be changed. You cannot always make the changes you want to. You may have to make choices that allow you to satisfy your needs in other ways.

■ *Martin feels good about himself when he teaches a friend how to build a model.*

Martin is doing some things he enjoys. Martin would like to do other things, too. He would like to ride a bicycle and to ice-skate. But Martin cannot do those things because he was born with a heart that does not work as it should.

Martin cannot change this physical trait. He cannot do everything he would like to do. However, he has learned to do some things well. He spends time doing what he enjoys. For example, he enjoys building models and teaching his friends how to build them.

Martin has chosen ways to act that make him feel good about himself and bring him close to other people. Martin's choices help him meet his needs.

Everyone has some traits that cannot be changed. You might never be able to do all the things you want to do. It is important to think about things you can change in your life. In many ways, you can decide how to look, think, feel, and act. These choices will help you be the healthiest person you can be.

How Do People Decide
What the Best Choices Are?

Many of the choices you will make during your life will be to meet needs. Everyone must make choices.

■ *Bess must decide on the best way to get her health fair project done on time.*

Bess knew that she needed to finish a project for the health fair. She had three weeks to do it. She saw that she had to choose the best way to use her time to finish the project.

Bess listed some possible plans. Here is Bess's list:

- Get the project done as soon as possible.
- Wait until the last week to work on it.
- Spend some time on it each day.

Bess then asked herself some questions: Will I forget something if I try to hurry and get the project done? Can I finish it if I wait until the last week to work on it?

■ *Bess has decided to work on her health fair project a little each day after school.*

In order to complete her project on time, Bess had to change her plan. She had to work on the project every day after school and on weekends.

Will others who have done well on health projects have some ideas for planning my time? By answering these questions, Bess thought of some results of her possible choices.

Bess thought about the answers to her questions. She wanted her project to be the best it could be. She wanted others to learn important facts about health. Bess based her choice on her answers. She decided to work on her project for one hour each day until she finished it.

Sometimes people have to change their choices. Bess had to change her plans because her first choice did not work out. She soon found that one hour each day after school was not going to be enough for her to finish the project on time. She decided to work on the weekends as well.

Bess followed four steps for making her choices:

1. She found out all about her possible choices.
2. She thought about the results of each possible choice.
3. She made what seemed to be the best choice.
4. She thought about what would happen as a result of her choice.

Having steps to follow can help you make choices. You will be making many choices during your life. Many of these choices will have an effect on your wellness. You will want all your choices to be responsible ones. Knowing that you can make choices helps your self-esteem. You will know that you are able to carry out a plan that works well for you. Others will know that you did the best you could.

REVIEW
SECTION 4

REMEMBER?

1. What is one example of something you can do if your needs are not being met?
2. What need can making changes help you meet?
3. Name, in order, four steps for making choices.

THINK!

4. Why is it important to notice the results of a decision?
5. How might *knowing* you can make wise choices help your self-esteem?

Making Wellness Choices

Angela had been looking forward to the day when her school pictures would arrive. Today was that day. Angela's teacher, Mrs. Alcott, handed Angela an envelope with her pictures in it. Angela peeked at the pictures and closed the envelope quickly. She was unhappy because her eyes were closed in her pictures. Now Angela does not want her friends to see the pictures. She thinks her friends might laugh at her. Angela's friend Carmen wants to trade pictures.

? What could Angela say to Carmen? Explain your wellness choice.

People in Health

An Interview with a Classroom Teacher

> *Marcia Blair is an elementary-school teacher in Chicago, Illinois. She teaches fourth-grade students several subjects, including health.*

What are some of the topics you teach in health?

My classes study the food groups and how the body works. We learn about the importance of exercise, rest, sleep, and good posture. We talk about caring for the body. Students learn that they need to take care of their bodies if they want them to work well. My main goal in teaching health, however, is helping students understand self-esteem. I want them to know what it is like to feel good about themselves.

Why is self-esteem so important for students?

When students have high self-esteem, they like themselves. When students like themselves, they know that they are special. They know it is all right to be different, too. Students discover their talents and take pride in their work. When students are happy with themselves, they work better with other people. They enjoy meeting people who have different customs and different ways of thinking. As a result, they have positive self-concepts and good feelings about their world.

■ *Students who are happy with themselves work better with others.*

How do you help students feel good about themselves?

When possible, I like to have students work in groups. As students work together, they discover each other's talents and help each other with their classwork. They also help each other to feel good. This helps them meet their social and emotional needs as people. Sometimes I like to have the whole class make choices together. We learn that life is full of choices and that we sometimes need help in making our choices.

When did you know you wanted to be a teacher?

I have always been interested in helping people. In school I saw that my teachers were able to help students. I liked the way they encouraged students to be the best they could be. I remember one teacher saying that a person with self-esteem could expect good things to happen. That idea stuck with me. That is what I try to give my students when I teach health.

What is the hardest part of being a teacher?

The hardest part is not being able to help all my students who have problems. Sometimes a student is upset but has a hard time saying why. I work with students like that and try to find out what the problem might be. I talk with parents and other teachers. I cannot help all my students as much as I would like.

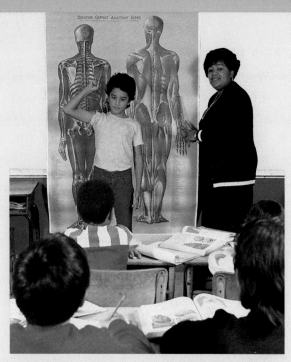

■ *Ms. Blair helps her students learn and grow in self-esteem.*

What do you like best about being a teacher?

The reward comes when I see my students learning something new. When I see it in their eyes, I know I made the right choice about being a teacher. I have helped them learn and grow both in knowledge and in self-esteem. I have helped them gain the skills they will need to be happy in the world.

Learn more about people who work as teachers in schools. Interview a teacher. Or write for information to the National Education Association, 1201 Sixteenth Street, N.W., Washington, DC 20036.

21

CHAPTER
REVIEW

Main Ideas

- Your physical, mental, social, and emotional traits combine to make you special.
- Your personality is made up of the ways you think, act, and feel.
- Learning more about your personality traits can help you develop a positive self-concept.
- All people have weaknesses and strengths.
- All people are special because of the differences in their traits.
- Everyone has physical, mental, social, and emotional needs.
- Many of the choices you will make during your life will be to satisfy needs.
- There are steps you can follow to help you make choices.

Key Words

Write the numbers 1 to 11 in your health notebook or on a separate sheet of paper. After each number, copy the sentence and fill in the missing term. Page numbers in ( ) tell you where to look in the chapter if you need help.

special (2)   strength (7)
trait (3)   weakness (7)
wellness (3)   self-esteem (8)
self-concept (3)   need (10)
emotions (6)   healthful (10)
personality (7)

1. The way you think about yourself is your ___?___ .

2. Something that a person must meet or satisfy to be healthy is a ___?___ .

3. A good feeling about yourself is called ___?___ .

4. A ___?___ is something about you that shows what you are like.

5. The ways you think, act, and feel make up your ___?___ .

6. A ___?___ is something you do well.

7. To be ___?___ is to be one of a kind.

8. A ___?___ is something you do not do well.

9. A high level of health you can reach is ___?___ .

10. *Feelings* is another word for ___?___ .

11. Something that is ___?___ is good for your health.

Remembering What You Learned

Page numbers in ( ) tell you where to look in the chapter if you need help.

1. What are four kinds of traits that make a person special? (3–6)

2. How can you keep your body healthy? (4)

3. What are four different ways of feeling? (6)

4. What are three things that your personality depends on? (7)

5. What does it mean to have self-esteem? (8)

6. Name three things that shape your self-esteem. (8)

7. What are four basic physical needs that all people must meet to stay alive? (11)

8. What does it mean to have a mental need? (11)

9. What are three different emotional needs? (12)

10. What can a person do if his or her needs are not being met? (14)

11. What might a person have to do if he or she has a trait that cannot be changed? (15–16)

12. Describe the steps for making a choice. (18)

Thinking About What You Learned

1. What are four ways in which you could compare yourself to your classmates?

2. Why is being able to "learn by doing" a mental trait?

3. How might an emotional trait have an effect on your self-concept?

4. What are some ways in which people can find out about their weaknesses?

5. What should a person do after he or she makes a choice and acts on it?

Writing About What You Learned

1. All people have a need to feel good about themselves. If you are aware of your strengths and weaknesses, you can take steps to feel good about yourself. Write two paragraphs about yourself. In the first paragraph, describe one of your traits that you think is a strength. Describe how it helps your self-concept. In the second paragraph, describe a weakness that you can change. Tell how you feel about the weakness. Describe how you can start to change it. Include one way a parent or another adult can help you improve the trait.

2. Long ago a wise person advised people who are angry to count to ten before they speak. Write a paragraph telling how you think this might help a person who is angry.

Applying What You Learned

PHYSICAL EDUCATION

Tell a parent or guardian how practicing and becoming better at sports skills, such as dribbling or kicking a ball, helps you feel good about yourself.

ART

Draw a picture of the way you see yourself. Include in the drawing things that show your physical, emotional, mental, and social traits.

Modified True or False

Write the numbers 1 to 15 in your health notebook or on a separate sheet of paper. After each number, write *true* or *false* to describe the sentence. If the sentence is false, also write a term that replaces the underlined term and makes the sentence true.

1. <u>Everybody</u> thinks and acts exactly the way you do.

2. A high level of health that you can reach is called <u>healthful</u>.

3. The way you think about yourself is your <u>self-concept</u>.

4. Your body size is a <u>mental</u> trait.

5. Love, worry, anger, and happiness are all <u>emotions</u>.

6. A <u>trait</u> is something a person must meet or satisfy to be healthy.

7. Shelter is a <u>physical</u> need.

8. The ways you look, think, act, and feel are <u>needs</u>.

9. Being talkative is a <u>social</u> trait.

10. You cannot see all of your <u>physical</u> traits.

11. Interrupting people when they are talking is a <u>strength</u>.

12. No one has a <u>personality</u> that is just like yours.

13. The need to feel loved is a <u>physical</u> need.

14. Sometimes you can meet your needs by changing your <u>actions</u>.

15. Being good at math is a <u>mental</u> trait.

Short Answer

Write the numbers 16 to 23 on your paper. Write a complete sentence to answer each question.

16. How do your emotional needs affect your self-esteem?

17. How is a personality formed?

18. Describe a physical trait that can be seen only with special medical equipment.

19. List the four things everyone must have.

20. Describe two ways you can learn more about your weaknesses.

21. Describe the four steps a person can take to make a wise choice.

22. How is your self-concept related to your personality?

23. How is your self-esteem related to your needs?

Essay

Write the numbers 24 and 25 on your paper. Write paragraphs with complete sentences to answer each question.

24. Sara is a new student in your class. She never speaks in class and does not smile often. Explain how you could help Sara's self-esteem.

25. Write about the different traits of someone you admire. Be sure to include physical traits, mental traits, social traits, and emotional traits.

ACTIVITIES FOR HOME OR SCHOOL

Projects to Do

1. Make your own coat of arms. You can use symbols from photographs, drawings, or pictures in magazines to describe what you like to show others about yourself.

2. Most stories are about a problem that someone has and how it is solved. Choose a story to read in which the main character solves a problem. On a piece of paper, write the steps for making a wise choice. Leave several spaces between the steps. As you read the story, look for words that relate to the steps for making a wise choice. In the spaces you left after each step, write the words that relate to that step.

Information to Find

1. Crying is one way that people show their emotions. Find out how crying helps people deal with a sad time in their lives. Also, find out why some people cry when they are happy. You may want to ask your school nurse or counselor.

2. Researchers have found that daydreaming now and then can be very useful to some people. Some researchers think daydreaming can improve a person's ability to use his or her imagination. Daydreaming may be useful in other ways, too. Find out how daydreaming can be a useful intellectual trait.

■ *Thomas Edison invented many things that make life enjoyable.*

3. Many people have had to live with traits that kept them from doing certain things. Thomas Edison, once a poor student, became a famous inventor. Find out about Thomas Edison. How did he learn to live with a negative intellectual trait? What choices did he have to make to start his career?

Books to Read

Here are some books you can look for in your school library or the public library to find more information about your personality and needs.

de Regniers, Beatrice Schenk. *The Way I Feel . . . Sometimes*. Clarion Books.

Swenson, Judy Harris, and Roxane Kunz. *No One Like Me*. Dillon Press.

Thomas, Marlo, and Friends. *Free to Be . . . A Family*. Bantam Books.

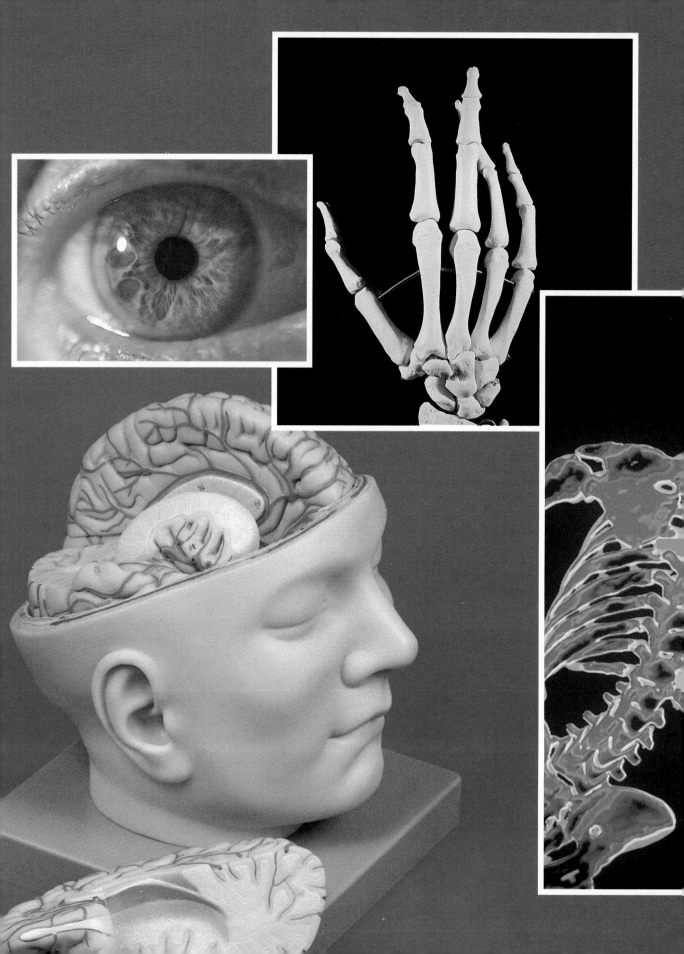

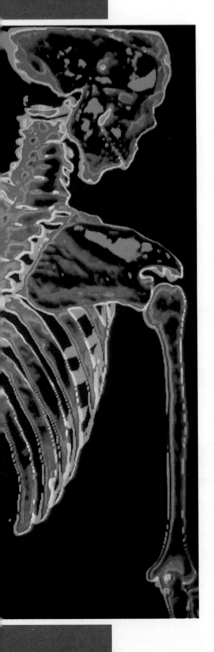

CHAPTER 2

ABOUT YOUR BODY

There is more to you than meets the eye. Under your skin is a world you never get to see. It is a world of muscles, bones, blood, tubes, and many other kinds of parts.

The world outside your body is full of things to see, hear, touch, smell, and taste. The world within your body helps you know the world outside. Your brain and all the other parts of your body work together to help you live and enjoy life. Keeping your body parts healthy takes work. Your job is to practice good health habits to help yourself reach wellness.

GETTING READY TO LEARN

Key Questions
- Why is it important to learn how your body works?
- Why is it important to know how you feel about your body?

Main Chapter Sections

1 The Parts of Your Body

Your body is made up of many different parts. Each part of your body does a certain job. Some parts work by themselves. Other parts work together. But each part of your body, no matter how small, has a job to do. When all the parts of your body are working as they should, you are healthy.

What Are Cells?

cell (SEHL), the smallest working part of your body.

The smallest working part of your body is called a **cell.** Cells might be called the building blocks of your body. Every part of your body is made of cells. Your bones are made of bone cells. Your skin is made of skin cells. Your whole body is made of many kinds of tiny, living cells.

■ *Your body uses food to produce new cells, such as the skin cells shown below.*

One cell is too small to see with only your eyes. In fact, hundreds of cells would fit on the head of a pin. You can see a cell if you look at it through a microscope. A microscope makes small things look bigger.

Cells might also be called energy warehouses for your body. **Energy** is the ability your body has to do things. Certain foods give you energy. The parts of food that give you energy are stored in cells.

When your body needs energy to walk, run, and even move your arms, the cells use their supply of energy. Your body also needs energy to do things you do not think about doing, such as breathing and sleeping. Cells supply the parts of the body with the energy they need to do their jobs.

What Are Tissues?

Your body has many different kinds of cells. Groups of the same kinds of cells work together to do the same job. Skin cells, for example, are round and flat. They fit together tightly. Skin cells work together to cover and protect your body. Your skin is made of many skin cells working together.

Groups of the same kinds of cells working together are **tissues.** Skin is one kind of tissue in your body. Bones and muscles are two other kinds of tissues. Your body is made up of many kinds of tissues.

energy (EHN uhr jee), the ability your body has to do things.

tissues (TIHSH OOZ), groups of the same kinds of cells working together.

■ Skin tissue, left, is made of skin cells. Bone tissue, right, is made of bone cells.

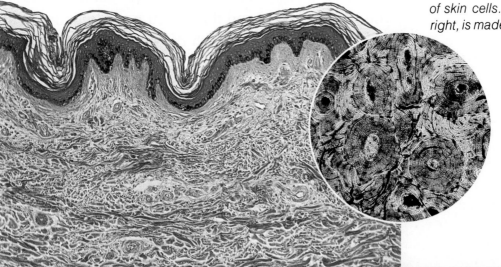
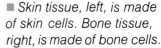

29

What Are Organs?

Tissues in your body also work together in groups. Groups of tissues that work together are **organs.** Each organ has a certain job. Your heart is an organ. It has the job of pumping your blood. Like all organs, the heart is made up of several kinds of tissues. Your stomach, your brain, and your eyes are some of your other organs.

■ *The heart is one of the most important organs in your body. It pumps blood to every cell.*

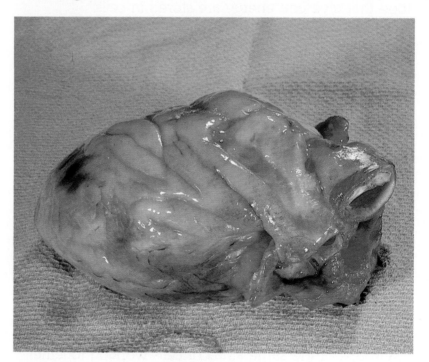

What Are Body Systems?

Your organs help you do the things you need to do to stay alive and healthy. You need to eat and breathe. You need to move and think. You need to understand the world around you. Each of your organs helps with one or more of those jobs. But no organ does the whole job by itself. Several organs work together to meet each of your body's needs.

Organs working together make up a **body system.** Different body systems take care of different needs. One body system, for example, helps you breathe. Other body systems help you move.

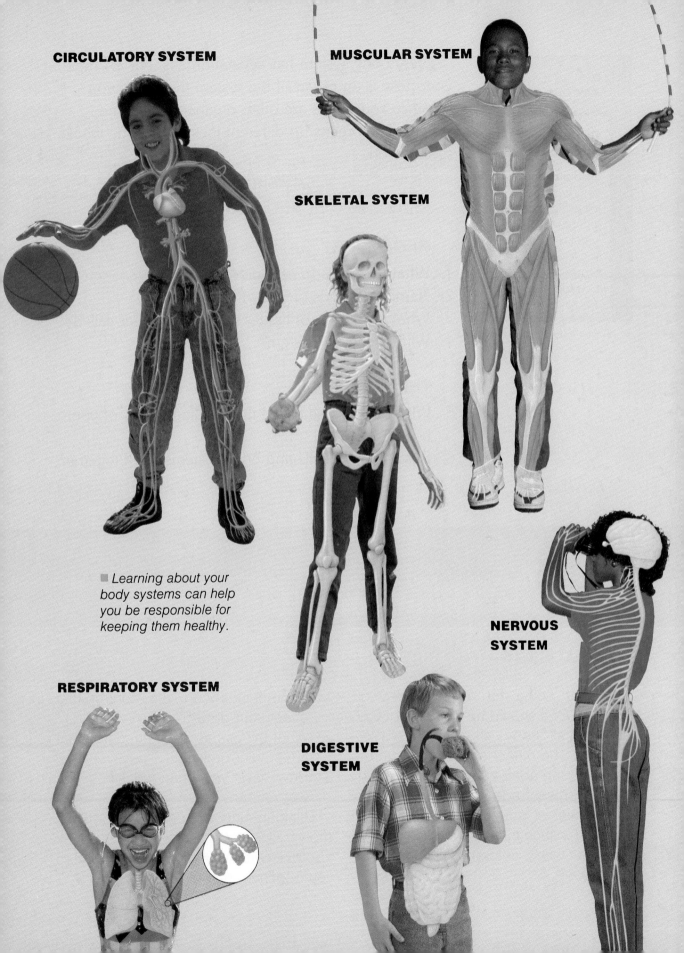

CIRCULATORY SYSTEM

MUSCULAR SYSTEM

SKELETAL SYSTEM

■ *Learning about your body systems can help you be responsible for keeping them healthy.*

NERVOUS SYSTEM

RESPIRATORY SYSTEM

DIGESTIVE SYSTEM

Every body system has several organs. For example, your nose is an organ of the system that helps you breathe. Your lungs are other organs of the same system. The organs do different jobs to help the whole system work.

STOP REVIEW
SECTION 1

REMEMBER?

1. What two jobs do cells do for your body?
2. Name two kinds of body tissue.
3. What is a group of tissues working together called?
4. What is a body system?

THINK!

5. Why can cells be called the building blocks of your body?
6. Describe how cells and body systems work together.

Thinking About Your Health

How Are You Growing?

Ask at home for four pictures of yourself. One should be a picture of you as a small baby, six months old or younger. The others should be pictures of you at the ages of three and six and at your present age. Place the pictures on a sheet of paper. Write the correct age under each picture. Then look at the pictures and answer the following questions:

1. What things can you control that affect your growth?
2. What things can you not control that affect your growth?
3. How have you changed since you were a baby?

Think about how much your body has grown since you were a baby. Think about how much your body will grow as you become an adult.

32

Health Close-up

Growing Up

Part of growing up involves physical growth. As people grow, they get taller. They gain weight. Their arms and legs get longer. Their hands get bigger. Even their heads get larger. It takes many years for all their body parts to reach their full size.

Growing up, however, means much more than getting bigger in size. While people are growing physically, they are also growing in other ways. Mental, emotional, and social growth are taking place along with physical growth. People continue to grow and change in many ways after they reach the physical size and age at which they are called adults.

Growing people gain new knowledge in many areas. They learn more about school subjects, such as language and science. They also learn about earning money and using it wisely. They learn to use information to make wise choices. They learn personal health care skills from family members and health workers. People never stop learning.

Growing people learn to express their emotions in healthful ways. They watch as family members show and describe different feelings. They learn to understand their own feelings. They learn why they feel certain ways at certain times. By understanding their feelings, people can better understand their actions. The way people act depends often on how they feel.

A growing person learns to act in ways that help other people feel good. A growing person uses new knowledge to act more responsibly in social groups. Your family and your school are two very important social groups. As you grow, you take on more duties at home. You help your family keep your home clean and safe. In school you are expected to be polite to other students and adults. Taking care of your duties without being reminded is a sign of social growth.

■ *Learning how to meet new people is part of growing up.*

Thinking Beyond

1. What do you think it means to be an adult?
2. Why do families and communities give adults privileges that are different from the privileges of young people?

33

2 Your Skeletal and Muscular Systems

Look at your hand. You can move your hand in many ways. You can swing your thumb all around, and you can curl all your fingers. Many other parts of your body can bend, twist, and move, too.

Two body systems help you move the way you do. One is your skeletal system. It gives your body its basic size and shape. The other system is your muscular system. It helps your body move. Both systems also help protect parts of the body.

What Gives Your Body Its Shape?

skeleton (SKEHL uht uhn), all the bones in your body.

joint (JOYNT), a place where two bones meet.

■ *The bones of a hinge joint and a ball-and-socket joint move in certain directions. Immovable joints connect bones, but do not let the bones move.*

The bones in your body make up your skeletal system, or **skeleton.** Your skeleton gives your body its shape. Without your skeleton, your body would be soft, like a caterpillar's body. Because you have a skeleton, you can stand up. You can sit, walk, or run without losing your shape.

Bones are stiff, like pencils. They cannot bend. Your body can bend in many places, though, because there are places in your skeleton where bones meet. Where two bones meet, you have a **joint.** Your skeleton has many joints.

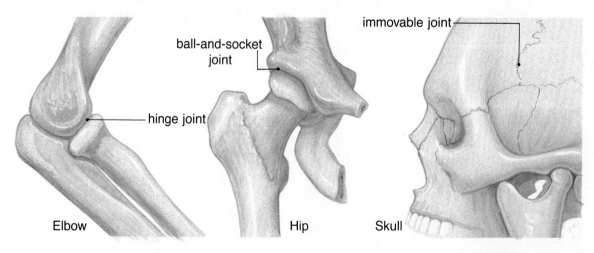

ball-and-socket joint

immovable joint

hinge joint

Elbow

Hip

Skull

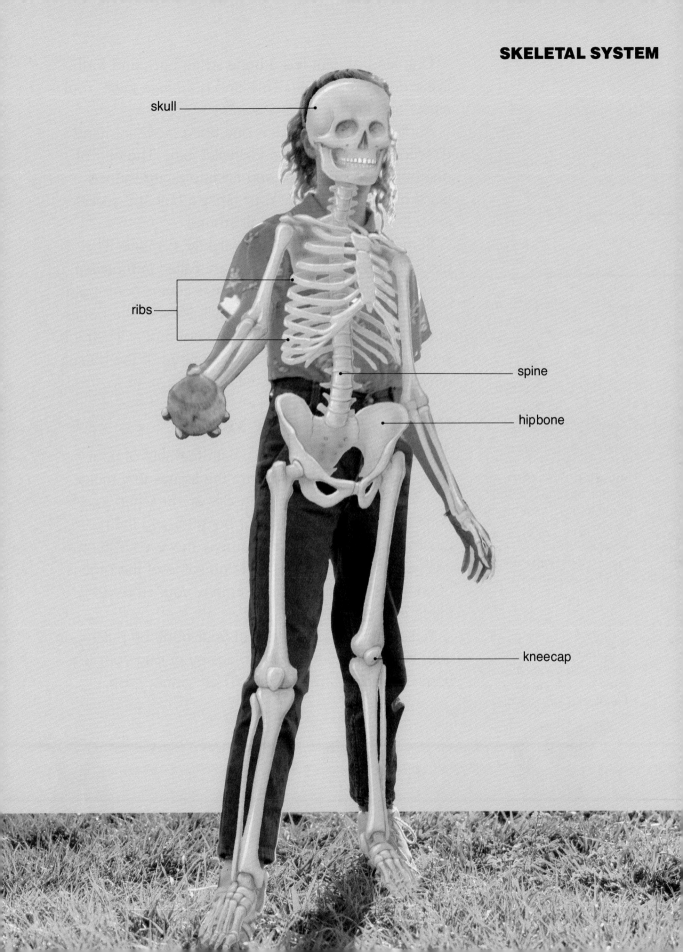

SKELETAL SYSTEM

skull

ribs

spine

hipbone

kneecap

One kind of joint lets a bone swing back and forth like a door on a hinge. This kind is a *hinge joint.* Your elbow and knee are hinge joints.

Another kind of joint lets one bone move in many directions. This is a *ball-and-socket joint.* The end of one bone is round. This end fits into a cup-shaped place on another bone. Your hip is a ball-and-socket joint. It lets your leg swing all around.

Some bones fit together too tightly to move. The places where such bones meet are called *immovable joints.* A rounded set of eight bones covers your brain. This set of bones is called the skull. Most of the bones in the skull lock together. They do not move. Their job is to protect the brain from being injured. If the bones moved, they could not do their job.

How Does Your Body Move?

Your bones can move only with the help of your muscular system. **Muscles** are the tissues that make up your muscular system. Muscles are attached to bones and other parts of your body to help them move. Some muscles, for example, move your eyes as you read. Other muscles make up some of the organs of your body systems. For example, your stomach is made of muscle.

Muscles move some parts of your body by pulling on your bones. They move your legs by pulling your leg bones. Muscles can only pull. They cannot push.

muscles (MUHS uhlz), tissues attached to body parts to help them move.

■ *Certain muscles pull on the arm bones as each boy tries to force the other's arm down.*

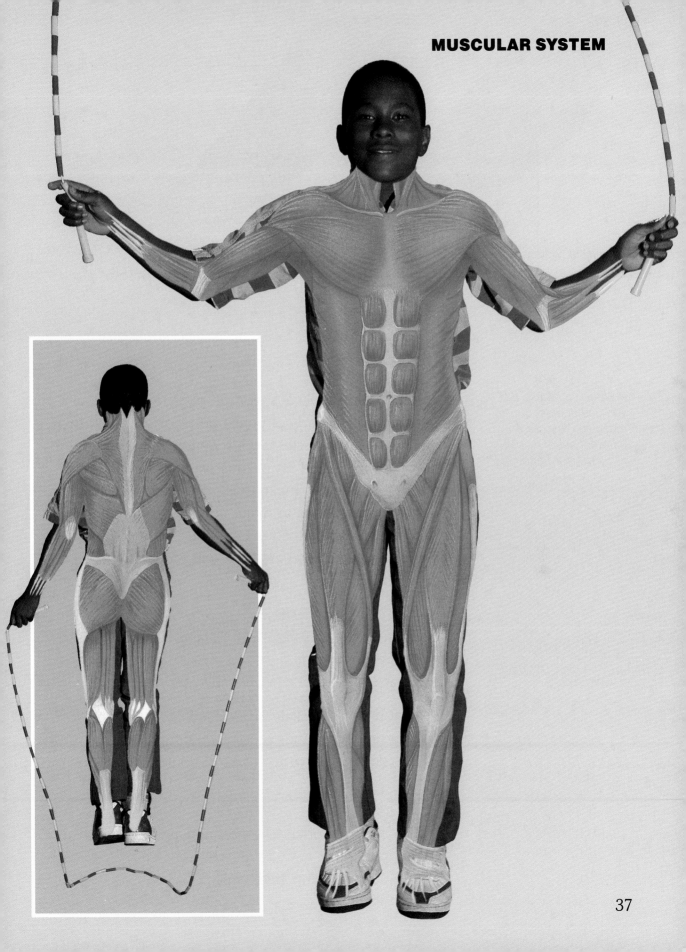

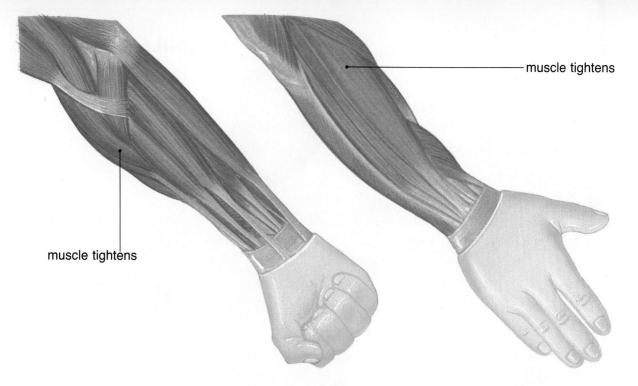

muscle tightens

muscle tightens

■ *When you make a fist you use one set of muscles. You use a different set of muscles to open your hand.*

Muscles almost always work in pairs to move your bones and other parts of your body. For example, two different sets of muscles work together when you open and close a fist. One set of muscles pulls the fingers of your hand closed to make a fist. Another set of muscles pulls the same bones to make your fingers straighten.

Your bones and muscles help you run, walk, and play. They help you every time you move any part of your body.

REVIEW
SECTION 2

REMEMBER?

1. What does your skeleton do?
2. What are three kinds of joints in your skeleton?
3. How do muscles move parts of your body?

THINK!

4. What might happen to someone who could not use a leg muscle?
5. How do your joints help you move?

3 Your Digestive and Respiratory Systems

You must eat because your cells need parts of food called **nutrients.** Cells need nutrients to grow and to be active. Your digestive system breaks up food so that your cells can use the nutrients in the food you eat.

Your cells also need a gas called **oxygen.** Cells need oxygen to use nutrients. You get oxygen from the air you breathe. Your respiratory system controls your breathing. It helps you get oxygen from the air. It also helps you get rid of a gas called *carbon dioxide.* Carbon dioxide is a gas that your cells make but cannot use.

What Happens When You Eat?

Several organs make up your digestive system. Most are hollow tubes. The tubes are connected end to end. Food moves from one tube to the next. Each organ pushes the food to make it move. Some of the organs of the digestive system make liquids that help digest food. Those liquids are called **digestive juices.**

KEY WORDS

nutrients
oxygen
digestive juices
esophagus
stomach
small intestine
large intestine
trachea
lungs
alveoli

nutrients (NOO tree uhnts), parts of food the body needs to grow and be active.

oxygen (AHK sih juhn), a gas needed by your cells.

digestive juices (dy JEHS tihv • JOOS uhz), liquids that help digest food.

■ *Your digestive system turns food, like this apple, into nutrients your body can use.*

39

DIGESTIVE SYSTEM

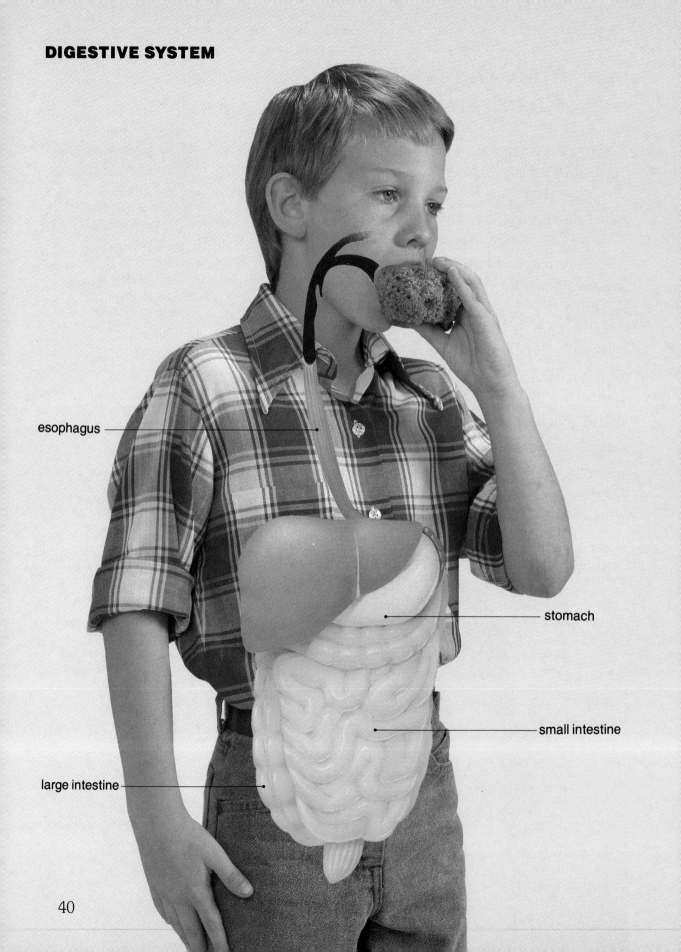

esophagus

stomach

small intestine

large intestine

When you eat, you put food into your mouth. Your teeth break your food into smaller pieces as you chew. Then you swallow. Your food passes into your esophagus. The **esophagus** is a tube made of muscle. It squeezes food down into your body, the way you might squeeze toothpaste out of a tube.

Your esophagus pushes the food into your stomach. Your **stomach** is an organ with openings at both ends. Its wall is made up of muscles. The muscles squeeze and mash your food. Digestive juices help break up your food, too. Most food stays in your stomach for a few hours.

When food leaves your stomach, it passes into your small intestine. Your **small intestine** is a hollow tube that gives off digestive juices. Like your stomach, your small intestine has a wall of muscle. This muscle squeezes your food and keeps it moving. Most digestion takes place in the small intestine.

Your small intestine is only as wide as a finger. But in someone your age, the small intestine is about 13 feet (4 meters) long. That is more than twice as tall as you are! The small intestine is all folded up inside your body. Nutrients move into the blood through the thin wall of your small intestine.

The food you eat has many parts that your body cannot digest or use. Materials that your body cannot digest or use are called *wastes*. The wastes from your food move into your large intestine. Your **large intestine** is wider and shorter than your small intestine. Your large intestine is nearly 4 feet (1.2 meters) long. The wastes enter your large intestine as a thick liquid. The large intestine removes the water from the wastes. Wastes are then stored in the large intestine until they leave the body.

Wastes leave your body through an opening at the lower end of the large intestine. An act of moving wastes out of your body is called a *bowel movement*.

esophagus (ih SAHF uh guhs), a tube made of muscle that squeezes food down into the stomach.

stomach (STUHM uhk), a digestive organ that squeezes and mashes food.

small intestine (SMAWL • ihn TEHS tuhn), a hollow tube in which most digestion takes place.

large intestine (LAHRJ • ihn TEHS tuhn), a hollow tube in which wastes are stored until they leave your body.

RESPIRATORY SYSTEM

alveoli

trachea

lungs

What Happens When You Breathe?

The air you breathe enters your body through your nose. Some air may also enter through your mouth. Your nose, however, warms the air that enters it. Tiny hairs and the moist walls inside your nose remove some of the dust and dirt from the air.

The air then moves into a tube called the **trachea,** or windpipe. This tube goes from your nose and mouth into your chest. There your trachea branches into two parts. Each branch goes into one of your two lungs. Your **lungs** are large respiratory organs inside your chest. They are spongy, pink organs.

Inside your lungs are thousands of treelike branches. At the ends of the branches are tiny air sacs called **alveoli.** The alveoli are like small balloons. They fill with air when you breathe in. Oxygen in the air passes through the walls of the alveoli into the blood. At the same time, carbon dioxide in the blood moves into the alveoli. Your cells make carbon dioxide, which your cells cannot use. The body gets rid of this waste gas when you breathe out.

trachea (TRAY kee uh), a tube that goes from your nose and mouth down into your chest; windpipe.

lungs (LUHNGZ), spongy respiratory organs inside your chest.

alveoli (al VEE uh ly), tiny air sacs in your lungs.

REVIEW SECTION 3

REMEMBER?

1. Trace the path of food through the digestive system.
2. Describe what happens when you breathe in and out.
3. What do the alveoli do?

THINK!

4. How do muscles and digestive juices work together to help your body digest food?
5. How might breathing smoky, dusty air affect your respiratory system?

4 Your Circulatory System

Look at your feet. They are far away from your small intestine and from your lungs. Yet cells in your feet need nutrients and oxygen to stay alive. Nutrients and oxygen must be carried to all your cells. Your circulatory system does this important job. This same body system also carries wastes away from each cell. All cells have to get rid of their wastes.

Your circulatory system is made up of three main parts. They are your blood, your heart, and your blood vessels.

What Is Your Blood Made Of?

blood (BLUHD), a liquid that carries nutrients and oxygen to your cells.

Your **blood** is like a river carrying nutrients and oxygen to your cells. Your blood moves through your body without stopping. Most of your blood is a clear liquid. In fact, your blood is made mostly of water. Your blood also has cells floating in it.

■ *Your blood contains red blood cells, white blood cells, and platelets.*

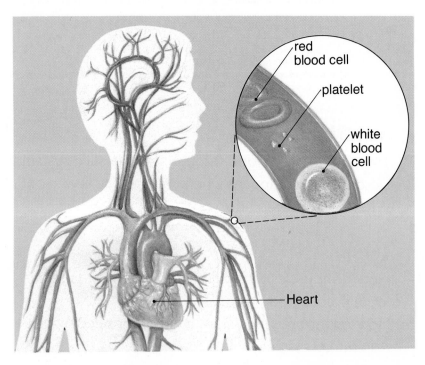

red blood cell

platelet

white blood cell

Heart

44

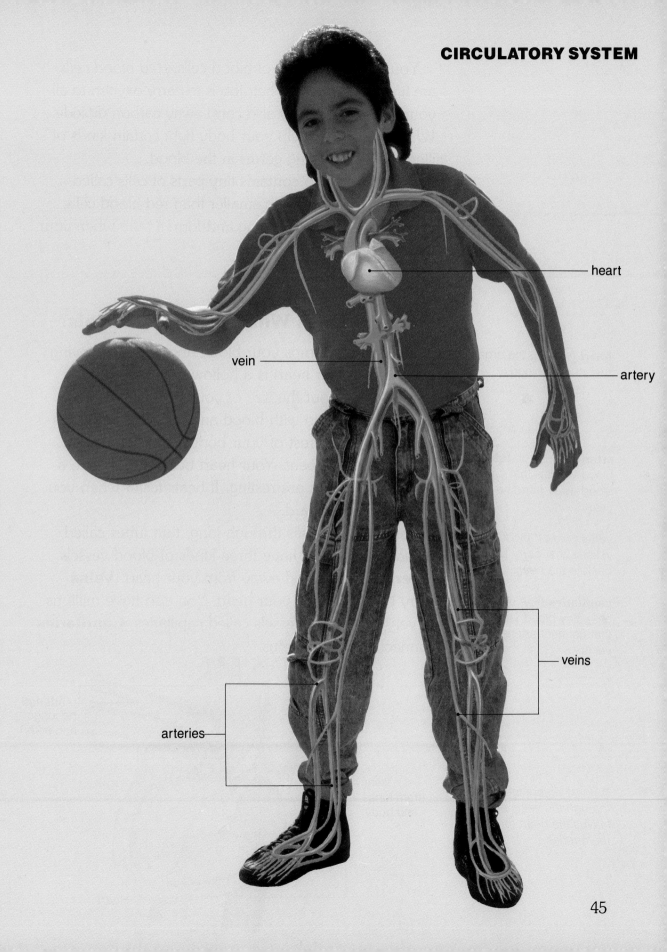

heart

vein

artery

veins

arteries

You have two kinds of blood cells. *Red blood cells* are tiny, round cells. Their job is to carry oxygen to all your other cells. They also carry away carbon dioxide. *White blood cells* help your body fight certain kinds of illnesses by attacking germs in the blood.

Your blood also contains tiny parts of cells called *platelets*. They are even smaller than red blood cells. Platelets help slow bleeding and form a scab when your skin gets cut.

What Happens When Your Heart Beats?

heart (HAHRT), the organ that pumps blood.

Your **heart** pumps your blood and keeps it moving at all times. Your heart is a hollow organ made of muscle. It is about the size of your fist. Your heart works by filling up with blood and then squeezing the blood out to the rest of your body. The squeezing is called your *heartbeat*. Your heart beats about once a second when you are resting. It beats faster when you move and work hard.

arteries (AHRT uh reez), blood vessels that carry blood away from the heart.

veins (VAYNZ), blood vessels that carry blood back to the heart.

capillaries (KAP uh lehr eez), tiny blood vessels that connect arteries to veins.

Your blood moves through long, thin tubes called *blood vessels*. You have three kinds of blood vessels. **Arteries** carry blood away from your heart. **Veins** carry blood back to your heart. You also have millions of very tiny blood vessels called capillaries. **Capillaries** connect arteries to veins.

■ *Blood enters the heart through the veins and leaves the heart through the arteries.*

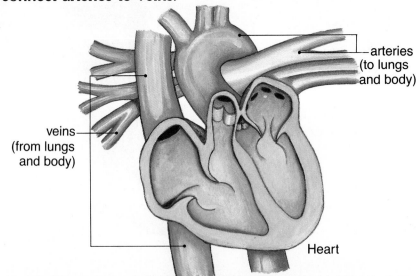

arteries (to lungs and body)

veins (from lungs and body)

Heart

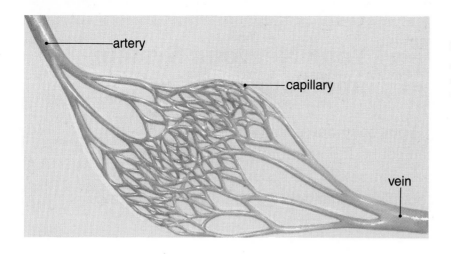
artery

capillary

vein

■ *Every cell in your body gets oxygen and nutrients from the capillaries.*

Of the three kinds of blood vessels, capillaries have the thinnest walls. The walls of capillaries are so thin that nutrients and oxygen can move through them. Capillaries in your small intestine let nutrients into your blood. Capillaries in the alveoli of your lungs let oxygen into your blood. Capillaries near your cells let nutrients and oxygen out of your blood and into your cells. Capillaries also carry wastes away from your cells. Every cell in your body has a capillary near it.

Your circulatory system helps keep your cells alive. It brings your cells everything they need and takes away wastes they cannot use.

 **REVIEW**
SECTION 4

REMEMBER?

1. What are the three main parts of the circulatory system?
2. What are the two kinds of blood cells?
3. What are the three kinds of blood vessels?

THINK!

4. How does the circulatory system help keep your body healthy?
5. Why is the circulatory system called a *system*?

5 Your Nervous System and Your Senses

Your body does many more things than you can count. It does more than the biggest and best computer. One system inside your body controls the many things you do. That system is your nervous system.

What Makes Your Body Parts Work Together?

Your nervous system is made up of three main parts. They are your brain, your nerves, and your spinal cord. All the parts of your nervous system are made of special cells called *nerve cells.*

Your **brain** tells all other parts of your body what to do. It is the organ that you use to remember, think, feel, and plan.

The brain is like several computers all working at once. It is a busy message center. It receives messages from all over your body. It sends messages to all parts of your body, too.

Messages move to and from your brain through nerves. **Nerves** are bundles of nerve cells. Nerves connect all parts of your body with your brain. Some nerves, such as those in parts of your face, connect directly with your brain. Other nerves are connected with your brain by a large group of nerves called the **spinal cord.**

Your spinal cord is in the center of bones in your back. The top of your spinal cord connects with your brain. A stack of bones called the *spine* protects it. Some people call the spine the backbone.

Nerves branch out from your spinal cord and go to all parts of your body. They go to your organs, arms, chest, legs, and feet. The nerves carry messages from

brain (BRAYN), the organ that you use to remember, think, feel, and plan.

nerves (NURVZ), bundles of nerve cells that carry messages.

spinal cord (SPYN uhl • KAWRD), a large group of nerves down the center of your back that connects with your brain.

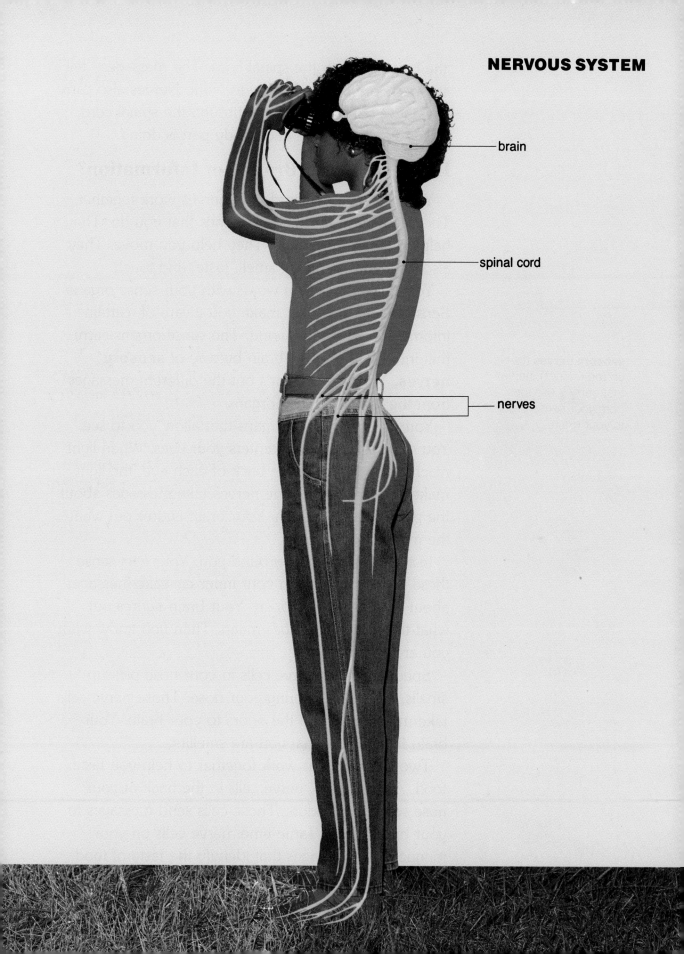

NERVOUS SYSTEM

brain

spinal cord

nerves

the brain through the spinal cord. The messages "tell" the parts of your body how to work. Nerves also carry messages back to the brain through the spinal cord, telling the brain what each body part is doing.

How Does Your Brain Get Information?

Your brain, spinal cord, and nerves work together. They allow you to do all the things that you do. They help you learn and think. They help you move. They also help you see, hear, smell, taste, and touch.

Your nervous system works with your sense organs. *Sense organs* sense, or make you aware of, certain information about the world. The sense organs carry that information to the brain by way of **sensory nerves.** Your brain figures out the different messages from the different sense organs.

Your eyes are sense organs that allow you to see. You see only when light enters your eyes. When light reaches the nerves at the back of each eye, the light makes a little picture. The nerves take messages about the picture to your brain. Your brain figures out what the messages mean.

Listen to the sounds around you. Your ears sense these sounds. Nerves in your inner ear take messages about sounds to your brain. Your brain figures out what the sound messages mean. Then you know what you are hearing.

Special sensory nerve cells in your nose pick up smells, or odors, entering your nose. Those nerve cells take messages about the odors to your brain. Your brain figures out what you are smelling.

Two sense organs work together to help you taste food. As you chew, nerve cells in the back of your nose sense food odors. Those cells send messages to your brain. At the same time, nerve cells on your tongue send messages that identify the taste of food. What you taste is really a mixture of taste and smell.

sensory nerves (SEHNS uh ree • NURVZ), nerves that carry messages from your sense organs to your brain.

50

6 Your Body Grows

Look at these pictures of Mark. The picture on the left was taken nine years ago. Mark's body was tiny then. The picture on the right shows what Mark looks like now. His body has grown.

You may not notice yourself growing from day to day. But you have grown a lot since you were born, and you are still growing.

How Does Your Body Grow?

Your body gains size by making more and more cells. Your body grew from one fertilized cell. When it began, your body was smaller than a grain of salt. Then your one cell turned into two cells. Your two cells became four cells. The four became eight. The eight became sixteen. The cells remained tiny. But they kept increasing in number.

Now you have more cells than you can count. Your body is making new cells all the time. And old, worn-out cells are always dying. As you continue to grow, your body will continue to make more cells. Parts of your body, such as your hair and nails, will make new cells all your life.

■ *Your body grows in size as the number of its cells increases.*

How Fast Do You and Others Grow?

Look at the picture of some of Mark's classmates. All the students are about the same age. Yet they are not all the same size. Some are taller and some are shorter. The shapes of their bodies are different, too.

Differences like these are normal at any age. People grow in different ways. Faye has been growing faster than Phyllis. But Phyllis may catch up with Faye this year. No one grows at the same speed all the time.

Growing follows a pattern, however. People grow quickly at certain times. At other times they grow more slowly.

■ *You are probably bigger than some of your classmates and smaller than others. Differences in size are normal among people your age because people grow at different rates.*

HEIGHT AND AGE

71 inches	180 centimeters
63 inches	160 centimeters
55 inches	140 centimeters
47 inches	120 centimeters
39 inches	100 centimeters
32 inches	80 centimeters
24 inches	60 centimeters
16 inches	40 centimeters
8 inches	20 centimeters
0 inch	0 centimeter

Ages   9   11   13

■ *Girls grow earlier than boys, but boys catch up a little later.*

The chart "Height and Age" shows growing patterns for girls and boys. The growing pattern for girls is a little different from the growing pattern for boys. At your age, for example, girls often begin growing faster than boys. Girls usually are taller than boys around the age of 11 or 12. Then growing begins to slow down in most girls. Growing speeds up in many boys. Within a few years, most boys are taller than most girls.

 **REVIEW SECTION 6**

REMEMBER?

1. How does your body grow in size?
2. At what age are most girls taller than most boys?

THINK!

3. Why are some people taller or shorter than others of the same age?
4. What kinds of feelings might people have about how their bodies grow?

FOR THE CURIOUS

Around the age of 11 or 12, the average boy is eight-tenths as tall as he will be as an adult. The average girl at this age is nine-tenths as tall as she will be as an adult.

An Interview with a Pediatrician

> Howard Taras knows how young people grow and develop. He is a pediatrician. A pediatrician is a special kind of physician. Dr. Taras treats babies, children, and teenagers and helps them stay healthy. He also teaches at a medical school in San Diego, California.

What do pediatricians do?

Pediatricians treat children who are ill or injured. But they do more than that. Pediatricians are concerned about the total child. They are interested in everything from a child's feelings to how a child learns in school. Pediatricians want to help parents keep their children totally healthy as the children grow up.

What made you decide to become a physician?

Before I went to medical school, I worked in a hospital as a volunteer. I did not get paid for my work. I was there because I wanted to learn. I saw what happens in a hospital. I saw physicians making decisions and using their learning to help people. I knew then that I wanted to do more in a hospital than I could do as a volunteer.

What made you decide to become a pediatrician?

Most physicians decide on a special kind of study after being in medical school a few years. I decided before I started my medical training. I chose to become a pediatrician because I liked the pediatrician who cared for me.

How long did it take you to become a pediatrician?

After high school, it took a total of 11 years. I went to college for 4 years. Then I studied in medical school for 4 years to become a physician. I needed another 3 years of special study to become a pediatrician.

Why do you enjoy being a pediatrician?

I enjoy the children who are my patients. It is wonderful to see children

■ A pediatrician helps children stay healthy with regular check-ups.

grow up over the years. I enjoy teaching children good health habits. I teach children about both exercise and nutrition. Showing them how to stay healthy can help them keep from becoming ill. I enjoy knowing that I am helping children in these ways.

Besides helping patients, what else do you do?

I teach medical students. I teach physicians who want to become pediatricians. Each week I also work a half day in the public schools in San Diego.

What do you do in the public schools?

I help teachers and school nurses who teach health. I tell them about all that is new in medicine, health, and safety. I also help parents and principals decide when it is safe for children who have been ill to return to school. At each school, I talk with the students. Sometimes I talk with children who are having trouble in school. I try to find out the causes of their problems. I handle a lot of different health matters in the schools.

What makes you feel good about being a pediatrician?

Helping children who are ill is the best reward for a pediatrician. I see many children with different kinds of diseases and injuries. To see a child become healthy again is any pediatrician's greatest reward.

Medical Teaching

■ Dr. Taras teaches medical students who want to become pediatricians. He also teaches young people about health.

Learn more about how pediatricians help keep children healthy. Interview a pediatrician. Or write for information to the American Academy of Pediatrics, 141 Northwest Point Boulevard, P.O. Box 927, Elk Grove Village, IL 60009.

57

Main Ideas

- Your body has many different parts. Each part has a certain job to do.
- Your skeletal system gives your body its basic size and shape.
- Your muscular system works with your skeletal system to help you move.
- Your digestive system changes food so that you can get nutrients from it.
- Your respiratory system helps you get oxygen and get rid of carbon dioxide.
- Your circulatory system carries nutrients and oxygen to all your cells.
- Your nervous system and your senses work together to give you information that helps you protect your health.
- People have different growth patterns.

Key Words

Write the numbers 1 to 15 in your health notebook or on a separate sheet of paper. After each number, copy the sentence and fill in the missing term. Page numbers in ( ) tell you where to look in the chapter if you need help.

cell (28)	nutrients (39)
energy (29)	oxygen (39)
tissues (29)	digestive juices
organs (30)	(39)
body system (30)	esophagus (41)
skeleton (34)	stomach (41)
joint (34)	small intestine (41)
muscles (36)	large intestine (41)

1. Tissues that help you move are called ___?___ .

2. Your ___?___ is a digestive organ that squeezes and mashes food.

3. The smallest working part of your body is called a ___?___ .

4. Groups of the same kinds of cells working together are ___?___ .

5. Organs working together are a ___?___ .

6. You must eat because your cells need parts of food called ___?___ .

7. Your bones make up your ___?___ .

8. Your ___?___ is a hollow tube in which most digestion takes place.

9. Where two bones meet, you have a ___?___ .

10. You must breathe because your cells need a gas called ___?___ .

11. Wastes from food are stored in the ___?___ until they leave your body.

12. The ability your body has to do things is called ___?___ .

13. Groups of tissues that work together are ___?___ .

14. Some of the organs of the digestive system make liquids, called ___?___ , that help digest food.

15. A tube made of muscle that pushes food down into your stomach is called your ___?___ .

Write the numbers 16 to 27 on your paper. After each number, write a sentence that defines the term. Page numbers in ( ) tell you where to look in the chapter if you need help.

16. trachea (43)
17. lungs (43)
18. alveoli (43)
19. blood (44)
20. heart (46)
21. arteries (46)
22. veins (46)
23. capillaries (46)
24. brain (48)
25. nerves (48)
26. spinal cord (48)
27. sensory nerves (50)

Remembering What You Learned

Page numbers in ( ) tell you where to look in the chapter if you need help.

1. What do cells do in your body? (28–29)

2. How are tissues different from organs? (29–30)

3. What two systems in your body help you move? (34)

4. Where in your body do you have a hinge joint? (36)

5. What must happen to the food you eat before it can be used by your cells? (39)

6. What gas do you breathe in? What gas do you breathe out? (39)

7. What happens when your heart beats? (46)

8. What organ might you call the message center of your body? (48)

9. What protects your spinal cord? (48)

10. What is a job of the nerves that branch out from your spinal cord to all parts of your body? (48–50)

Thinking About What You Learned

1. How might a muscle injury affect a joint?

2. Why are muscles important to the digestive system?

3. How might breathing through your nose in cold weather help you?

4. Why are the walls of capillaries thin?

5. How are nerves like telephone wires?

Writing About What You Learned

Some machines have parts that look similar to body parts. For example, some machines have an armlike part that picks things up. Think of a machine you have seen. Write a paragraph comparing a part or parts of the machine with a part or parts of your body.

Applying What You Learned

MATHEMATICS

Measure your own height and the height of someone in your class who is either taller or shorter than you. Figure the average of the two heights. Measure four other classmates. Average their heights. Try to figure the average height for your whole class.

Modified True or False

Write the numbers 1 to 15 in your health notebook or on a separate sheet of paper. After each number, write *true* or *false* to describe the sentence. If the sentence is false, also write a term that replaces the underlined term and makes the sentence true.

1. The smallest working part of your body is called a <u>tissue</u>.
2. The small intestine is <u>longer</u> than the large intestine.
3. A <u>joint</u> connects two bones.
4. A body system is a group of <u>cells</u> working together.
5. When you swallow food, it moves down the <u>trachea</u>.
6. Arteries are blood vessels that carry blood <u>away from</u> the heart.
7. If you had no <u>sensory nerves</u>, you would be unable to taste food.
8. Your nervous system is made up of <u>five</u> parts.
9. <u>Energy</u> is the ability your body has to do things.
10. Your hip is a <u>hinge</u> joint.
11. Without <u>muscles</u>, you would be unable to move.
12. Swallowed food is pushed from the esophagus to the <u>large intestine</u>.
13. There are <u>two</u> kinds of blood cells.
14. If you have just run a race, your heart beats <u>slowly</u>.
15. Every cell has a <u>vein</u> near it.

Short Answer

Write the numbers 16 to 23 on your paper. Write a complete sentence to answer each question.

16. Explain why your circulatory system needs both veins and arteries.
17. Describe how you can grow even though your cells never get big enough to be seen without a microscope.
18. How is a hinge joint different from a ball-and-socket joint?
19. What do the two kinds of blood cells do?
20. How do cells get energy?
21. Name two ways muscles work in your body.
22. In what organ in the digestive system do nutrients enter the blood?
23. Name two ways waste products are removed from your body.

Essay

Write the numbers 24 and 25 on your paper. Write paragraphs with complete sentences to answer each question.

24. Describe the journey of a piece of food from the time it enters your mouth to the time when any waste products leave your body.
25. Describe what problems you might have if your brain were unable to receive messages from the nerve cells that sense odors.

ACTIVITIES FOR HOME OR SCHOOL

Projects to Do

1. Digestive juices contain acids that help you digest food. Vinegar is an acid, too. Soak several kinds of food in vinegar for a day. Use a piece of meat, a piece of bread, and a green vegetable. How does each kind of food change? Which kind of food might someone digest most easily?

2. Blindfold a friend. Ask your friend to hold his or her nose. Feed your friend a slice of an apple and a slice of an onion. Can your friend tell which is which? Then have your friend blindfold you. Try the test yourself. Which senses do you need in order to taste food?

3. Make a model of one of the organs of the body. You might use clay, papier-mâché, or some other kind of material. On a sheet of paper, write about what you can do to help keep the real organ healthy.

Information to Find

1. What does a fish heart look like? What does a reptile heart look like? A mammal heart? Use library books or an encyclopedia to find out about each one.

2. What does a nerve cell look like? In what way does its shape help it carry messages? Look in an encyclopedia to find out more about nerve cells.

3. How sharp is a dog's sense of smell? How do dogs use their sense of smell? What animals besides dogs have good senses of smell? An animal doctor might be able to answer your questions.

4. List the names of at least five organs in your body. To which body system does each organ belong? Do some organs belong to more than one body system? Library books about body systems might be a source for this information.

Books to Read

Here are some books you can look for in your school library or the public library to find more information about your body and how it grows.

Crump, Donald J. *Your Wonderful Body!* National Geographic Society.

Miller, Jonathan, and David Pelham. *The Human Body.* Viking Press.

Townsend, Anne. *Marvelous Me: All About the Human Body.* Lion Publishers.

■ *This model shows what the human brain looks like.*

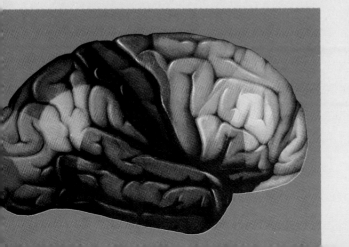

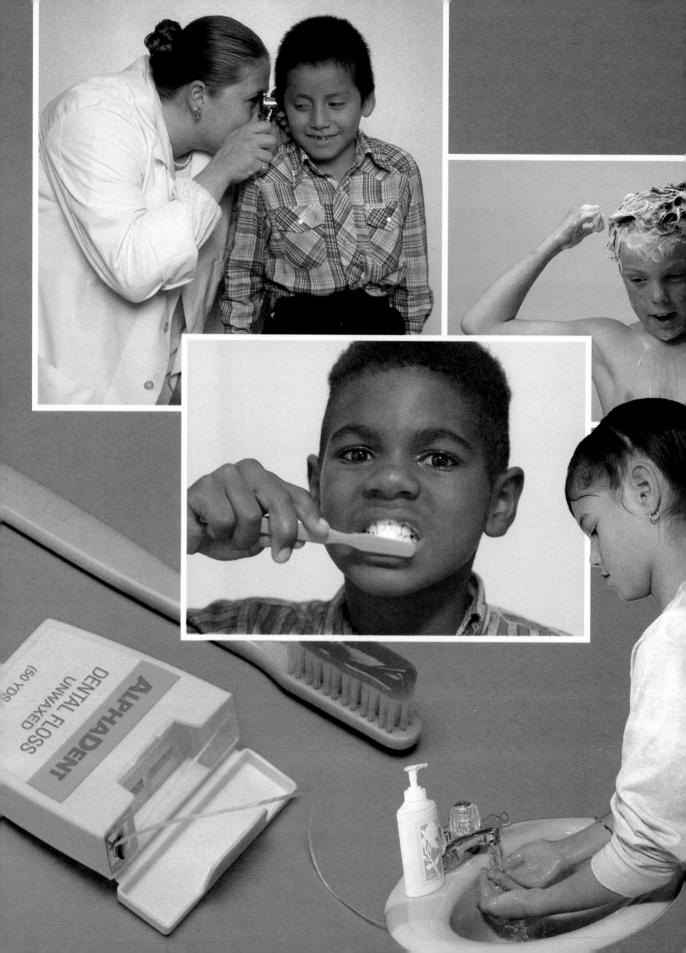

CHAPTER 3

TAKING CARE OF YOUR HEALTH

You are important to your own good health. Having good daily health habits and making use of health care helpers will help keep your body working at its best.

At one time, it was thought that only physicians, nurses, and dentists kept people healthy. Now we know that our safety and good health also depend on our own health choices. This change puts more responsibility on each of us. With good health information and health habits, you can handle the duty of keeping yourself healthy. You can also help others stay healthy.

GETTING READY TO LEARN

Key Questions

- Why is it important to learn how to care for your body?
- What can you do to have better health habits?
- How can you learn to make healthful choices in caring for your body?
- What can you do to become more responsible for taking care of your own body?

Main Chapter Sections

1 Your Teeth
2 Taking Care of Your Teeth and Gums
3 Taking Care of Your Vision
4 Taking Care of Your Hearing
5 Deciding About Health Products

1 Your Teeth

You need your teeth to eat many of the foods you enjoy. Chewing your food grinds it and begins to get it ready to be digested. You could live, of course, without your teeth. But all you could eat would be liquids and very soft foods.

Teeth are also important for the way you look. Have you ever seen a person with a missing front tooth? Often the person tries to hide it or seems to smile oddly. The way your teeth look can affect the way you feel about yourself.

KEY WORDS

incisors
cuspids
bicuspids
molars
crown
gums
root
enamel
dentin
pulp

■ *Imagine eating these foods without teeth. Teeth help you enjoy a variety of good foods.*

How Many Teeth Do You Have?

You were born with two sets of teeth. Your first set of teeth began growing in when you were about 6 months old. Those teeth were your *primary teeth*.

You had only 20 of those teeth. You probably have lost some of them already. You probably will lose the last one when you are 12 or 13.

As your first teeth are lost, your second set grows in. The new teeth are your *permanent teeth.* There are 32 teeth in the permanent set. Your first permanent tooth most likely grew in a year or two ago. You should have your full set of permanent teeth by your late teens. Ideally, your permanent teeth should last the rest of your life. If you lose one of them, your body cannot grow another. You may need a false tooth to replace it.

What Kinds of Teeth Do You Have?

You have four kinds of teeth. Each kind has a different shape and works in a different way. To chew properly, you need all four kinds.

To take a bite of most food, you use teeth in the front of your mouth. These teeth have sharp, straight edges. They are **incisors.** You have eight incisors. Four are in your upper jaw. Four are in your lower jaw.

FOR THE
CURIOUS

Not all people lose all their primary teeth. Some people have one or more primary teeth as adults.

incisors (ihn SY zuhrz), teeth with sharp, straight edges that cut your food.

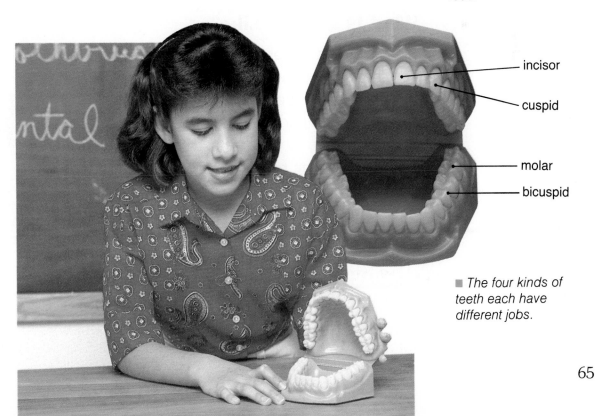

incisor

cuspid

molar

bicuspid

■ *The four kinds of teeth each have different jobs.*

65

cuspids (KUHS puhdz), teeth with one point that tear your food.

bicuspids (by KUHS puhdz), teeth with two points that grind and crush your food.

molars (MOH luhrz), wide teeth in the back of your mouth that crush and grind your food.

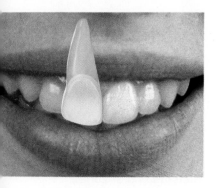

■ *Each incisor has a root that keeps the tooth in place.*

crown (KROWN), the part of a tooth you can see.

gums (GUHMZ), pink tissue around your teeth.

root (ROOT), the hidden part of a tooth.

enamel (ihn AM uhl), the hard outer layer of a tooth.

dentin (DEHNT uhn), the thick layer under the enamel.

The upper and lower incisors work together, like the blades of scissors. You use your incisors mainly to cut your food.

The teeth on both sides of the incisors tear your food. These teeth come to a point. They are called **cuspids.** You have two cuspids in your upper jaw and two in your lower jaw.

When you chew a bite of food, your tongue moves the food toward your back teeth. Some back teeth have two points. They are called **bicuspids.** You may not have any bicuspids yet. Other teeth do their job for now. In a few years, you will probably have eight bicuspids.

Your **molars** are the wide teeth in the very back of your mouth. Each molar is broad and has several points. When you chew, the upper and lower molars press against each other. They crush and grind the food between them. The more a bite of food is chewed, the more it is being broken into smaller pieces. The smaller the pieces of food, the easier they are to digest.

What Is a Tooth Like?

Smile into a mirror and look at one of your teeth. You are looking at only part of the tooth. The part you can see is called the **crown.** More than half of the tooth is hidden under your gums. Your **gums** are the pink tissue around your teeth. The hidden part of the tooth is called the **root.** The roots of your teeth are in your jawbone and are covered by pink gums.

A tooth has three layers. Each layer is different. The picture shows the different layers of a tooth.

The **enamel** is the outer layer. It is a thin, hard shell around the tooth. Enamel is even harder than bone. It protects the tooth during chewing. **Dentin** is a thick layer under the enamel. Dentin is hard, too. But it is not as hard as enamel.

66

Dentin and enamel are made by the living part of the tooth. The living part is the **pulp.** It is in a hollow space in the very middle of the tooth. The pulp is made of soft tissue and has nerves and blood vessels. The pulp keeps the rest of the tooth healthy by carrying nutrients to the tooth.

pulp (PUHLP), the soft tissue in the middle of a tooth; contains nerves and blood vessels.

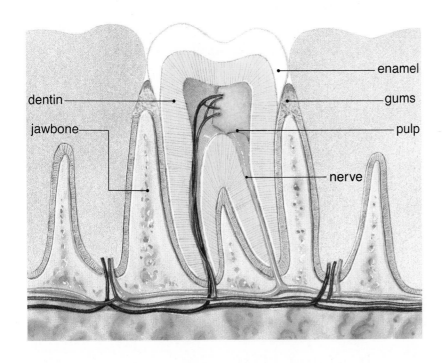

■ *Enamel and dentin protect the pulp and nerves in your teeth.*

STOP REVIEW SECTION 1

REMEMBER?

1. What are primary teeth?
2. What is your second set of teeth called?
3. Name the four kinds of teeth.
4. What are the names of the three layers of a tooth?

THINK!

5. How might you feel about your appearance if you lost a permanent incisor?
6. Why do you need to chew certain foods with your molars?

2 Taking Care of Your Teeth and Gums

decay (dih KAY), to rot.

If you do not take good care of your teeth, they can rot, or **decay**. Decayed teeth look bad. They also can cause you a lot of pain. You may even lose a tooth that is decayed. Taking good care of your teeth can help keep you from getting tooth decay.

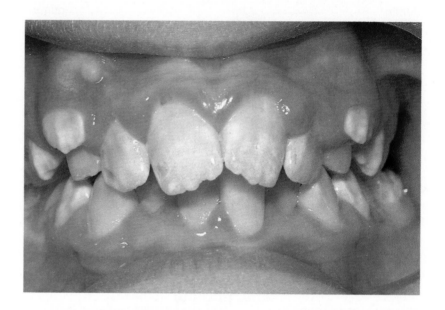

■ *Having good dental health habits may prevent permanent teeth from growing in crooked.*

You cannot chew or talk as well as you should if you are missing any of your teeth. Even if you lose only one tooth, that loss can make a difference. If you lose a permanent tooth, you cannot grow another one to take its place.

You should take good care of your primary teeth, too. They are important even though permanent teeth will take their place. If you let your primary teeth decay, they may be lost too soon. Because of this change, your permanent teeth might grow in crooked. Or your top and bottom teeth might not meet as they should. You might find it difficult to chew.

How Do Tooth and Gum Problems Happen?

Tooth decay begins after you eat. Bits of food left on and between teeth attract certain germs in your mouth. When food and germs mix, they form a clear, sticky film on your teeth. That film is called **plaque.**

Germs live in plaque, feeding on the sugar in food. The germs make an acid that can slowly decay tooth enamel. As tooth enamel is destroyed, a hole forms in your tooth. The hole is called a **cavity.** Unless it is cleaned out and filled by a dentist, a cavity will keep growing bigger and deeper. In time, the whole tooth may be destroyed.

Plaque can harm your gums, too. If plaque stays on your teeth too long, it forms calculus (tartar). **Calculus** is a hard, colored substance that collects on teeth. Calculus causes a space to form between teeth and gums.

plaque (PLAK), a clear, sticky mixture of food and germs that forms a film on teeth.

cavity (KAV uht ee), a hole that forms in a tooth because of decay.

calculus (KAL kyuh luhs), a hard, colored material that collects on teeth.

Stages of tooth decay

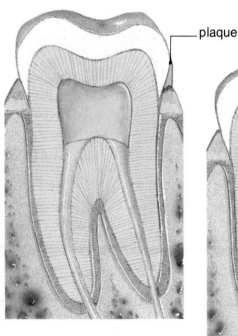

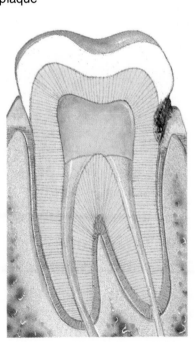
plaque

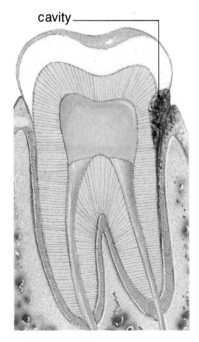
cavity

■ *Germs in plaque can eat through the enamel, dentin, and pulp of a tooth, causing a painful cavity.*

69

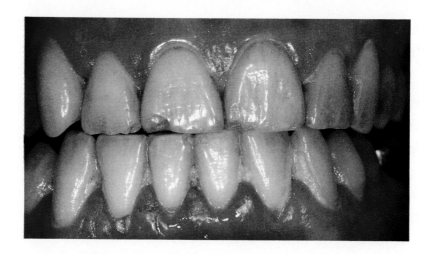

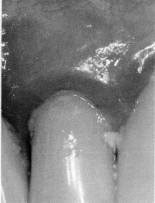

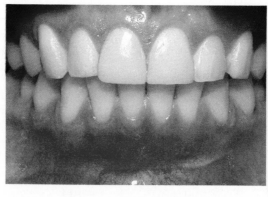

Calculus collects between teeth and gums. It allows germs to grow, causing gum trouble.

Germs grow in the space. The result can be painful gum problems.

When gums are damaged, they look red instead of pink. They often bleed when you brush your teeth. In some cases, the jawbone holding the teeth in place becomes diseased. Then the teeth become loose and may even fall out. Gum trouble often causes adults to lose healthy teeth.

Healthy gums, left, are important for keeping teeth healthy. Unhealthy gums, right, may cause teeth to become loose and fall out.

How Can You Keep Your Teeth and Gums Healthy?

Plaque causes health problems for both teeth and gums. But you can make choices to keep problems from happening. Cleaning plaque from your teeth daily is an important first step.

Look at the pictures of Jack and Martha cleaning their teeth. Jack is using toothpaste on a soft-bristled toothbrush. Martha has brushed her teeth already. Now she is using dental floss. **Dental floss** is a kind of strong thread used for cleaning between teeth. Flossing helps remove plaque and food that stick between teeth and along the edge of the gums. Dental floss can clean places that a toothbrush cannot reach.

dental floss (DEHNT uhl • FLAWS), strong thread used for cleaning between teeth.

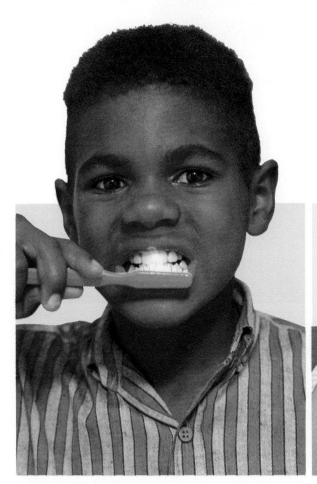

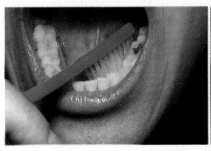
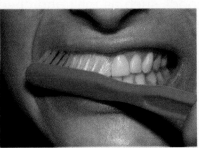

■ When Martha flosses her teeth, she cleans the spaces between her teeth and gums. When Jack brushes, he cleans the surfaces of his teeth. Holding a toothbrush at an angle is the best position for cleaning teeth.

71

You should completely clean your teeth at least once a day with a toothbrush and floss. The best time is at bedtime. You should brush your teeth after every meal, if possible. If you cannot brush after a meal, rinse your mouth with water. This will remove some of the bits of food.

■ *You should floss your teeth carefully so you do not cut your gums. Holding the floss properly (above) helps you floss properly.*

fluoride (FLUR yd), a substance that helps tooth enamel stay hard.

Your drinking water may have safe amounts of fluoride. **Fluoride** is a substance that helps tooth enamel stay hard. Your toothpaste may also have it. Fluoride helps keep tooth decay from happening. Dentists and the American Dental Association say that people of all ages should use fluoride.

Besides cleaning their teeth, Jack and Martha choose other ways to help keep their teeth healthy. They eat foods such as milk and cheese to make their teeth strong. They also try not to eat sticky foods with sugar. Jack and Martha know that eating food with sugar or having it in their mouths for a long time can harm their teeth and gums. Instead, Jack and Martha eat crunchy foods such as carrots and celery for snacks. These foods help clean their teeth as they eat.

Why Is a Dental Checkup Important?

Even when you take proper care of your teeth, you may still get a cavity. If you do not have a cavity filled right away, it can cause a toothache. But if you visit your dentist when he or she says you should, you may never get a toothache. Your dentist can find and fill a cavity when it is small. Then the cavity never becomes large.

Your dentist may have a *dental hygienist* clean your teeth and tell you how to care for them. By using special tools, the hygienist can clean your teeth better than you can.

Many people visit a dentist at least once a year. At your age, it might be wise to visit one every six months. That is because you are losing one set of teeth and growing another set. A dentist can watch out for possible problems.

Taking care of your teeth and gums is important for your health. Healthy teeth can help make you look and feel good. Healthy gums and flossed teeth also help keep your breath pleasant. If you develop a habit now of taking care of your teeth, they should last you the rest of your life.

■ *Visiting a dentist is one way you can help take good care of your health.*

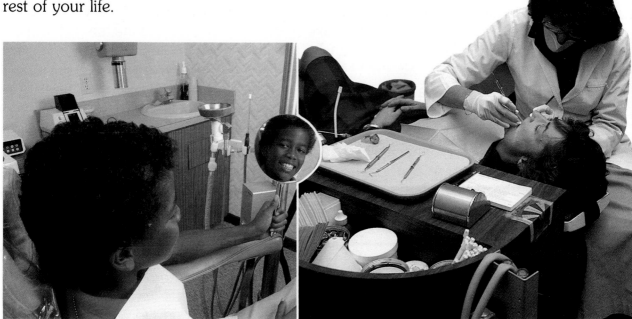

73

REMEMBER?

1. How is a cavity formed?
2. What is dental floss used for?
3. What foods help build strong teeth?
4. What kinds of foods can harm your teeth?

THINK!

5. How might you know if you have a cavity?
6. What kinds of snack foods are best for your teeth?

Health Close-up

Repairing a Tooth with Plastic

A chipped or broken tooth can ruin a nice smile. It can also cause dental problems. What can be done to make the tooth look as it did before it was damaged?

Dentists can repair a damaged front tooth in different ways. One way is called *bonding*. Bonding is a way to repair a tooth by using a substance called *resin*. Resin is a sticky liquid plastic.

Dentists can often bond a tooth without drilling into it. The enamel around the damaged part of the tooth is painted with a special liquid. This liquid makes the enamel rough, like sandpaper. Resin is then painted in layers onto the rough surface until it fills the damaged area. After the resin gets hard, the dentist polishes it to make it smooth. The tooth then looks as it did before it was damaged.

Thinking Beyond

1. How might a chipped tooth cause other health problems?
2. Why is repair important to a person with a chipped tooth?

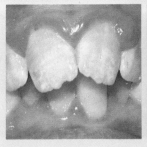
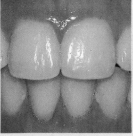

Taking Care of Your Vision

Your *eyes* are parts of your body that help you *see*. The ability to *see* is called *vision*. Knowing how your eyes work, how to care for them, and when to get an eye test will help you take care of your vision.

retina

cornea

lens

pupil

eye muscle

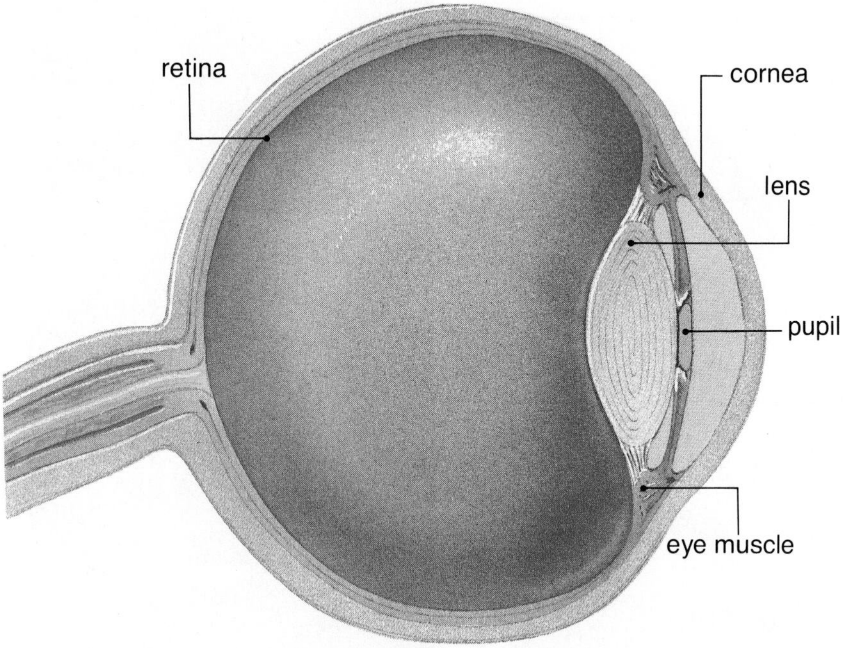

■ *The many parts of the eye work together to help you see.*

How Do Vision Problems Happen?

Your eyes work much the way a camera does. When light enters a camera, an image, or picture, is made on film. You can see only when light enters your eye. The light makes a little image of what you are looking at. The image is made on the back of your eye. When you see well, the image is sharp and clear.

In some people's eyes, the light that enters comes into focus before it reaches the back of the eye. It does so because the eye has grown too long from front to back. For such people, faraway things are not clear. Only nearby things are clear. A person with this vision problem is said to be **nearsighted.**

nearsighted (NIHR syt uhd), unable to see faraway things clearly.

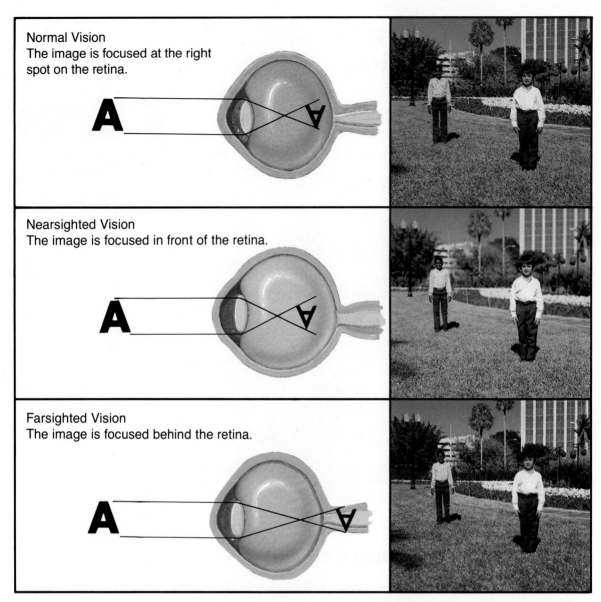

Normal Vision
The image is focused at the right spot on the retina.

Nearsighted Vision
The image is focused in front of the retina.

Farsighted Vision
The image is focused behind the retina.

In other people's eyes, the light that enters reaches the back of the eye before it comes into focus. It does so because the eye is too short from front to back. For such people, nearby things are not clear. Only faraway things are clear. A person with this vision problem is said to be **farsighted.**

Eyeglass lenses or contact lenses can correct either of those vision problems. The lenses cause the light entering each eye to focus where it should on the back of the eye. Then the person can see sharp, clear images.

farsighted (FAHR syt uhd), unable to see nearby things clearly.

What Are Some Signs of Vision Problems?

You cannot keep your eyes from becoming nearsighted or farsighted. Those problems can happen in people who take good care of their eyes. People often do not know they have such vision problems until they have their eyes tested.

Most vision problems begin very slowly. In school, students may notice they have trouble seeing the words in their books. They might also have trouble reading words written on the chalkboard.

As a vision problem becomes worse, some people will squint to change a blurry image. Some may tip their heads to find a way to see more clearly. Each action is a sign that the eyes and vision should be checked. If you happen to have any of these signs, ask to have your vision checked. Tell an adult at home, your teacher, or your school nurse. People who have their eyes checked every year or two are taking responsibility for their vision.

MYTH AND **FACT**

Myth: Blindness, or total vision loss, cannot be prevented.

Fact: As many as nine out of ten cases of blindness are unnecessary. Most eye diseases and accidents that cause blindness can be prevented by taking care of the eyes.

■ *Having your eyes checked regularly is a way to take responsibility for your vision.*

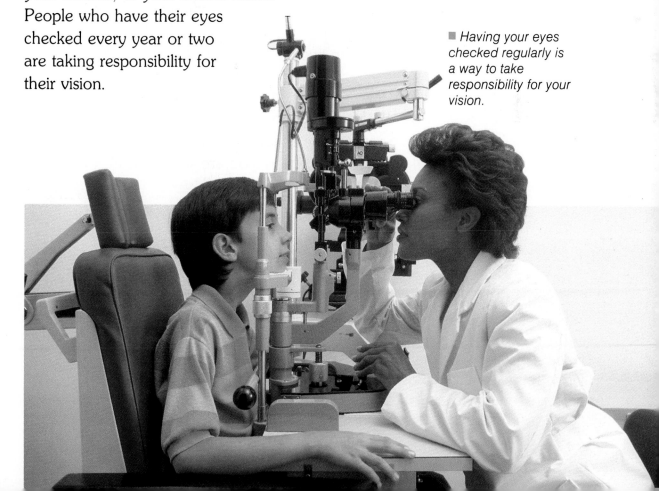

How Can You Protect Your Vision?

Taking care of your eyes is important to staying healthy. The following are some eye-care tips:

- For comfort, choose a level of light in which you can read or work without squinting. Avoid *glare,* or uncomfortably bright light.
- Wear sunglasses outdoors on bright days to stop glare that can cause eye irritation.
- Wear safety glasses or goggles when mowing the lawn or working with tools.
- If you feel as if something is in your eye, ask an adult for help. Do not try to remove it yourself. You might scratch the surface of your eye.

 **REVIEW SECTION 3**

REMEMBER?

1. How is being nearsighted different from being farsighted?
2. What are two ways to protect your vision?

THINK!

3. Why is having your eyes checked every year or two a responsible action?
4. How do you know you are seeing well?

Making Wellness Choices

Karen enjoys reading for pleasure, but she has not been reading much lately. She says that the words on the page look blurry. To make the words look clear again she needs to squint. Too much squinting gives her a headache. Karen misses not being able to enjoy her reading.

 What could she do? Explain your wellness choice.

Taking Care of Your Hearing

Your ears are the parts of your body that give you the ability to hear. If you could not hear properly, you would have trouble understanding what people were saying to you. Having good hearing is important for learning and for your safety.

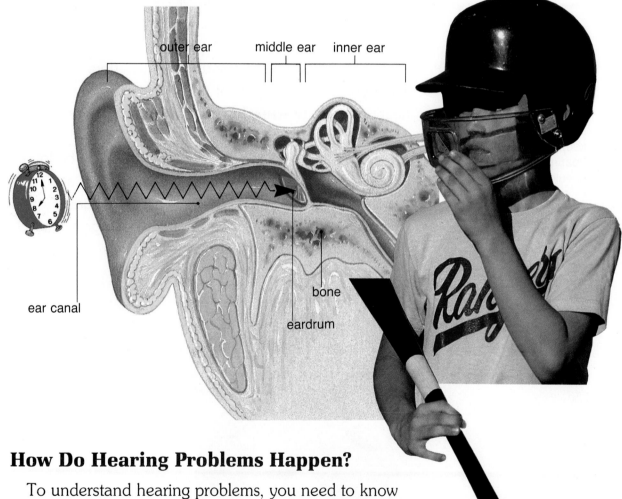

outer ear   middle ear   inner ear

ear canal

bone

eardrum

How Do Hearing Problems Happen?

To understand hearing problems, you need to know how people hear. Anything that makes a sound causes air to move in a certain way. That movement is a back-and-forth motion called *vibration*. Before you can hear a sound, a vibration of tiny bits of air must reach your outer ear. The outer ear is the part people can see.

■ *The batting helmet this boy is wearing protects the delicate structures inside his ear.*

79

eardrum (IHR druhm), a thin piece of flexible tissue that separates the outer ear from the middle ear.

The sound then passes through a tube that is called the *ear canal.* The sound pushes against your eardrum and causes it to vibrate. The **eardrum** is a thin piece of flexible tissue. It separates your outer ear from your middle ear.

A chain of three tiny bones in your middle ear picks up a vibration and passes it to your inner ear. This part of your ear has a coiled tube filled with a liquid much like seawater. The liquid picks up the vibration, changing it into a certain kind of electric signal. Nerves carry the signal to your brain. You then *hear* the sound.

Sometimes not all of a sound reaches your inner ear. Then you hear only part of the sound. You have a hearing loss. **Hearing loss** keeps you from hearing sounds as you should.

hearing loss (HIHR ihng • LAWS), a condition that keeps people from hearing sounds as they should.

earwax (IHR waks), a substance made by the ears to help protect them.

Hearing loss may last a short time, or it may be long lasting. One cause of short-term hearing loss is a buildup of earwax. **Earwax** is a substance made by your ears to protect them. It traps dust that gets inside the ear canal. Sometimes too much earwax is made.

■ *Using a special instrument, a physician can see if earwax is blocking your ear canal.*

It builds up in front of the eardrum. Then only some sounds can reach the eardrum. If this happens to you, a physician can clean your ear canal for you.

Some hearing loss is long lasting. Very loud noises, such as a firecracker blowing up near your ear, can damage the inner ear. Sounds that are not so loud can also harm the inner ear if they are heard often over a long time. For example, people who work around noisy machinery sometimes suffer hearing loss. Listening to music so loud that your ears hurt can cause hearing loss, too. Protecting your hearing is one way you can take responsibility for your own health.

■ *Keeping the volume low while listening to music may prevent hearing loss.*

What Are Some Signs of Hearing Problems?

People might not know they have a hearing loss until they have their ears tested. Like most vision problems, hearing loss can begin slowly. In school, students may at first have trouble understanding their teacher's words. As hearing loss becomes worse, voices sound blurry. Voices sound like static on a radio.

If there seems to be hearing loss, some choices need to be made. One important step is to decide to do something about it. If you have a hearing problem, you can talk with a parent, a teacher, or a school nurse and ask to have your ears tested. Your school nurse can check your hearing and inspect your ears to see if you need to see a physician. People who have their hearing checked are acting in a responsible way to care for their health.

How Can You Protect Your Hearing?

You can choose to help prevent hearing loss. You can follow these tips for ear care:

- Keep your outer ears clean. Wash only your outer ears with a wet cloth every day.
- Never stick *any object* into your ear.
- Never shout into anyone's ear. Loud noises can damage the inner ear.
- If you listen to music through headphones, keep the volume low.
- Never slap anyone on the ear. The pressure can damage the eardrum.

REVIEW
SECTION 4

REMEMBER?

1. What does an eardrum do?
2. How do the tiny bones in the middle ear help you hear?
3. What are some causes of long-lasting hearing loss?
4. What are two things you can do to protect your hearing?

THINK!

5. How might you know if you had a hearing problem?
6. Why is taking care of your hearing important to learning?

5 Deciding About Health Products

Making good choices to take care of your body helps you reach wellness. Choosing to take proper care of your body is your responsibility to yourself.

For now, your parents make most of your health choices for you. They choose your physician and your dentist. They also select most of the health products you use, such as toothpaste and soap. As you get older, adults will use more of your ideas when buying things for you. At some point, you will begin making your own choices about health products. You will want to choose wisely.

■ *You can make health decisions with a parent or guardian. Getting an adult's help can help you learn to take responsibility for your own health.*

How Can You Be a Wise Health Consumer?

A **health consumer** is someone who buys things that help take care of the body. A wise health consumer is someone who follows a plan for making choices about what to buy. You can be a wise health consumer by following these steps:

1. Find out all you can about the choices you could make.
2. Think of the results of each possible choice.
3. Make what seems to be the best choice.
4. Think about what happens as a result of your choice.

Wise health consumers know when a choice must be made. They know about the different kinds of products and services available. They also know where to get facts to make their choices. Wise health consumers depend on different sources for health facts. A young person's starting place for health facts should be a parent or other trusted adult.

■ Following these four steps can help you make wise health choices.

MAKE WISE HEALTH CHOICES
1. FIND OUT ALL YOU CAN ABOUT YOUR CHOICES.
2. THINK ABOUT THE RESULTS OF EACH POSSIBLE CHOICE.
3. MAKE WHAT SEEMS TO BE THE BEST CHOICE.
4. THINK ABOUT WHAT HAPPENS AS A RESULT OF YOUR CHOICE.

What Different Kinds of Health Products Are There?

Many of the health products your parents might buy for you are used to keep your body clean. Shampoo and soap are examples of health products that are cleaning aids.

Bandages and medicines are health products, too. They are used to treat an injury or illness. Such health products can protect your body from further harm or illness.

Most health products are either for cleaning or protecting the body. Certain kinds are for both, however. Toothpaste is a health product that can both clean and protect. While it cleans your teeth, it helps protect them from decay.

Some toothpastes are better than others at one of those jobs. Fluoride toothpastes that have been approved by the American Dental Association are best for protecting teeth from decay. A tooth-cleaning paste of baking soda and salt can clean your teeth. It does not have fluoride, however. Fluoride, you remember, is a substance that helps keep tooth enamel hard. As a wise consumer, you need to choose the product that best meets your health need for clean *and* strong teeth.

■ *There are many kinds of health products. Choosing the best products for your needs takes thought and responsibility.*

85

What Can You Learn from Labels?

A wise health consumer needs to be able to tell the difference between kinds of products that clean or protect the body. Being able to tell the difference can help you in making choices. A package label often gives you some of the facts you need.

The following helpful facts are given on most packages:

- kind of health product
- name of product
- quantity, or amount
- cost
- ingredients
- directions for use
- warnings about use

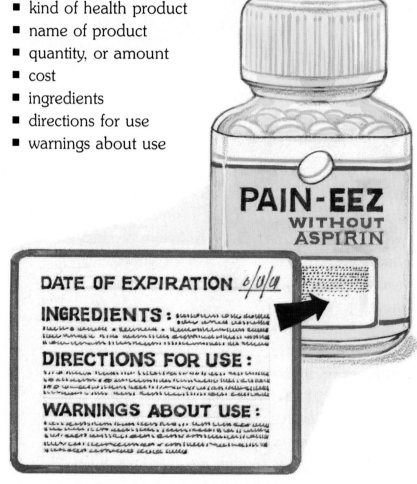

■ *A responsible health consumer always reads the labels on health products before using them.*

Some information on a package label may not be very helpful. Sometimes such words as *new, improved,* or *better than ever* are used. They tell you very little about the product or how it is to be used. Those words are there only to help sell the product. They are there to try to get you to make a certain choice.

What Can You Learn from Advertising?

Advertising is telling about something or praising something to many people. One helpful use of advertising is to make consumers aware of different and new kinds of products and services. Often the goal of advertising is to get you to switch to a new product.

Commercials on television and radio are advertising paid for by the company trying to sell a product or service. Commercials use pictures and songs to make people want to buy new things. Not all information given in commercials is helpful. Take the example of a mouthwash that is said to "kill germs."

advertising (AD vuhr tyz ihng), telling about something or praising something to many people.

commercials (kuh MUR shuhlz), forms of advertising on television or radio.

■ *When you look at an advertisement, try to learn something about the product.*

The commercial tries to make a person believe that the mouthwash meets a health need. But that may not be true. Talking to your parents about the commercials you see and hear is a way to learn how to make use of advertising.

Not all advertising is directed toward selling a product or service. Some gives consumers hints on how to stay healthy. Some tells consumers about a new health worker who lives in your community. You can use that information to become a wise health consumer. Knowing that you can learn how to use advertising wisely can help raise your self-esteem.

■ *Some kinds of advertising may not be easily understood. Asking a parent or guardian about advertisements can help you better understand them.*

88

REMEMBER?

1. What steps can you follow in making choices about health products?
2. Name two kinds of health products.
3. What helpful information is given on most health product packages?
4. Why is it important to find out as much information as you can about a health product before making a choice?
5. What is one goal of advertising?

THINK!

6. How might product labels and advertising help wise consumers?
7. Why do wise consumers base their choices on more information than just advertising?

Thinking About Your Health

How Do You Care for Your Own Health?

If you practice several daily health habits, you can increase your wellness. How do you know if you are making wise choices in caring for your health? If you say "sometimes" or "never" to any of the following statements, you might not be. You might need to talk with a parent, guardian, school nurse, or teacher about caring for your health.

- I brush my teeth at least one time each day.
- I use dental floss each day.
- I tell someone if my eyes bother me or if I cannot see well.
- I tell someone if my ears bother me or if I cannot hear well.
- I get regular dental, vision, and hearing checkups.

People in Health

An Interview with a School Nurse

Concepción "Connie" Gutierrez, R.N., knows about good health habits and about taking care of people's health. She is a school nurse in Austin, Texas.

What does the *R.N.* after your name mean?

R.N. stands for *registered nurse*. Registered nurses must take special training. They also need to pass a state nursing test. Many registered nurses work in hospitals. Some work with physicians at their offices. Others are school nurses.

How is a school nurse different from a hospital nurse?

A nurse in a hospital takes care of people who are ill or injured. As a school nurse, I work mainly with healthy children. Most school nurses test children's hearing and vision. They check on students who are absent for health reasons. Some school nurses teach health classes, like first aid and disease prevention. School nurses also help children who are hurt or not feeling well. I can judge if they need to go home to rest or see a physician. Most often I can help them feel better so they can stay in school.

What do you like most about being a school nurse?

I like it when students say, "I'm glad you're here." I like it when children feel they can trust me. Children might come to me when they are in trouble. If they have a fight, they come to talk with me. If they feel lonely or angry, they know they can talk to me. I like it when I can help children feel good, whether they are ill or not.

■ *Students who feel lonely or angry can talk to the school nurse.*

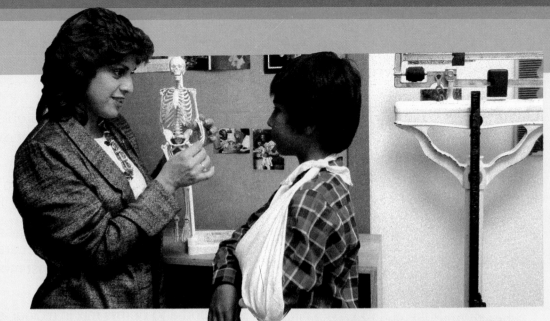

■ *School nurses test hearing and vision. They also check for other health problems.*

When did you first think about becoming a school nurse?

When I was in elementary school, I was often ill with stomach problems. My school nurse was always very kind to me. She helped me and listened to what I had to say. I wanted to grow up to be like her.

Once you were old enough, what kind of training did you need to become a nurse?

Not long ago, nurses needed only a high school diploma. They could then take training at a hospital. Today most nurses need to go to college first. I took nursing classes at the University of Texas in El Paso. After I passed the state test for nursing, I worked in a hospital for two years. Then I became a school nurse. I think it was a good idea to work in a hospital first. It helped me learn how to take care of people.

What would you tell a boy or girl who is thinking about becoming a school nurse?

I would tell him or her that the most important part of being a nurse is caring about other people. Nursing is helping other people. That is the biggest reason people become nurses. That is my reason. I wanted to care for other people.

How can a student begin to prepare to become a nurse?

When a student is in high school, he or she can become a hospital volunteer. Then the student will be able to see what nurses do every day. For anyone thinking of becoming a nurse, that is a good way to start.

Learn more about people who work as nurses in schools and hospitals. Write for information to the American Nurses' Association, 600 Maryland Avenue, S.W., Suite 100-W, Washington, DC 20024.

Main Ideas

- You can keep your teeth and gums healthy by practicing good health habits and by eating healthful foods.
- Good eye-care habits can help prevent some vision problems.
- You can prevent certain hearing problems by having good ear-care habits.
- Once you see that you need to choose a health product, you need to follow a plan for choosing which products to buy.
- Package labels and advertising of health products can help consumers by giving helpful information.
- Wise consumers do not depend on only one source of information when choosing health products.

Key Words

Write the numbers 1 to 14 in your health notebook or on a separate sheet of paper. After each number, copy the sentence and fill in the missing term. Page numbers in ( ) tell you where to look in the chapter if you need help.

decay (68)
plaque (69)
cavity (69)
calculus (69)
dental floss (71)
fluoride (72)
nearsighted (75)
farsighted (76)

eardrum (80)
hearing loss (80)
earwax (80)
health consumer (84)
advertising (87)
commercials (87)

1. Your teeth can rot, or ___?___, if you do not take good care of them.

2. A person with a vision problem in which faraway things are not clear is called ___?___ .

3. A person who is not able to hear sounds as he or she should has a ___?___ .

4. Forms of advertising that are not always helpful to a consumer are called ___?___ .

5. Food and germs mix in a clear, sticky film on your teeth called ___?___ .

6. A person with a vision problem in which nearby things are not clear is ___?___ .

7. A thin piece of flexible tissue that separates the outer ear from the middle ear is called the ___?___ .

8. A hole in a tooth is called a ___?___ .

9. A strong thread used for cleaning between teeth is called ___?___ .

10. A substance that is made by your ears to help protect them is called ___?___ .

11. Someone who buys things to help in taking care of the body is called a ___?___ .

12. A hard, colored material that collects on teeth and makes a space between the teeth and gums is called ___?___ .

13. A substance that helps tooth enamel stay hard is ___?___ .

14. In ___?___ a person tells about something in order to sell it.

Write the numbers 15 to 24 on your paper. After each number, write a sentence that defines the term. Page numbers in ( ) tell you where to look in the chapter if you need help.

15. incisors (65)   **20.** gums (66)
16. cuspids (66)   **21.** root (66)
17. bicuspids (66)   **22.** enamel (66)
18. molars (66)   **23.** dentin (66)
19. crown (66)   **24.** pulp (67)

Remembering What You Learned

Page numbers in ( ) tell you where to look in the chapter if you need help.

1. What kinds of teeth do people have? (65–66)

2. What are the five main parts of each tooth? (66–67)

3. What might cause a cavity? (69)

4. Name two products used to clean your teeth. (71)

5. What are two signs of a vision problem? (77)

6. Name three things you can do to protect your vision. (78)

7. Name two signs of a hearing problem. (81)

8. Name three things you can do to protect your hearing. (82)

9. What steps can you follow to make wise choices about health products? (84)

10. What can you learn about a product from its advertising? (88)

Thinking About What You Learned

1. What might be some results of taking good care of your teeth and gums?

2. How might you make life easier for friends or family members who have hearing problems?

3. Why does a wise consumer gather information about a product before buying it?

4. Why does a wise consumer carefully think about what is being said in advertising?

Writing About What You Learned

1. Write about how doing each of the following things could harm your teeth or gums:
   - chewing on a pen or pencil
   - chewing sweetened bubble gum
   - chewing ice
   - playing a rough sport, such as hockey or football, without mouth protection

2. Pretend you have a friend who does not want to brush or floss his or her teeth. Write a letter to your friend explaining why it is important to take good care of the teeth.

Applying What You Learned

ART

Draw pictures of the parts of a tooth, an eye, or an ear. Write the correct name for each part on the drawing.

Modified True or False

Write the numbers 1 to 15 in your health notebook or on a separate sheet of paper. After each number, write *true* or *false* to describe the sentence. If the sentence is false, also write a term that replaces the underlined term and makes the sentence true.

1. The part of a tooth that you can see is called the <u>root</u>.

2. When you use dental floss, you are trying to prevent a buildup of <u>plaque</u>.

3. Your <u>inner ear</u> is separated from your middle ear by the eardrum.

4. By developing good health habits and learning health information, you can help keep yourself <u>healthy</u>.

5. Your <u>molars</u> cut up food inside your mouth.

6. Hard, colored material that collects on teeth is <u>dentin</u>.

7. A person who must sit near the front of the class to read the chalkboard may be <u>nearsighted</u>.

8. <u>Earwax</u> is a substance made by the ear to help protect it.

9. If you listen to music through headphones, keep the volume <u>high</u>.

10. <u>Commercials</u> are a kind of advertising.

11. Soft tissue in the middle of a tooth is called <u>pulp</u>.

12. You can <u>see</u> a sound.

13. Wise health consumers depend on <u>one</u> source of information when choosing health products.

14. Fluoride is a substance that helps keep tooth <u>calculus</u> hard.

15. There are three bones in your <u>middle ear</u>.

Short Answer

Write the numbers 16 to 23 on your paper. Write a complete sentence to answer each question.

16. What are two signs of a hearing problem?

17. Describe the two sets of teeth you have.

18. What should a toothpaste do?

19. What is the difference between being nearsighted and farsighted?

20. How does plaque form?

21. What are two ways you can protect your vision?

22. What do commercials tell you about a product?

23. How does dental floss help you?

Essay

Write the numbers 24 and 25 on your paper. Write paragraphs with complete sentences to answer each question.

24. Describe how you hear sound.

25. Explain how you would go about choosing a toothpaste.

Projects to Do

1. Ask a family member to help you make a scrapbook of health advertising. Look for examples in newspapers, magazines, and fliers. Place only one ad on each page in your scrapbook. Then read each advertisement and think about answers to the following questions. What information is given? What does the advertisement say the product will do for your health? What parts of the advertisement just try to sell the product?

2. You can check your dental health habits by keeping a chart for one week. Make a chart like the one in the picture. Place it near where you keep your toothbrush. At the end of each day, fill in your chart. How did you clean your teeth after each meal? Write *b* for brushing, *f* for flossing, and *r* for rinsing. Your chart should help you see how you can improve your tooth-care habits.

Dental Health Habits	S	M	T	W	TH	F	S
Morning	b f						
Noon	r						
Night	b						

Information to Find

1. Many products are made to help protect people's health. Many are alike, and the companies that make them compete for sales. Select a health product that is made by many companies. Find advertisements for several brands. Compare the information given to see how the advertisements are alike and how they are different.

2. Why is the eardrum a delicate part of the ear? How deep is it inside the ear? How can it be protected from injury? Look for library books about the human body, and read about the ear.

3. Prepare a report for your class about fluoride and the way it helps your teeth. Look in library books about teeth, or ask your dentist for information about fluoride.

Books to Read

Here are some books and a magazine you can look for in your school library or the public library to find more information about personal health and consumer choices.

Iveson-Iveson, Joan. *Your Nose and Ears*. Franklin Watts.

Penny Power. Consumers Union of the United States. 1980–present.

Ward, Brian. *Dental Care*. Franklin Watts.

White, Laurence B., and Ray Broekel. *Optical Illusions*. Franklin Watts.

CHAPTER 4

MAKING HEALTHFUL FOOD CHOICES

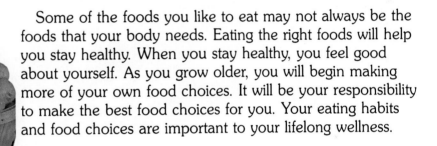

Some of the foods you like to eat may not always be the foods that your body needs. Eating the right foods will help you stay healthy. When you stay healthy, you feel good about yourself. As you grow older, you will begin making more of your own food choices. It will be your responsibility to make the best food choices for you. Your eating habits and food choices are important to your lifelong wellness.

GETTING READY TO LEARN

Key Questions

- Why is it important to learn about food?
- What can you do to have more healthful eating habits?
- How can you learn to make healthful food choices?
- What can you do to be more responsible for the foods you choose to eat?

Main Chapter Sections

1 Food Helps You Grow and Gives You Energy
2 Variety and Balance in the Foods You Eat
3 Deciding What to Eat

1 Food Helps You Grow and Gives You Energy

Daniel's parents make sure that he gets all the foods he needs to stay healthy. Like Daniel, you need food for growth, for energy, and for helping your body work as it should. The parts of food that help your body grow and work and that give you energy are called *nutrients*.

KEY WORDS

carbohydrates
fats
proteins
vitamin
minerals
fiber

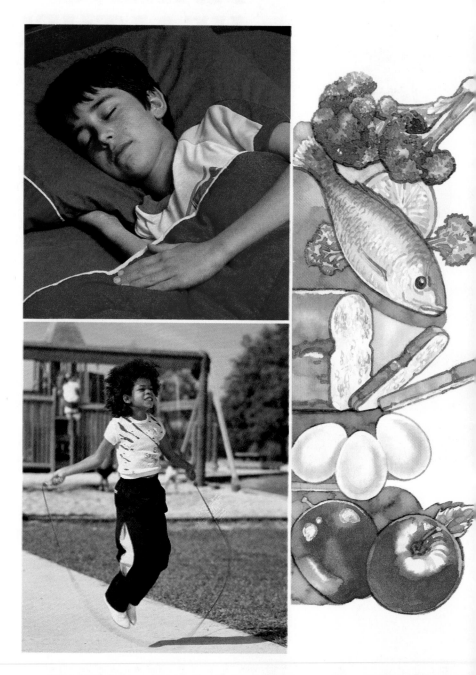

■ *You need sleep, exercise, and proper nutrients for good health. To get all the nutrients you need, you must eat many different kinds of foods.*

98

What Are the Energy Nutrients?

Three kinds of nutrients in foods give you energy. The energy nutrients are carbohydrates, fats, and proteins. You can get all the energy you need for good health by eating a variety of foods.

When Amanda drinks orange juice, she gets energy from the carbohydrates in it. **Carbohydrates** should be the nutrients that are your main source of energy each day. They give you energy to help you grow and be active. All fruits, vegetables, breads, and cereals are good sources of carbohydrates. Milk and other dairy foods also give you carbohydrates.

Fats are the nutrients that give you the greatest amount of energy. When you eat meat, eggs, and cheese, you get energy from the fats in these foods. Margarine, mayonnaise, and vegetable oil also have fats in them. Your body uses fats to provide the energy you need to be active.

Proteins are energy nutrients, too. But your body also uses proteins mainly to repair body cells and build new cells for growth. Because you are growing, you need to eat foods high in proteins every day. Meat, fish, eggs, nuts, and milk and other dairy foods all have a lot of the proteins you need.

Your body needs a variety of foods with carbohydrates, fats, and proteins. When you eat enough energy nutrients, your body can work at its best. When your body works at its best, you feel well and strong.

carbohydrates (kahr boh HY drayts), nutrients that should be your main source of energy.

fats, nutrients that give you the greatest amount of energy.

proteins (PROH teenz), energy nutrients that the body uses for growth and to repair cells.

■ *Energy nutrients in orange juice help Amanda grow and be active. But Amanda also needs fats and proteins.*

vitamin (VYT uh muhn), a nutrient that helps cause a specific reaction in the body.

How Do Vitamins and Minerals Help You?

In addition to energy nutrients, your body needs vitamins and minerals. Vitamins and minerals are nutrients, but they do not give you energy. They help your body in other ways.

Vitamins. Each **vitamin** helps cause a specific reaction in the body. Vitamins with the letter names A and C, for example, work in different ways.

Vitamin A works with other nutrients to help you see well in dim light. Vitamin A also helps your bone cells grow and stay healthy. This vitamin helps keep your skin smooth and soft, too. Vitamin C works with other nutrients to help keep your gums and other body tissues healthy.

Look at the table called "Some Vitamins for Good Health." It lists some vitamins and the foods that are good sources of these vitamins. The table also tells how different kinds of vitamins help you.

SOME VITAMINS FOR GOOD HEALTH

Vitamin	Sources	What It Does
Vitamin A	carrots, milk, sweet potatoes	helps you see in dim light; helps keep bone cells and skin healthy
Vitamin B_1	breads, pork, whole-grain cereals	helps in digestion; helps nerves work
Vitamin B_2	meat, cheese, eggs	helps cells make energy; helps keep skin and hair healthy
Vitamin B_{12}	meat, fish	helps your nervous system
Vitamin C	orange juice, broccoli, strawberries, tomatoes	helps keep your gums and other tissues healthy
Vitamin D	saltwater fish, eggs, fortified milk	helps build strong bones and teeth

SOME MINERALS FOR GOOD HEALTH

Mineral	Sources	What It Does
Calcium	milk, cheese, yogurt	builds bones and teeth; helps blood to clot
Iron	dark green vegetables, peas, beans, meat	carries oxygen in the blood
Phosphorus	meat, peas, beans, whole grains	builds bones and teeth; helps your body use energy
Potassium	baked potatoes, lima beans, oranges	helps nerves and muscles work
Zinc	eggs, seafood, grains, nuts	helps nerves and muscles work

Minerals. Minerals are another kind of nutrient your body needs to help it grow and stay healthy. **Minerals** are nutrients used by the body in doing many things. They help the body work well. Two important minerals are calcium and iron.

The body uses calcium to help build bones and teeth and to make them strong. You have more calcium in your body than any other mineral. Many foods are good sources of calcium. Drinking milk and eating cheese or yogurt give you a lot of calcium.

Iron is a mineral that is in your blood. It helps carry oxygen in your red blood cells to all your other cells. Oxygen helps your cells use the energy nutrients they need. Dark green vegetables, peas, beans, whole grains, and meat, especially liver, have iron.

The table called "Some Minerals for Good Health" lists several minerals. It lists good sources for minerals in the foods you eat or drink. The table also has information on how your body uses each of the different minerals.

minerals (MIHN uh ruhlz), nutrients such as calcium and iron that the body uses to help it grow and work.

101

How Do Water and Fiber Help Your Body?

Did you know that water is also a nutrient? Water is such an important nutrient that the body cannot live long without it. Most of your body is made of water. It is a part of every single cell. Water helps your body use other nutrients in food. It does this by breaking down the food and carrying the nutrients to where they are needed in the body.

When you drink milk or juice and even when you eat most foods, your body takes in water. Apples and many other fruits, for example, have a lot of water in them. To work well, your body needs at least 8 glasses (almost 2 liters) of water each day.

Fiber is also part of many foods you eat. **Fiber** is the "woody" substance in plants. It is needed by the body even though it cannot be digested. Fiber helps the

fiber (FY buhr), a substance that is in some food and helps keep the body's digestive system healthy.

■ You can see the water in apples when they are crushed for juice. You can feel the fiber in apples by touching their skins.

body by helping move waste through the digestive system. Fiber helps keep this body system working as it should.

Many different foods have fiber. Almost all fruits and vegetables have fiber. Fiber is also in popcorn, whole grains, and cooked dry beans and peas. If you eat some of these foods daily, you will get the fiber your body needs for good health.

■ *Fiber is found in many foods, such as celery, beans, and popcorn. Break a celery stalk in two, and see the fiber.*

STOP REVIEW SECTION 1

REMEMBER?

1. Why do you need food?
2. Which foods give you energy nutrients?
3. How are vitamins and minerals different from each other?
4. Name two foods high in fiber.

THINK!

5. Why do you need water to live?
6. How can vitamins, minerals, water, and fiber help you without giving you energy?

103

2 Variety and Balance in the Foods You Eat

diet (DY uht), the combination of foods you eat each day.

■ *How might you put the foods on this table into groups?*

How can you be sure you get the nutrients your body needs for good health? Dividing foods into food groups can help you plan your diet. Your **diet** is the combination of foods you eat each day.

What Are the Food Groups?

Terri has been asked to put the foods on the table into groups. How might she do this? Terri might group the foods by size or color. Or she might group the foods into those she likes and those she does not like. But there is another way to group foods. Terri can group foods by their nutrients. Learning why foods are grouped this way will help Terri make wise food choices now and all through her life.

Look at the picture of the foods in the pyramid. It shows how the foods you eat are divided into five

basic food groups. Each group makes up part of this food pyramid. Here are the five food groups:

- Milk, Yogurt, and Cheese Group
- Meat, Poultry, Fish, Dry Beans, Eggs, and Nuts Group
- Vegetable Group
- Fruit Group
- Bread, Cereal, Rice, and Pasta Group

Food Guide Pyramid
A Guide to Daily Food Choices

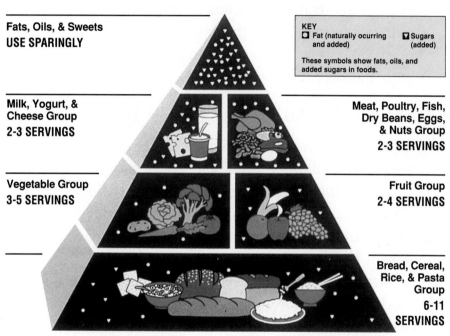

Fats, Oils, & Sweets
USE SPARINGLY

KEY
☐ Fat (naturally ocurring and added)   ▼ Sugars (added)

These symbols show fats, oils, and added sugars in foods.

Milk, Yogurt, & Cheese Group
2-3 SERVINGS

Meat, Poultry, Fish, Dry Beans, Eggs, & Nuts Group
2-3 SERVINGS

Vegetable Group
3-5 SERVINGS

Fruit Group
2-4 SERVINGS

Bread, Cereal, Rice, & Pasta Group
6-11 SERVINGS

Source: U.S. Department of Agriculture

Foods in the Fruit Group and the Vegetable Group contain carbohydrates, vitamins, minerals, and fiber. The Meat, Poultry, Fish, Dry Beans, Eggs, and Nuts Group gives you mostly proteins and fats, along with vitamins, minerals, and fiber. The Milk, Yogurt, and Cheese Group provides nutrients for building strong bones and teeth. Foods in this group are a major source of proteins, water, vitamins, and minerals—mainly calcium. The Bread, Cereal, Rice, and Pasta Group gives your body carbohydrates as well as vitamins, minerals, and fiber.

balanced diet (BAL uhnst • DY uht), the most healthful amounts of foods from the five basic food groups.

Foods from the five basic food groups need to be your first choices in planning your diet. After that, you might select a few other foods. These other foods are sometimes grouped together as the Fats, Oils, and Sweets Group. Fats, oils, and sweets have fewer nutrients than foods in the five basic food groups. Foods in the Fats, Oils, and Sweets Group are high in fats and carbohydrates but low in proteins, vitamins, and minerals. These foods include cakes, cookies, salad dressings, and sweetened soft drinks. Eating too many of these foods may keep you from eating enough nutrients from foods in the five basic groups. Eating too much fat can cause you to gain extra weight. Eating a lot of sweets can raise your chances of tooth decay.

How Can You Balance Your Diet?

The food pyramid can help you plan meals having a variety of healthful foods. You can be sure that you are getting all the nutrients you need by eating foods from all the groups. When you eat the right amounts of foods from the five basic food groups each day, you have a **balanced diet.**

Yesterday Luis ate foods from each of the five basic food groups. For breakfast Luis had a bowl of cereal, two slices of toast, half a grapefruit, and a glass of orange juice. At lunchtime Luis ate a turkey sandwich, carrots, a pear, and had a glass of milk. For dinner Luis had broiled fish, green beans, a baked potato, and a glass of milk. He enjoyed eating a muffin for dessert.

Luis tried to have a balance of nutrients needed for good health. How will Luis know that he had a balanced diet?

■ The five basic food groups can help you plan meals with variety and a balance of nutrients.

The table shows how many servings from each food group you need to eat each day to have a balanced diet. A **serving** is the amount of a food that one person would be likely to eat during a meal.

serving (SUR vihng), an amount of food someone would be likely to eat during a meal.

A GUIDE FOR DAILY FOOD CHOICES

Food Group	Number of servings	Examples of servings
Bread, Cereal, Rice, and Pasta	6– 11 servings	1 slice bread 1 ounce dry cereal 1/2 cup cooked cereal, rice or pasta
Vegetable	3– 5 servings	1 cup raw, leafy vegetables 1/2 cup cooked or chopped raw vegetables 3/4 cup vegetable juice
Fruit	2– 4 servings	1 medium-sized apple, banana, or orange 1/2 cup chopped, cooked, or canned fruit 3/4 cup fruit juice
Milk, Yogurt, and Cheese	2– 3 servings	1 cup milk or yogurt 1 1/2 ounce natural cheese 2 ounces processed cheese
Meat, Poultry, Fish, Dry Beans, Eggs, and Nuts	2– 3 servings	2–3 ounces cooked lean meat, poultry, or fish 1/2 cup cooked dry beans, 1 egg, or 2 tablespoons peanut butter count as 1 ounce lean meat

REVIEW
SECTION 2

REMEMBER?

1. What are the five basic food groups?
2. What is a person's diet?
3. What is a balanced diet?

THINK!

4. Why is it important to know about the food groups?
5. Why is it not healthy to eat just one kind of food?

Health Close-up

Pioneer Snacks

Think back to a time in history when most snacks did not come in packages. What did people eat then as snacks? To answer this question, think of some of the snack foods that children of early pioneers ate.

Pioneer children ate some of the very same snacks that you eat. They liked fresh or dried fruits, such as berries, apples, and apricots. These are foods with a variety of nutrients.

Think about the snacks you eat today. You have a much larger variety of fruits from which to choose. Pineapples, bananas, and fresh oranges would have been a real treat for pioneer children. Most of them never heard of these foods. At the time, these fruits were grown in countries far from the United States.

Another difference between today and long ago is that in the past, children could eat fruits only when they were ripe enough to be picked or after they had been dried. Because of modern ways of freezing and canning foods, you can now eat most fruits all year.

Unlike pioneer children, you have snack food choices other than fruits. You have to decide every day whether or not you should eat certain packaged snack foods. Some snack foods help you stay healthy. Others do not. Make a list of the snacks that you eat most often in one week. Are these snack foods healthful?

Thinking Beyond

1. Name two snacks you eat that pioneer children did not have.
2. How might eating certain snacks help you stay healthy?

■ *You have many more snack choices today than children in pioneer days had.*

3 Deciding What to Eat

Knowing about nutrients, food groups, and a balanced diet should help you understand why you need to eat healthful foods. It should also help you know the kinds of food you need to eat to stay healthy. But even when you know these things, making decisions about food is not always easy.

How Can You Make Wise Food Choices?

Have you ever thought about *how* people decide what food to buy or eat? Sometimes people make choices so fast that they do not think about what they are doing. Here are some steps you can follow to make wise food choices:

1. Find out all you can about the choices you could make.
2. Think of the results of each possible choice.
3. Make what seems to be the best choice.
4. Think about what happens as a result of your choice.

**REAL-LIFE
SKILL**

Making a Balanced Snack

Prepare a snack from foods in several food groups. On pieces of celery, spread peanut butter and add raisins. On other celery pieces, spread ricotta cheese made with skim milk and add a topping of unsweetened pineapple. Serve with whole-wheat crackers.

■ *People learn about foods from family, friends, and other sources of information, such as labels.*

109

Maria sees that she needs to make a choice about what to drink with her lunch. She first finds out about different drinks she could choose. She does this by gathering facts about each kind of drink. She looks at the drink list and asks herself some questions: Have I ever bought this drink before? What do I know about this drink? By answering questions such as these, Maria gets the facts she needs to make a wise choice.

Sometimes people can get more facts from a parent or friend. The more facts Maria has, the better prepared she is to make a choice. With facts, Maria can begin to think about the results of each possible choice. She asks herself, How will each drink keep me healthy?

Maria chooses the drink she thinks is best for her health. She chooses low-fat milk. When Maria tastes the low-fat milk, she says that she likes this kind of milk. Maria thinks about her choice. She seems happy with it and the way she made her choice.

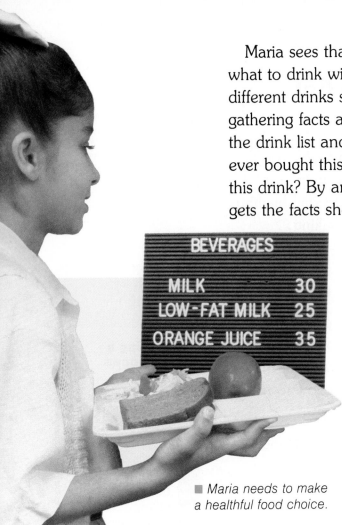

BEVERAGES

MILK · · 30
LOW-FAT MILK 25
ORANGE JUICE 35

■ *Maria needs to make a healthful food choice.*

Making Wellness Choices

Justin is preparing for a weekend outing with his Scout troop. Mr. Boles, the scoutmaster, has made plans for the outing. The troop will spend two nights at a ranch west of the city. Mr. Boles told Justin and the troop that he needs their help with the meals. They are pleased about this. It shows that Mr. Boles trusts them.

The troop will eat two dinners, two lunches, and two breakfasts on the outing. Mr. Boles asked the troop to plan meals that contain a variety of foods. The meals must also be balanced.

? What could Justin and his Scout troop plan for each meal? Explain your wellness choice.

Where Can You Find Facts About Food?

Jason goes shopping for food with his mother and father. Together, they make decisions about what their family will eat during the next several days. For example, Jason's family often decides to buy potatoes. Jason's parents know that baked potatoes have carbohydrates, minerals, and vitamins. The skin of a potato has fiber, too. Many of the food choices Jason's parents make for the family are based on what they know about the nutrients in foods.

How can you find out which nutrients are in a package of food? Look at the label. Food labels give nutrition facts.

■ *Families make many food choices each time they shop at the grocery store.*

Nutrition is the way your body uses food. Nutrition facts on food labels tell how much of each nutrient is in the food. The label also shows the serving size needed to get each amount of a nutrient.

Food labels also give information about ingredients. **Ingredients** are materials used to make the food. The ingredients are listed in a certain order. The list begins with the ingredient there is the most of. It ends with the ingredient there is the least of. The list must include everything that is in the food.

ingredients (ihn GREED ee uhnts), materials used to make a food product.

Food labels may also describe how the food can help you plan a healthful diet. The label may say "good source of fiber," "low fat," or "fat free."

Reading food labels can help you learn to choose foods you need to stay healthy.

Thinking About Your Health

Are You Making Healthful Food Choices?

How do you know if you are making wise food choices? You might not be if any of the following statements describe you. If they do, talk about improving your food choices with a parent, guardian, school nurse, or teacher.

- You eat few fresh fruits and vegetables.

- You do not eat breakfast every morning.
- You most often eat sweet cereal as your breakfast food.
- You eat only a few kinds of food.
- Sweetened soft drinks are your favorite snacks.

112

Some food package labels have more information. They tell you where the food was packaged. Many of the foods that Jason's parents buy come from places far away from their home. Fresh foods, such as potatoes, are packed in boxes or bags that show where the foods were grown. Most potatoes come from either Idaho or Maine. Most oranges come from Florida, Texas, or California. Texas onions, cabbages, watermelons, and beef are sold all over the country. So are Washington apples, Louisiana rice, Georgia peanuts, and Iowa pork.

■ *Sometimes food choices depend on where people live.*

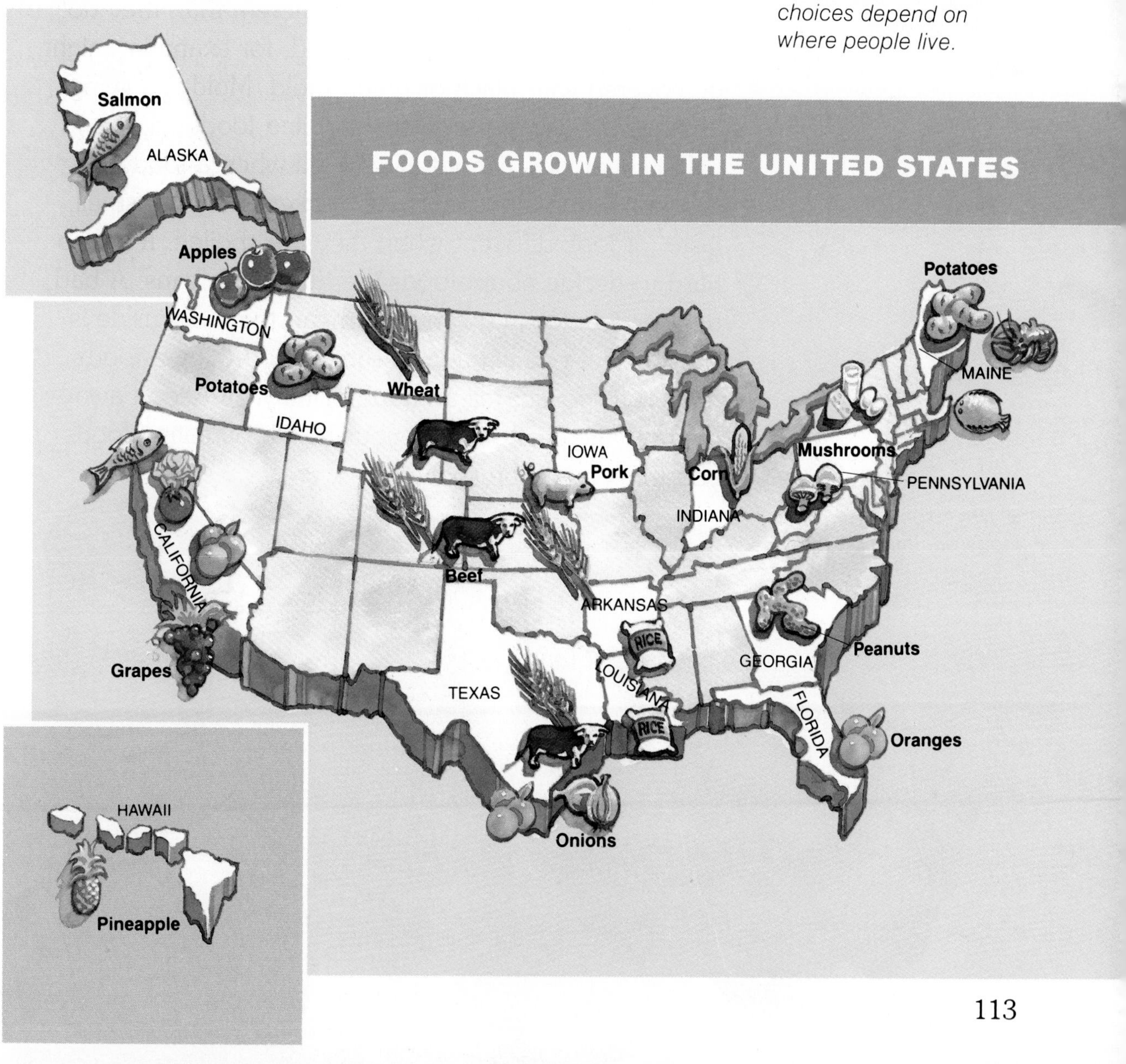

FOODS GROWN IN THE UNITED STATES

Salmon
ALASKA

Apples
WASHINGTON

Potatoes
IDAHO

Wheat

IOWA
Pork

Corn
INDIANA

Potatoes
MAINE

Mushrooms
PENNSYLVANIA

Beef

ARKANSAS

CALIFORNIA

Grapes

TEXAS

RICE
LOUISIANA

RICE

GEORGIA

Peanuts

FLORIDA

Oranges

Onions

HAWAII

Pineapple

How Can You Avoid Unsafe Foods?

Maria drinks low-fat milk at home and at school. One day she poured a glass of cold milk at home. She soon noticed that the milk did not smell as it should. Maria decided not to drink the milk. She asked her father why the milk had a bad smell. Her father smelled the milk and told Maria that it was spoiled. Spoiled food is food that is not safe to eat or drink because it can make you ill. Milk will spoil if it is not kept in a refrigerator at home and at the store.

Spoiled milk has a bad smell and does not taste good. Other spoiled foods look different than they do when they are fresh. Spoiled bread, for example, might be covered with black or green mold. Mold is a living organism that grows on some spoiled foods.

However, you cannot always tell when a food is spoiled. Some foods, such as chicken, may not smell, taste, or look different when they are spoiled. It is also hard to decide about foods that are inside cans. A bad dent or a bulge in a can may mean the food inside is spoiled, but you cannot be sure. If you think a food might be spoiled, tell an adult or throw the food away. Do not take chances with your health by eating foods you think might be spoiled.

■ Some food naturally spoils after a few days. The date printed on this carton tells you the milk should be sold on or before that date.

■ Why might these foods be unsafe to eat?

114

Food that is not handled properly can become spoiled. Here are some tips for making sure the food you will eat does not spoil:

- Always wash your hands before touching food you are preparing and before you eat.
- Always use clean eating and drinking utensils.
- Keep foods such as milk and meat in the refrigerator.
- Refrigerate leftovers right away.
- Do not eat any food that looks spoiled or smells different from the way it normally does.

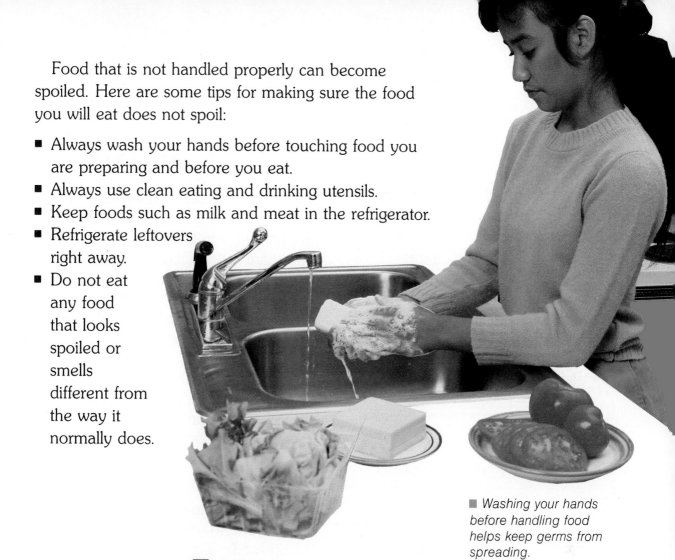

■ *Washing your hands before handling food helps keep germs from spreading.*

STOP **REVIEW SECTION 3**

REMEMBER?

1. What information do food package labels provide?
2. List in order four steps for making a wise food choice.
3. How might a can look if the food inside is spoiled?

THINK!

4. How might knowing how to read a food label help you buy wisely?
5. Suppose you bought meat, eggs, canned soup, flour, and oatmeal at the grocery store. Which of these foods need special storage when you get home? Why?

People in Health

An Interview with a Clinical Dietitian

Stephanie Mullican knows about food and good health. She is a clinical dietitian at a hospital in Orlando, Florida.

What does a clinical dietitian do?

A clinical dietitian helps people in hospitals. I work as part of a health care team to decide on the best nutrition plan for each of the patients.

■ *A clinical dietitian knows the importance of good nutrition for a healthy body.*

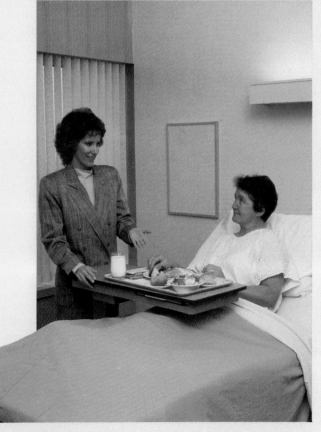

How would you describe the hardest part of your job?

Teaching about proper diet is the hardest part. Many people in hospitals are not ready to learn about diet. So we take care of their food needs for them. While they are in the hospital, we decide what they may eat. When these people go home, they are on their own. Before they leave the hospital, I visit with them and sometimes with the people who will prepare their meals at home. Teaching people about proper diet means talking about what people eat and how they prepare their food. It may change what the whole family is served.

What is the biggest surprise you have found in your work?

This would be the number of young people I see with high levels of fat in their diets. A great many young people between the ages of 9 and 11 eat a high-fat diet. It is clear to me that they do not have balanced diets. To stay healthy, they need to have a variety of foods each day.

When did you know you wanted to be a dietitian?

I first became interested in nutrition in junior high school. I suppose that was because I was overweight. I am still learning new things about food all the time. I make wiser food choices today than I did in the past.

■ *Stephanie Mullican is a clinical dietitian. She tells people that a balanced diet helps keep them healthy.*

How did you become a clinical dietitian?

I went to school at Florida State University. Then I worked as a student dietitian at a hospital in South Carolina. My job was to check all the food for the patients. I made sure that the right food went to the right person. After that, I took a national test. To become a registered dietitian, you must pass a test given by the American Dietetic Association. Even after you pass the test, you must keep taking classes. There is always something new to learn.

What subjects did you study in school?

I studied chemistry and biology to learn how the body works. I took classes about nutrition. Because food is bought and sold, I studied business and economics. I also learned how and why people make food choices. I took cooking classes, and I even learned the history of foods and eating habits.

What do you think young people should know about your job?

They should understand that a clinical dietitian is part of a larger health care team. The whole team—which includes physicians, nurses, and others—works together to help people in hospitals. A dietitian knows that it is important to live what you teach. If people are to believe what I tell them, they must see me as a good example for proper nutrition.

Learn more about people who work as dietitians in schools, hospitals, and businesses. Interview a dietitian. Or write for information to the American Dietetic Association, 216 W. Jackson Boulevard, Suite 800, Chicago, IL 60606-6995.

Main Ideas

- Your body gets the energy it needs from foods you eat.
- Different foods give your body different nutrients.
- Your body needs different kinds of nutrients to grow and stay healthy.
- You can get the nutrients you need by eating balanced meals. Balanced meals contain foods from each of the five basic food groups.
- Wise food choices need careful thought based on information and understanding.
- Deciding not to eat a food that might be spoiled is a wise food choice, too.

Key Words

Write the numbers 1 to 11 in your health notebook or on a separate sheet of paper. After each number, copy the sentence and fill in the missing term. Page numbers in ( ) tell you where to look in the chapter if you need help.

carbohydrates (99)   diet (104)
fats (99)   balanced diet
proteins (99)   (106)
vitamin (100)   serving (107)
minerals (101)   nutrition (112)
fiber (102)   ingredients (112)

1. Your _____?_____ is the food you eat each day.

2. Materials that are used to make food products are _____?_____ .

3. A substance that helps the body by moving waste through the digestive system is _____?_____ .

4. Calcium is one of many _____?_____ that your body needs.

5. A _____?_____ causes specific reactions to happen in the body.

6. The energy nutrients that your body uses to build and repair cells are _____?_____ .

7. The nutrients that should be your main source of energy are called _____?_____ .

8. The way your body uses food is called _____?_____ .

9. The nutrients that contain the most energy are _____?_____ .

10. An amount of food someone would be likely to eat during a meal is a _____?_____ .

11. When you eat the right amounts of foods from the five basic food groups each day, you have a _____?_____ .

Remembering What You Learned

Page numbers in ( ) tell you where to look in the chapter if you need help.

1. Name six kinds of nutrients you need to stay healthy. (99–102)

2. What does the nutrient found in orange juice give you? (99)

3. Name three foods that contain proteins. (99)

4. What parts of the body are helped most by vitamin A? (100)

5. What parts of the body are helped most by the mineral calcium? (101)

6. What does water do for the body? (102)

7. How does fiber help the body? (103)

8. What are the five basic food groups? (105)

9. List the number of daily servings that you need to eat from each food group to have a balanced diet. (107)

10. What are the steps you might take in making a healthful food choice? (109)

11. What two kinds of information are on most food packages? (112)

12. Describe five actions you can take to make sure the food you will eat does not spoil. (115)

Thinking About What You Learned

1. If you could design a perfect food, what would it be like?

2. What might happen to a person who ate nothing but foods from one or two food groups? Explain your answer.

3. Make up a shopping list for one day's balanced diet. Keep in mind each of the five basic food groups and the recommended number of servings for each.

4. Why is it important to know how to make wise food choices?

5. Why are food package labels important?

Writing About What You Learned

1. Interview three people about their favorite and least favorite foods. Ask the people you interview to explain their choices. In a paragraph or two, write what you learned about food choices.

2. Write an essay about why a person might choose to be a school dietitian. Use the "People in Health" interview to help organize your ideas.

Applying What You Learned

SOCIAL STUDIES

Relate foods to states and regions covered in your social studies class. Consider how geography influences people's choices of foods to buy and eat.

LANGUAGE ARTS

Take part in group discussions about snack-food choices by answering the following question: Why do many people snack on foods in the Fats, Oils, and Sweets Group?

Modified True or False

Write the numbers 1 to 15 in your health notebook or on a separate sheet of paper. After each number, write *true* or *false* to describe the sentence. If the sentence is false, also write a term that replaces the underlined term and makes the sentence true.

1. Most of your body is made of <u>fiber</u>.
2. Food that smells or tastes bad is <u>fresh</u>.
3. While you are growing, your body needs food high in <u>proteins</u>.
4. Vitamin <u>C</u> helps keep your gums and other tissues healthy.
5. Milk, cheese, and yogurt are sources of <u>calcium</u>.
6. The combination of foods you eat each day is your <u>diet</u>.
7. Carbohydrates, fats, and proteins are <u>energy</u> nutrients.
8. Iron is a <u>vitamin</u>.
9. One slice of bread is one serving from the <u>Bread, Cereal, Rice, and Pasta Group</u>.
10. <u>Water</u> is a nutrient that your body cannot live long without.
11. There are <u>five</u> basic food groups.
12. Vitamin C is found in <u>meat</u>.
13. Choosing a drink because it <u>tastes sweet</u> is a wise food choice.
14. Flour is an <u>ingredient</u> of bread.
15. The greatest amount of energy comes from foods with <u>proteins</u>.

Short Answer

Write the numbers 16 to 23 on your paper. Write a complete sentence to answer each question.

16. How does iron keep you healthy?
17. What are the steps you can follow to make wise food choices?
18. Why is it important to eat foods from all five food groups?
19. Why is an apple with peanut butter a more healthful snack than a piece of cake and a sweetened soft drink?
20. How can you get proteins without drinking milk or eating eggs?
21. Why are vitamins important to your health?
22. Name three ways you can tell that a food might be spoiled.
23. What kinds of foods might cause you to gain weight?

Essay

Write the numbers 24 and 25 on your paper. Write paragraphs with complete sentences to answer each question.

24. Amy often feels tired in class because she does not eat breakfast. Explain why a healthful breakfast may help Amy be more active.
25. John's family does not eat meat. Describe how John can still have a balanced diet without eating meat.

ACTIVITIES FOR HOME OR SCHOOL

Projects to Do

1. Ask a family member to help you make a salad that is rich in different nutrients. Look in cookbooks for ideas, or make up your own idea for a salad. Some foods you might want to use are spinach, mushrooms, tomatoes, celery, cheese, sunflower seeds, raisins, hard-boiled eggs, and cooked chicken. Choose a dressing such as oil and vinegar, or yogurt and dill, to go with the salad. Serve the salad at one of your family's meals.

2. Using a map of your state, show where different kinds of foods are grown or produced. Label each area with the name of the food and some nutritional information about the food. You might wish to bring to school samples of these foods for a classroom learning center.

3. Make a food display in the school cafeteria for younger students. Arrange food pictures on paper plates to show balanced meals. Add cutouts of healthful drinks.

Information to Find

1. Find out about the kinds of meals people ate at different times in history. How do they compare with balanced meals today? Library books about the history of food may have this information.

2. The next time you watch television or read a magazine, list the different

■ *You can pass on what you learned about nutrition by making your family a salad that is rich in nutrients.*

foods you see advertised. Decide in which food groups these foods belong. Are most of the foods in the five basic food groups?

3. Learn more about the peanut. Is it really a nut? What kinds of food products are made with peanuts? What nutrients are in peanuts?

Books to Read

Here are some books you can look for in your school library or the public library to find more information about food and nutrition.

Horwitz, Joshua. *Night Markets: Bringing Food to the City*. T. Y. Crowell.

Showers, Paul. *What Happens to a Hamburger*. Harper & Row, revised edition.

Smaridge, Norah. *What's on Your Plate?* Abingdon Press.

122

EXERCISE, REST, AND SLEEP

Fitness is for everyone. All people need healthy bodies that work at their best. People need healthy hearts and lungs. They need strong muscles and bones. People meet their fitness needs with proper exercise, posture, rest, and sleep. How you choose to meet your fitness needs can affect your health while you are young. The way you meet your fitness needs now can also affect your wellness for a lifetime.

GETTING READY TO LEARN

Key Questions

- Why is it important to learn about exercise, rest, and sleep?
- How do you feel about the ways you exercise, rest, and sleep?
- How can you learn to make healthful exercise, rest, and sleep choices?
- What can you do to have more healthful exercise, rest, and sleep habits?

Main Chapter Sections

1 Building an Active You
2 Exercising to Be Fit
3 Rest and Sleep
4 Choices You Make to Be Fit

1 Building an Active You

Think about the things you like to do at play. Do you like to run? Perhaps you like to swim, skate, or play ball with friends. All those things can be fun. Being active at play can also help you stay healthy.

What Is Exercise?

Most of Danny's days are active. She walks to school. She plays kickball at recess. During physical education class this month, her class is doing fitness training. After school she takes swimming lessons. All those activities make Danny's body work hard. Any activity that makes the body work hard is called **exercise.**

KEY WORDS

exercise
physical fitness
pulse

exercise (EHK suhr syz), any activity that makes the body work hard.

■ Exercising with your friends is fun. Exercises such as running and climbing help you stay healthy.

When your body works hard during play, you are exercising. Exercise can make your heart and other muscles strong. It makes you breathe faster and more deeply. It makes oxygen and nutrients in your blood move faster through your circulatory system to all the cells in your body.

■ *You are never too young or too old to exercise. It is good for people of all ages.*

■ *All people benefit from exercise.*

Daily play and exercise help you reach physical fitness. **Physical fitness** means having your body work the best it can. When your body works at its best, you are physically fit. Being physically fit helps you look and feel healthy. Looking and feeling healthy help you build a positive self-concept.

physical fitness (FIHZ ih kuhl • FIHT nuhs), the condition in which your body works the best that it can.

How Can Physical Fitness Help You?

Having physical fitness means you have enough energy to do your daily work. You can play in lively games without tiring too quickly. Reaching physical fitness is something you have to do yourself. You are responsible for keeping your body healthy by having it work at its best.

■ *Exercise increases the heartbeat rate, which can be measured as your pulse. A pulse is the flow of blood through certain blood vessels, such as those in the wrist.*

Your body works best when it has the energy and oxygen it needs. You get energy from nutrients in the food you eat. You get oxygen from air you breathe. Your circulatory system carries nutrients and oxygen to your cells, tissues, and organs.

Your heart pumps blood throughout your body. Active play and exercise make your heart strong. Then it can work its best. Each time your heart beats, it pushes blood through your circulatory system. A fit heart beats more slowly because it can pump more blood each time it beats. This push of blood through your blood vessels with each heartbeat creates your **pulse.**

Before Mrs. Jenkins had begun playing tennis three times a week, she counted her pulse while she was sitting quietly. She found that her heart beat about 70 times a minute. After playing tennis for three months, three or four times every week, Mrs. Jenkins has a heart rate of only 60 times a minute when she is sitting still. The slower pulse rate shows that her heart has become stronger. Regular exercise has made Mrs. Jenkins's heart muscle stronger, and she is more physically fit.

REAL-LIFE
SKILL

Taking Your Pulse

Gently press your first and second fingers against the inside of your wrist below your thumb. You should be able to feel your heart beating. Count the heartbeats you feel in one minute. This number is your pulse.

pulse (PUHLS), the push of blood through your blood vessels with each heartbeat.

🛑 **STOP** REVIEW
SECTION 1

REMEMBER?

1. Why is playing kickball exercise?
2. How is a fit heart different from a heart that is not fit?

THINK!

3. How can exercise affect your self-concept?
4. Why should exercise be an important part of your life?

Health Close-up

The Food-Exercise Connection

There is a connection between food and exercise. You can see this in many ways. One way is in your weight.

The amount and kind of food you eat and the amount and kind of exercise you get need to be in balance. If they are in balance, your weight will stay about the same. If you eat more food than your body can use, you will gain weight. You will also gain weight if you do not exercise to use the food you eat.

If you do not eat enough food, your body will use some of its stored energy nutrients, mainly fats. You will then lose weight. If you need to change your weight, you can change the amount of food you eat. You can also change the amount of exercise you get. Before making any weight changes, however, you need to talk with a parent, a guardian, your school nurse, or a physician.

Thinking Beyond

1. How might the kinds of food you eat affect your weight?
2. How can you know if the amount of food you eat and the amount of exercise you get are in balance?

■ *To maintain a healthful weight, you need a balance of diet and exercise.*

2 Exercising to Be Fit

Yoshi, Neal, and Erica exercise each day. They know that exercise helps keep their bodies physically fit. Regular exercise helps Yoshi, Neal, and Erica to be physically fit in three important ways. First, exercise makes their muscles, including their hearts, stronger. It also makes them able to be active longer without getting tired. Finally, exercise makes it easier for them to move and twist their bodies.

<table>
<tr><td>**KEY WORDS**</td></tr>
<tr><td>muscle strength
posture
endurance
aerobic exercises
flexible
warm-up
cool-down</td></tr>
</table>

How Can Muscle Strength Help You?

Yoshi rides her bicycle about 20 minutes every day. When she rides her bicycle, she has fun. She is also exercising. Exercising each day helps Yoshi build muscle strength. When you have **muscle strength,** your body is able to apply force with its muscles.

muscle strength (MUHS uhl • STREHNGTH), the ability of the body to apply force with its muscles.

By riding her bicycle, Yoshi builds strength in her leg muscles. The more Yoshi exercises her leg muscles, the stronger her muscles become. Strong leg muscles make it easier for Yoshi to ride her bicycle up hills and for long distances. Also, Yoshi's heart becomes stronger as she rides her bicycle.

■ *Some forms of exercise increase muscle strength. Bicycling strengthens Yoshi's leg muscles and her heart.*

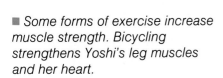

129

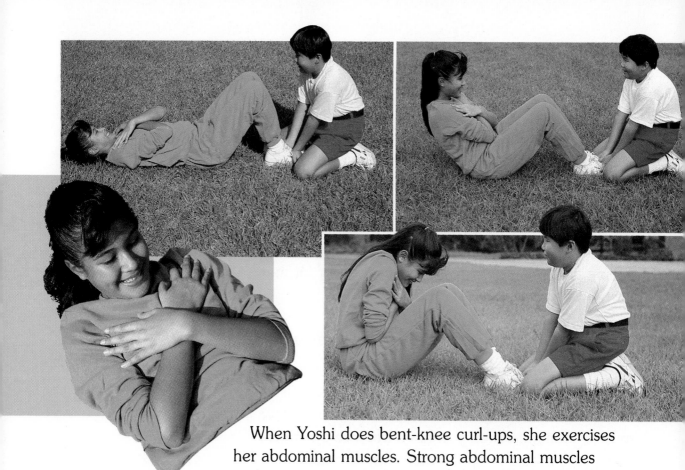

■ *Bent-knee curl-ups strengthen Yoshi's abdominal muscles.*

posture (PAHS chuhr), the way you hold your body.

When Yoshi does bent-knee curl-ups, she exercises her abdominal muscles. Strong abdominal muscles make it easier for Yoshi to sit up and lie back down again.

You need to be active in different ways to exercise different muscles. Then all your muscles become stronger.

You need strong muscles to have good posture. **Posture** is the way you hold your body. Strong muscles help hold your spine straight while you sit, walk, and stand. Strong muscles help your back and legs hold up your body weight. Good posture makes you look good. Standing, sitting, and walking with good posture also shows others that you feel good about yourself.

Weak muscles can cause poor posture. Weak muscles can get stiff easily. They can make parts of your body ache. They can also cause you to slump your shoulders or your back. Then your muscles may tire. Walking with poor posture also can make muscles sore.

Using good posture should be a daily habit. It is easier when you have strong muscles.

■ *Good posture helps you look and feel better. Poor posture shows you do not care about yourself.*

What Is Endurance?

Ten weeks ago, Neal could jump rope for only one minute. He became tired very quickly. He decided he would jump rope each day. He slowly raised the time he could jump rope to 5 minutes each day. He kept raising the time a little more each week. After eight weeks, Neal was jumping rope every day for 20 minutes without stopping.

Over the past ten weeks, Neal has improved his physical endurance. **Endurance** is the ability to be active a long time without getting too tired to keep going. Neal keeps up his endurance by jumping rope often and by being active in other ways.

Jumping rope helped build Neal's endurance by making his heart and his arm and leg muscles strong. It also helped his lungs move more air into and out of his body. The better Neal's lungs work, the better his body is able to work while exercising.

endurance (ihn DUR uhns), the ability to be active a long time without getting too tired to continue.

131

■ *Neal increases his endurance by jumping rope.*

Neal needs extra energy to jump rope for a long time. His muscles get energy from the nutrients stored in his body. As Neal jumps rope, he breathes faster and deeper. He breathes in extra oxygen. The oxygen is pumped to his muscles by a faster, stronger heartbeat (pulse). The quicker pulse sends stored nutrients to working muscles faster.

When Neal stops jumping rope, he still breathes hard, but only for a short time. Because he is doing less work, he needs less oxygen. Neal recovers quickly and breathes easily after exercising hard. He has good endurance.

Jumping rope is one of the activities that make your lungs and heart work hard. Many of these activities are fun. What other activities can make your lungs and heart work hard? Activities that cause you to breathe deeply and your heart to beat quickly for at least 20 minutes are called **aerobic exercises.** Aerobic exercises are done at a medium pace so that they can be done for a long time without stopping. Aerobic exercises help you build endurance. They make your

aerobic exercises (air OH bihk • EHK suhr syzuhz), activities that cause you to breathe deeply and your heart to beat quickly for at least 20 minutes.

132

heart, other muscles, and lungs physically fit. By doing 20 to 30 minutes of aerobic exercise at least three times a week, you can help make your body work at its best. You can develop endurance, and you can become physically fit.

■ *Distance running is another aerobic exercise that builds endurance.*

How Can Being Flexible Help You?

When Erica started learning to dance, she found it hard to bend, twist, and stretch. Her body felt stiff. Now she can move smoothly without feeling sore. Stretching before and after dancing helped Erica become more flexible. Being **flexible** means being able to move your joints easily and without tightness or pain.

Erica keeps up her flexibility by stretching before each time she dances. She sits on the floor with her legs straight. Then she bends forward. In that way, she stretches her leg muscles. Erica has learned that being flexible makes it less likely that her muscles will become sore or injured.

Stretching is part of Erica's warm-up before she dances. During a **warm-up,** you slowly start exercising.

flexible (FLEHK suh buhl), able to move your joints easily and without tightness or pain.

warm-up, activity done to start exercising slowly.

133

A five-minute warm-up gets your muscles ready to work. Stretching is part of a good warm-up. Stretching and other easy exercises increase the pulse little by little so that more blood flows to the muscles.

Erica also stretches after dancing. Stretching for five minutes after exercise acts as a cool-down activity.

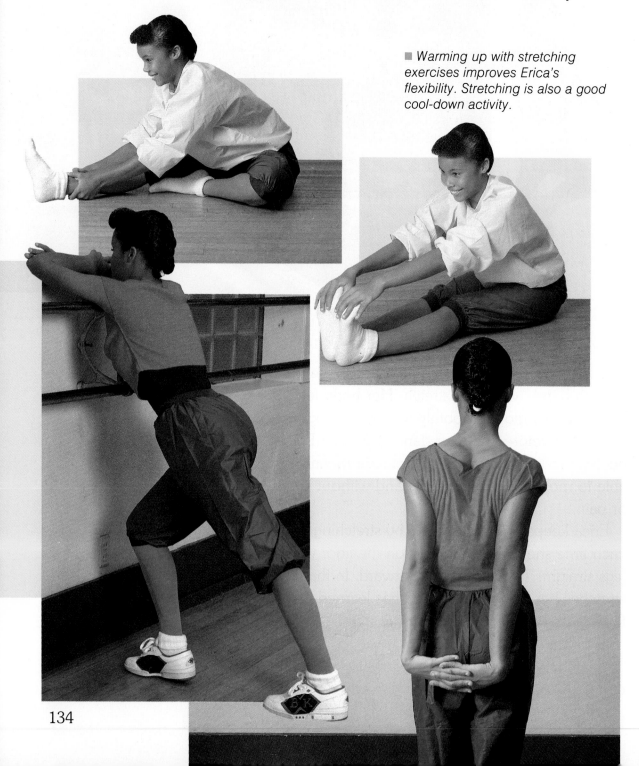

■ *Warming up with stretching exercises improves Erica's flexibility. Stretching is also a good cool-down activity.*

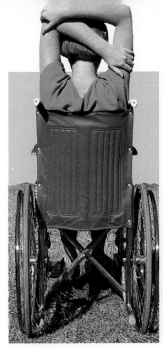

Stretching helps Melissa warm up her arms for the task of moving her wheelchair.

During a **cool-down,** you slowly stop exercising. Stretching, slowly pedaling a bicycle, or walking are good for a cool-down. A cool-down lets your muscles slowly relax as your pulse returns to normal.

You need to warm up before aerobic exercise and cool down afterwards. If you do, your play and exercise will be safer and more healthful.

cool-down, activity done when you slowly stop exercising.

STOP REVIEW SECTION 2

REMEMBER?

1. What are three important parts of fitness for everyone?
2. How do strong muscles help your posture?
3. What is the difference between a warm-up and a cool-down?

THINK!

4. How does riding a bicycle help build physical strength and endurance?
5. How might doing aerobic exercises help you become physically fit?

3 Rest and Sleep

No matter how fit you are, you still get tired. Just as your body needs regular exercise, it needs regular rest and sleep. While you rest and sleep, your body stores the energy it will use for work and play. After resting and sleeping, you have the energy you need to be active again. To help keep yourself physically fit, you need a daily balance of exercise, rest, and sleep.

Why Do You Need Rest and Quiet?

Kiyo is active most of the day. By late afternoon, she starts to feel tired. Feeling tired helps Kiyo's body protect itself from working too hard. It lets Kiyo know that her body needs rest.

When you rest, your body slows down and uses less energy. Resting gives your heart, other muscles, and lungs a chance to **relax,** or become calm. After you have been active for a long time, your muscles often get tight. They can feel sore. Resting helps your muscles relax. They loosen up and help your body get the rest it needs. As you rest, your pulse slows down, and you breathe slowly and easily.

Sitting quietly by yourself is one way of resting to relax. Other ways are reading for pleasure, playing board games with friends or parents, or even daydreaming after school.

KEY WORD

relax

■ *After an active day, Kiyo needs to rest to help relax her muscles.*

relax (rih LAKS), to become calm.

136

Every day, you also need the rest that comes only from sleep. When you sleep, your whole body rests, including your brain.

Why Do You Need Sleep?

Scientists do not know exactly why people need to sleep. But everyone must sleep for part of each day. If people go without sleep for a few days, they will become ill.

When you sleep, your whole body rests. But it does not stop working. It still uses energy, but less than when you are awake. When you sleep, your body is working to store energy for being active the next day.

You are responsible for staying fit by getting enough sleep. When you get enough sleep, you are helping to keep yourself healthy. How much sleep a person needs depends partly on age. When you were a baby, you needed more sleep than you do now. Most people your age need between 10 and 11 hours of sleep each night. Some adults need only between 5 and 6 hours of sleep.

One reason you need more sleep than older people is that you are probably more active than they are. Another reason is that your body is still growing. You need a lot of energy to be active and to grow.

■ *Sleep helps your whole body rest and store energy for the next day.*

137

REMEMBER?

1. About how many hours of sleep do people your age need each night?
2. Why do young people need more sleep than most adults?

THINK!

3. Suppose it is just after school and you feel tired. How might resting help you?
4. How might your body react to not getting enough sleep?

Thinking About Your Health

Are You Making Healthful Choices About Rest, Sleep, Posture, and Exercise?

Make a chart like the one shown here. On your chart, check off each day that you

1. take time to rest or relax during the day.
2. get at least 10 hours of sleep at night.
3. try to sit and stand straight and tall.
4. play actively for 20 to 30 minutes without stopping.

Think of yourself doing each activity. Describe on the chart how each activity affects your muscles and lungs. Think about how these activities help a person stay physically fit.

Healthful Choices Chart							
	Sunday	Monday	Tuesday	Wednesday	Thursday	Friday	Saturday
Rested + relaxed							
10-11 hours sleep							
Sit and stand tall							
Play actively 20-30 minutes							

4 Choices You Make to Be Fit

Maybe you want to play active games more often to help your body work at its best. You want to exercise more to feel good about yourself. But your body may not be used to the exercise. You need to increase the amount you exercise little by little. You need to get a good start so that you will enjoy your new health habit.

How Do You Start Exercising?

All people need active exercise. But people start exercising in different ways. Check with your parents, physical education teacher, or school nurse to find out what exercise to do and how much to do. Then increase slowly. Do just a little more exercise each day. After three or four weeks, you should be able to exercise for a longer time. You should be able to exercise for 20 to 30 minutes without resting.

If you choose the right kind of exercise, you will become stronger. You will have more endurance.

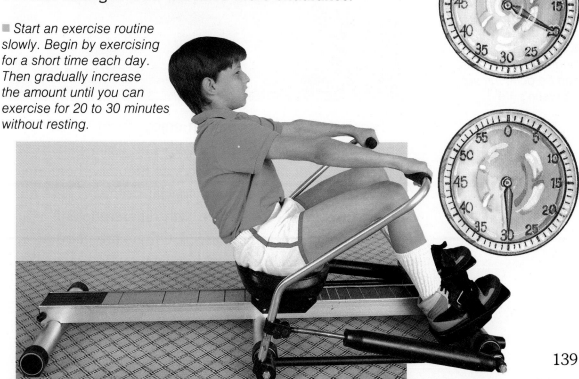

■ Start an exercise routine slowly. Begin by exercising for a short time each day. Then gradually increase the amount until you can exercise for 20 to 30 minutes without resting.

139

Making Choices About Play and Exercise

With a friend, choose a plan for regular exercise at home. Follow the steps for making choices to decide on the best kinds of activities for you. Also consider the amount of money needed for the activity.

Your body will become more flexible. It is possible to choose exercises that will help you build strength, endurance, and flexibility all at the same time. What, do you think, are some of those exercises?

Staying physically fit is an important responsibility for young people and adults. Choose activities you enjoy. Feeling good about what you do will make it easy for you to keep exercising. Some people choose activities that they will enjoy all their lives. Lynn's father learned to swim when he was in the fourth grade. He still makes time to swim several days a week. He goes swimming either before or after work. Lynn's father chose a way to stay fit that has helped him stay healthy as he grows older.

■ *Swimming is one kind of exercise that can be done throughout a person's life.*

There are exercises you can enjoy doing alone. Some exercises can be done with one other person or with a group of family members or friends. There are exercises that do not require special clothes. There are different exercises for people with different talents. Some people enjoy gymnastics. Others are good at tennis. People with physical handicaps also enjoy exercises that suit them. Some people who are blind can snow-ski. Some people in wheelchairs play basketball.

By setting a goal of daily exercise, you choose a way to stay healthy. Meeting your fitness goal will help you feel good about yourself. Exercise helps many people relax and feel good.

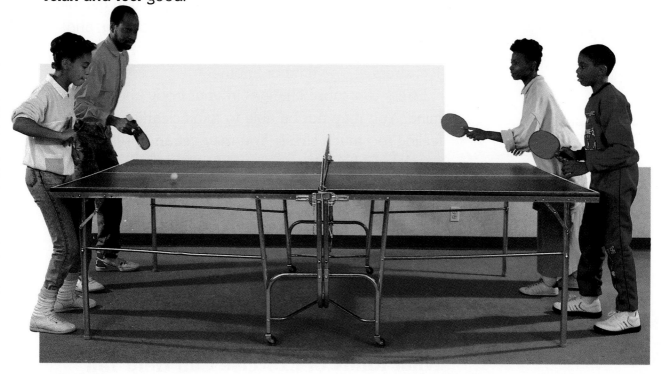

■ *Some games can be fun for the entire family, as well as help you relax.*

Making Wellness Choices

Alex is active with his classmates in physical education class. He runs, bends, and stretches. During recess he sometimes plays tag. Alex also likes to watch sports on television. He watches games on television for many hours each week. When friends ask him to play an active game, Alex always says he is too busy. Sometimes he tells his friends that he is too tired. He also says, "I don't need to play any games. I get plenty of exercise in physical education class."

? Is Alex making a wise decision? Why or why not? Explain your wellness choice.

141

How Can Exercise Help Fight Stress?

stress (STREHS), a tense feeling, as if you were about to run or fight.

Stress is a tense feeling that you get, as if you were about to run or fight. You can feel stress from things that bother you. You can feel stress when you get into an argument. You can feel stress before, during, and after an exciting time, such as a class play. All people feel stress at one time or another.

Stress can cause changes in your body and your mind. You may not be able to think clearly if you are feeling too much stress. You may get an upset stomach or a headache. Stress can make your heart beat faster than it should while you are sitting still. Your muscles may feel tight.

Exercise is a good way to ease the body changes that come from stress. It helps your body get rid of the tense feelings. Exercise can also help take your mind off what caused your stress. After exercise you feel better—more relaxed—and you can think more clearly.

What Kinds of Exercise Can Help You Build Fitness?

Lively sports are good exercise for your whole body. Riding your bicycle, running, fast walking, cross-country skiing, and swimming are all very good aerobic exercises if done for at least 20 minutes without stopping.

■ *Being upset with yourself, or with someone else, causes stress. Exercise can often get rid of stress and make you feel better.*

They make your muscles work hard. They make you breathe hard. They make your heart beat fast. They also help ease the effects of stress.

People who dance or do gymnastics build strength in addition to endurance. They become more flexible. They stretch, swing, and jump. Exercising in these ways helps keep their bodies fit.

You are responsible for helping to keep yourself healthy and fit. Choosing the best ways to keep yourself fit can help your body all your life. Being responsible for fitness habits can make you feel good about yourself.

■ *Gymnastics is a good activity to keep you fit. It builds muscle strength and endurance. It also increases flexibility.*

 **REVIEW**
SECTION 4

REMEMBER?

1. What should you do before changing your exercise habits? Why?
2. How does exercise help ease the effects of stress?

THINK!

3. What active exercises would you enjoy doing alone? With a friend? With a group?
4. Why is it important to choose physical activities that you can do all your life?

People in Health

An Interview with a Physical Education Teacher

Karen Kerley knows the importance of exercise. She is a physical education teacher at an elementary school in Schenectady, New York.

What do you do as a physical education teacher?

I teach up to eight physical education classes a day to elementary school students. I begin each class by having students do warm-up exercises. I always tell students what muscles they are warming up. That way they learn where different muscles are. After the warm-ups, I have students complete a lesson. The lesson depends on the activity or sport I am teaching that day. Some of the sports I teach during the year are cross-country running, soccer, touch football, floor hockey, basketball, and tumbling. After students have completed their day's lesson, I have them cool down by doing slower exercises. Near the end of class, I discuss with students what they have learned.

What happens to the body during exercise?

Exercise helps the blood flow faster through the heart and the rest of the body. Because the heart is a muscle, exercise makes it stronger. After a few weeks of exercise, the heart does not have to work as hard to pump blood. Also, exercise makes the lungs able to hold more air. The faster flow of blood and the greater intake of air mean more oxygen goes to the body's cells faster. Overall, exercise helps students' bodies

■ *Warming up is an important part of exercise.*

■ *Ms. Kerley enjoys teaching students how to improve their physical fitness.*

work more efficiently. That means they do not waste any effort.

How can students tell when their hearts and lungs are not wasting any effort?

If a student puts a hand to his or her chest after exercise, the student will feel that it takes less and less time for the heartbeat to return to normal. On the first day of exercise, it might take two or three minutes for the heartbeat to return to normal. After a few weeks, it may take only 30 seconds. The less time it takes the body's heartbeat and breathing to return to normal, the stronger the body is getting.

What does exercise do for students in addition to making the body fit?

Exercise often helps students build confidence in themselves. When they improve their physical condition, they often improve their self-esteem. When students see that they can practice and improve physically, they realize they can practice and improve in other areas of their lives as well. Some students will never be the best athletes in class, but at least they know they can get better at something. Also, students learn through sports to cooperate with one another. They learn to share in order to reach a goal.

What do you like most about being a physical education teacher?

I enjoy my job most when students realize that they have improved. Sometimes one student will point out the improvement in another student's skills. Other times a student might all of a sudden say, "I'm getting better!" Sometimes I can tell students feel they have improved—when I see the smiles on their faces.

Learn more about physical education teachers. Interview a physical education teacher. Or write for information to the American Alliance for Health, Physical Education, Recreation, and Dance, 1900 Association Drive, Reston, VA 22091.

Main Ideas

- Active play is exercise when it makes your body work hard.
- You can develop physical fitness through regular exercise.
- Daily exercise helps you build physical strength and endurance and helps you become flexible.
- Exercise helps make your muscles strong. Strong muscles help you have good posture.
- Rest and sleep help your body store the energy it will need for growing and being active.
- You need to develop good habits of exercise, rest, and sleep for good health all your life.
- You can help ease the effects of stress by exercising.

Key Words

Write the numbers 1 to 12 in your health notebook or on a separate sheet of paper. After each number, copy the sentence and fill in the missing term. Page numbers in ( ) tell you where to look in the chapter if you need help.

exercise (124)
physical fitness (125)
pulse (127)
muscle strength (129)
posture (130)
endurance (131)
aerobic exercises (132)
flexible (133)
warm-up (133)
cool-down (135)
relax (136)
stress (142)

1. The condition in which your body works at its best is called __?__ .

2. Your __?__ is the way you hold your body.

3. When you have __?__ , you are able to be active a long time without getting tired.

4. Any activity that makes your body work hard is __?__ .

5. Being __?__ means you can move at the joints easily.

6. During a __?__ , you slowly stop exercising.

7. Resting gives your muscles, your lungs, and your heart a chance to __?__ .

8. The push of blood through your blood vessels with each heartbeat is your __?__ .

9. The ability of the body to apply force with its muscles is __?__ .

10. Activities that cause you to breathe deeply for at least 20 minutes are __?__ .

11. A __?__ gets your muscles ready to work hard.

12. A feeling you get when something bothers you is called __?__ .

Remembering What You Learned

Page numbers in ( ) tell you where to look in the chapter if you need help.

1. How does physical fitness help your self-concept? (125)

2. List two things that a fit heart does. (127)

3. Where do your muscles get the extra energy they need during exercise? (127)

4. What are three ways that regular exercise can help your body? (129)

5. What kinds of exercise help your heart and lungs the most? (131–132)

6. What should you do right before and after exercising? (133–135)

7. How do tired feelings help your body protect itself? (136)

8. What are two ways of resting to relax? (136–137)

9. Why do young people often need more sleep than adults? (137)

10. Why is exercise a good way to ease the effects of stress? (142)

Thinking About What You Learned

1. In what ways is your need for physical fitness different from the needs of other members of your family? In what ways is it the same?

2. Suppose you have not ridden your bicycle for two weeks. You see a notice for a 10-mile (16-kilometer) bicycle ride to be held in your community. What should you do to prepare for the ride?

3. A good health goal is to have physical fitness all your life. What are some things you can do now to help yourself reach that goal?

4. Why is it important to do exercises that you enjoy?

5. How does being physically fit help your self-esteem?

Writing About What You Learned

1. Keep an exercise log for seven days. List all the kinds of exercise you get each day during the week. Maybe you walk to school or to the store. Maybe you play a team sport. Mark with the letters *S, F,* or *E* the exercises that helped your strength, flexibility, or endurance. Write three paragraphs in which you explain which exercises have helped you develop each kind of fitness.

2. Interview a handicapped person who exercises to stay physically fit. Ask what kinds of exercises help him or her stay physically fit.

Applying What You Learned

SOCIAL STUDIES

Tell how your play activities help you learn ways of getting along with others. Think about the need for rules in some games and the need for carrying out those rules.

PHYSICAL EDUCATION

List the activities you do in physical education class. Which activities help your fitness? Which activities help you learn skills for a sport?

Modified True or False

Write the numbers 1 to 15 in your health notebook or on a separate sheet of paper. After each number, write *true* or *false* to describe the sentence. If the sentence is false, also write a term that replaces the underlined term and makes the sentence true.

1. Strong muscles help your <u>posture</u>.

2. When you can move your joints easily and without pain, you are <u>fit</u>.

3. Any activity that makes your body work hard is called <u>stress</u>.

4. Riding a bicycle for 20 minutes is good <u>aerobic</u> exercise.

5. You need more <u>sleep</u> than your parents because you are growing.

6. Reading a book is one way to let your muscles <u>cool down</u>.

7. If you can run for 30 minutes without tiring, you show <u>muscle strength</u>.

8. Your <u>pulse</u> is the push of blood through your blood vessels with each heartbeat.

9. You <u>warm up</u> after you exercise.

10. You can become physically fit through <u>regular</u> exercise.

11. When you sleep, your body stores <u>energy</u>.

12. A person your age should get about <u>4 to 5</u> hours of sleep each night.

13. <u>Stress</u> makes you feel tense.

14. As you become physically fit, your pulse <u>slows</u>.

15. When your body is less active you need less <u>oxygen</u>.

Short Answer

Write the numbers 16 to 23 on your paper. Write a complete sentence to answer each question.

16. Give two ways of resting to relax.

17. Explain how aerobic exercise can lower your pulse.

18. What is the first thing to do when starting a new fitness program?

19. List two activities that will increase your flexibility.

20. Why is it important to do aerobic exercise at least three times a week?

21. How can exercising reduce stress?

22. How is your posture affected by exercise?

23. Who is most responsible for making sure you become physically fit?

Essay

Write the numbers 24 and 25 on your paper. Write paragraphs with complete sentences to answer each question.

24. Describe an exercise routine that will decrease your pulse and increase your endurance.

25. Diego's family lives in northern Alaska, where he is not able to go outside much during the winter. Describe how Diego can still get exercise year round. Include the amount of rest and sleep Diego should get as well.

Projects to Do

1. Plan a group-fitness week with your family or friends. Have each person make up a fitness exercise or event to include in the week. Try to include a variety of exercises to build endurance, strength, and flexibility.

2. Develop a plan for turning your classroom into a "Rainy-Day Fitness Center." With your class, invent an indoor marching drill that lasts 15 to 20 minutes. Use a drum or other instrument to keep rhythm.

3. Write down the number of hours of sleep you get each night for one week. Add up the figures, and then divide by seven. How many hours of sleep do you get, on the average, each night? How do you know that you are getting enough sleep?

4. Survey your class for exercise habits. Make a chart to show how many people do aerobic exercise at least three times a week. Mark on the chart the exercises that are good for endurance, strength, or flexibility.

Exercise Habits

Name	Activity	How Often	Benefits
Kim	dance	2 times/week	flexibility strength
Billy	running	3 times/week	endurance

Information to Find

1. Find out how physically fit you are compared with other fourth-grade boys and girls. Ask your physical education teacher about the FYT (*Fit Youth Today*) Program. Write the American Health and Fitness Foundation, 6225 U.S. Highway 290 East, Suite 114, Austin, TX 78723.

2. Learn more about fast walking. Find out why some people prefer fast walking to jogging or running. Use library books and magazines to help you find information on fast walking.

3. Find out about circuit training courses. What happens at the stations, or stopping places, on a circuit training course? Does your community have a course at a school or public park? If so, what does the course include?

Books to Read

Here are some books you can look for in your school library or the public library to find more information about exercise, physical fitness, rest, sleep, and posture.

Bains, Rae. *Health and Hygiene*. Troll Associates.

Richardson, Joy. *What Happens When You Sleep?* Gareth Stevens.

Vevers, Gwynne. *Your Body: Muscles and Movement*. Lothrop, Lee & Shepard.

■ *Taking a survey of how people exercise may help you form better exercise habits.*

GUARDING AGAINST DISEASE

Have you ever heard someone who is ill say, "I have a bug"? People who say that do not really mean that they have insects in their bodies. Another kind of tiny creature is making them ill. People's bodies have ways to keep out such "bugs" and to fight them.

Sometimes people have illnesses that are not caused by these tiny creatures. The body can become ill for many other reasons.

There are ways you can help keep yourself from becoming ill. Practicing good health habits is one way. To protect your wellness, you need to help your body control illness.

GETTING READY TO LEARN

Key Questions

- Why is it useful to learn about diseases?
- How well can a person avoid diseases?
- What can you do to have more healthful habits to protect yourself from disease?
- How can you take more responsibility for keeping disease from spreading?

Main Chapter Sections

1 Why People Become Ill
2 Communicable Diseases
3 Your Body Can Fight Communicable Diseases
4 Some Noncommunicable Diseases and Disorders

1 Why People Become Ill

Think of the people you see in school. Most of them go to school every day. They stay healthy most of the time. Their bodies work well more often than they do not. Your body probably works well most of the time, too. When your body is not working well, however, you feel ill.

KEY WORDS

disease
symptoms
treatment
communicable
    disease
noncommunicable
    disease
prevent
chronic
acute

■ *Your classmates stay healthy most of the time. However, sometimes illness keeps their bodies from working well.*

disease (dihz EEZ), a breakdown in the way your body works.

What Happens When Someone Gets Ill?

Sally is ill today. She has a cough and a sore throat. Her eyes are watery. Her body is warmer than usual. Sally has a disease. A **disease** is a breakdown in the way the body works. It means that some part of the body has stopped working as it should.

A disease may make a person feel discomfort and pain. A disease may cause other signs of illness.

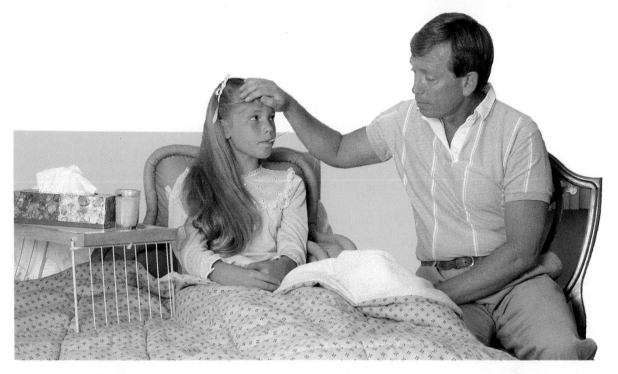

These signs of a disease are called its **symptoms.** Each disease has its own symptoms. The symptoms of a cold, for example, may be a cough, a sore throat, and a higher than normal body temperature.

When you have symptoms of a disease, you may need **treatment,** or care. Your parents might care for you at home. You might also need a physician's help. A physician can tell you what kind of disease you have. A physician can also tell your parents how to treat your disease. You might need to take medicine. Or your body might be strong enough to get well by itself in a short time.

■ *A fever is often a symptom of an illness. It is the body's way of fighting some diseases.*

symptoms (SIHMP tuhmz), signs and feelings of a disease.

treatment (TREET muhnt), care for a disease.

What Kinds of Disease Are There?

Can you remember the last time you had a cold? Did someone you know have a cold before you got yours? Did someone else you know get a cold right after you?

A cold can spread from one person to another. Your cold most likely spread from someone to you. In turn, you might have spread the cold to another person. A cold is one example of a communicable disease.

communicable disease
(kuh MYOO nih kuh buhl •
dihz EEZ), illness that
can be spread to a
person from someone or
something.

**noncommunicable
disease** (nahn kuh MYOO
nih kuh buhl • dihz EEZ),
illness that cannot be
spread from person to
person.

prevent (prih VEHNT), to
keep something from
happening.

■ *Some communicable
diseases can be spread
easily by coughing and
sneezing.*

A **communicable disease** is an illness that can be spread from person to person. Water, food, and animals can spread some communicable diseases to people.

Colds, chicken pox, and pinkeye are all communicable diseases. They can be treated by your parents, with help from the school nurse or your physician.

Not all diseases are spread from person to person. An illness or a health problem that cannot be spread from person to person is a **noncommunicable disease.** Examples of noncommunicable diseases are asthma and allergies.

Scientists who study disease do not always know why a person gets a certain noncommunicable disease. For some people, a family history of the disease is a reason. Scientists say that healthful living habits can help prevent some noncommunicable diseases. To **prevent** means to keep something from happening. Eating a balanced diet is one way to prevent certain diseases. Sleeping enough to feel rested and getting daily exercise will also help. Never smoking or chewing tobacco are two more ways of preventing many diseases.

Many diseases, such as cancer and heart disease, last a long time. Some might last for months or years. Any disease that continues for a long time, usually more than a month, is said to be **chronic.** Other diseases last a short time, usually less than a month. They are called **acute.** An earache is an acute illness. A cold is another example of an acute illness.

Scientists are always looking for ways to prevent diseases. Learning and practicing good health habits can help you protect yourself against diseases. Learning the early warning signs of diseases can help, too. Checking with a physician as soon as those early signs appear can help keep a disease under control.

chronic (KRAHN ihk), continuing for a long time, more than a month.

acute (uh KYOOT), present for a short time, a few days or weeks.

STOP

REVIEW
SECTION 1

REMEMBER?

1. When you think you have a disease, what might you need to do?
2. What is the difference between a communicable disease and a noncommunicable disease?
3. Name three healthful living habits that can help prevent some noncommunicable diseases.

THINK!

4. What is the difference between acute and chronic diseases?
5. Why would having a communicable disease keep a person from going to school?
6. How do good health habits help prevent some communicable and noncommunicable diseases?

■ *Tell a parent when you are not feeling well. A parent can decide if you need to see a physician.*

155

2 Communicable Diseases

Germs cause communicable diseases. Germs are microbes that can make you ill. **Microbes** are living things so small that they can be seen only with a microscope. Thousands of microbes would fit in a single drop of water.

Some microbes are helpful to people. Some are neither helpful nor harmful. Others can cause disease. When you have disease microbes in your body, you have an infection. An **infection** is the growth of disease microbes somewhere in your body. When your body has an infection, you can sometimes become ill.

microbes (MY krohbz), living things so small that they can be seen only with a microscope.

infection (ihn FEHK shuhn), the growth of disease microbes somewhere in your body.

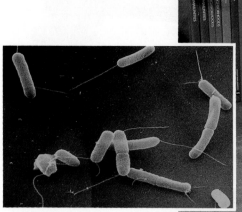

■ *Many of the microbes that cause disease, left, can be seen only with a microscope.*

What Kinds of Microbes Cause Disease?

Disease microbes can be grouped in many ways. Three main groups of disease microbes are viruses, bacteria, and fungi. Each group looks different from the others. Each kind of disease microbe in a group can cause a different communicable disease.

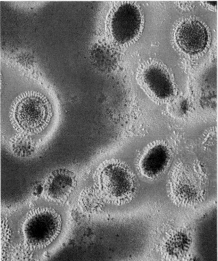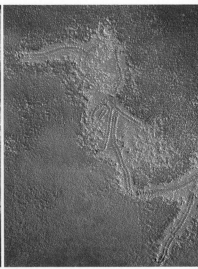

 Viruses are very small. Shown here are viruses that cause chicken pox, left; flu, center; and measles, right.

viruses (VY ruhs uhz), the smallest kind of disease microbes.

Viruses. The **viruses** make up one group of microbes. These are the smallest kind of disease microbes. A virus cannot live by itself. It needs to live inside the cells of some other creature. Some viruses live in people. Other viruses live in animals or in plants.

When a virus gets inside a living cell, it takes over the cell. It makes the cell stop doing its usual work. Instead, the cell starts making new viruses. When the cell is full of viruses, it breaks open. The viruses spill out and enter nearby healthy cells. Each of those cells then makes more viruses. In this way, one virus microbe soon turns into many virus microbes.

Some viruses cause diseases such as colds, chicken pox, and measles. Persons having some viruses that cause disease may not have any symptoms. HIV is one such virus. *HIV* stands for *human immunodeficiency virus.* This virus attacks certain blood cells and harms the body's ability to defend itself against other infections. HIV causes the disease AIDS. *AIDS* stands for *acquired immunodeficiency syndrome.* People with AIDS cannot fight off infections as well as healthy people can. These infections can be strong enough to cause a person's death.

MYTH
AND
FACT

Myth: A person can get AIDS by hugging or shaking hands.

Fact: The AIDS virus, HIV, is not spread by casual touching. People can work, play games, and attend school and parties with people who have AIDS without getting the disease.

157

bacteria (bak TIHR ee uh), very small microbes.

■ *Bacteria that cause strep throat are round. Other bacteria are rods or spirals.*

fever (FEE vuhr), a body temperature that is higher than normal.

■ *Harmful bacteria multiply very quickly inside the body. When their numbers become great, they cause signs of an illness.*

Bacteria. Other very small microbes make up a group called **bacteria.** (A single microbe of this kind is a *bacterium.*) A line of 1,000 bacteria could fit inside the period at the end of this sentence. The pictures show the different shapes of bacteria.

Bacteria are living cells. Like all living cells, bacteria need food and water to stay alive. Some bacteria need oxygen to live. Others can live where there is no oxygen.

When bacteria can meet their needs to stay alive, they grow. When one bacterium has grown to a certain size, it can divide into two cells. Then the two new cells grow and divide. They become four cells, and then the four become eight cells, and so on.

Most bacteria do not harm people. But if several of the same kind of bacteria grow in your body, an infection can develop. One kind of bacteria can cause a sore throat. Another kind of bacteria can cause an earache.

When bacteria cause an infection, you may get a fever. A **fever** is a body temperature that is higher than normal. When you have a fever, your skin may feel very warm to the touch. A fever is a useful reaction of the body. It can be an early warning sign that you are ill. A fever can slow the growth of disease microbes.

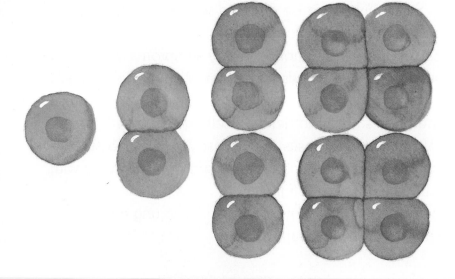

High fever, however, does more harm than good. It causes chills and weakness. It may take you longer to get better if you have an illness with a high fever.

Fungi. Microbes that live and grow like tiny plants are called **fungi**. (A single microbe of this kind is a *fungus.*) Fungi cannot move by themselves. They have to be carried by air, water, and even people. If fungi land in the right place, they can grow and multiply.

Many fungi often live together in large groups. Fungi do not need light in order to live. Some fungi grow best in warm, wet places. Others grow best in cool, dry places. Some fungi grow on or in the human body.

One fungus infection in the mouth is called *thrush.* *Athlete's foot* is a fungus infection of the skin between the toes. *Ringworm* is a skin infection caused by a kind of fungus, not a worm. Ringworm makes a circle-shaped patch, or "ring," where the fungi have infected the skin.

fungi (FUHN jy), microbes that live and grow like tiny plants.

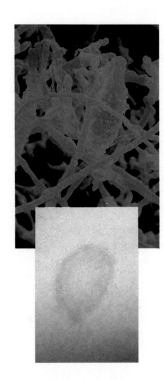

■ *Ringworm, bottom, is a skin disease caused by fungi, top. Ringworm is not caused by worms.*

SOME HUMAN DISEASES CAUSED BY MICROBES	
Microbes	**Diseases**
Viruses	AIDS chicken pox colds influenza (flu) measles
Bacteria	boils earache sore throat strep throat whooping cough (pertussis)
Fungi	athlete's foot ringworm thrush

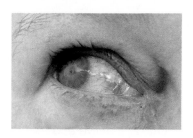

■ *Neil's eye is infected. The infection is called pinkeye. It can easily spread to other people.*

How Can People Prevent Disease?

Having a small number of disease microbes inside your body will usually not harm you. But a greater number of these microbes means a greater chance of becoming ill. Once you have found out how disease microbes are spread, you can take action to keep many of them away from your body. By knowing how microbes spread, you can help others avoid illness.

Neil had an eye infection. The infection, called *pinkeye,* was caused by bacteria. His eyes felt itchy, so he rubbed them. The bacteria got on his hands. Then they got on the chalk, the doorknobs, and the other things he touched at school.

Many of Neil's classmates touched those same things. They got pinkeye bacteria on their fingers. Then some of the classmates touched their eyes and faces. In a few days, they had pinkeye as well.

People who are ill can also breathe, sneeze, or cough disease microbes into the air and onto their hands. Then those microbes can get into your eyes, nose, and mouth. This might be the way you got your last cold. It might also be the way you spread your cold to someone else.

Making Wellness Choices

It is a warm summer day. Jason and Andrew have been playing in the park for a few hours. Jason is thirsty and wants a drink of water. The water fountains at the park are not working. Jason remembers that a stream runs through the park. Both boys walk to the stream. Andrew tells Jason it is not a good idea to drink from the stream. Jason agrees not to drink the water but wants to rinse his mouth out with it.

? Did Jason make a wise decision? Why or why not? What should the boys do? Explain your wellness choice.

Disease microbes can get into different systems of the body. A person might breathe in disease microbes through the respiratory system. Disease microbes might enter the circulatory system through a cut in the skin. A person putting a finger into his or her mouth might be putting disease microbes into the digestive system. Disease microbes can enter adults' bodies through intimate body contact.

If you are ill, you can avoid spreading your disease to others. You can stay home until you are well. You can be careful not to give food to anyone after you have touched it or started to eat it. You can make sure to wash your hands after using the rest room or after covering a cough. You can cover your mouth with a tissue when you cough or sneeze. Then you can put the tissue into the trash so that no one else handles it. You can be careful to keep your mouth off the drinking fountain spout. Tell your teacher if the fountain does not arch the water high enough for you to drink without touching the spout.

 **REVIEW SECTION 2**

REMEMBER?

1. What might happen if disease microbes enter your body?
2. What needs to happen in your body before an infection caused by bacteria can occur?
3. What are four actions you can take to prevent spreading disease microbes?

THINK!

4. Why should you be careful not to drink from the same glass that someone else used, even when you are both healthy?
5. Why can a fever be helpful to the body?

■ Using and disposing of tissues properly and washing your hands can stop the spread of some communicable diseases.

161

Avoiding Disease Microbes

Microbes are everywhere. Disease microbes can be spread in many ways. Communicable diseases can be spread by people. Water, food, animals, and insects can also spread disease to people.

You can avoid many diseases by drinking water that you know is safe. Ask your parents if your water at home comes from a community system or a well. The disease microbes in most community water systems have been killed. Health workers in your community can test the safety of water from wells.

Sometimes disease microbes grow on food. They can cause the food to spoil. You should eat only food that you know is safe. Do not eat any food that looks spoiled or smells different from the way it normally does. Some foods have disease microbes or chemicals on them when you buy them. You need to wash fresh fruits and vegetables before you eat them.

Animals and insects spread many diseases by biting people or other animals. Even healthy animals carry microbes in their mouths. Some animals, such as dogs, cats, and squirrels can spread rabies. Rabies is a dangerous disease that can be spread by animal bites. If any animal ever bites you, tell your parents or another adult at once. Wash the cut with soap and water. You may need to see a physician quickly.

Some insects, such as mosquitoes and ticks, can carry disease microbes in their bodies. If they bite you, they can put microbes into your body. Houseflies do not bite. But they are often covered with microbes. They shake off disease microbes anyplace they go. Try not to let flies land on your food or on anything else you put into your mouth.

Thinking Beyond

1. How might disease microbes from spoiled chicken enter your body?
2. How might disease microbes from a tick enter your body?

■ *Insects can spread certain diseases, so you need to wash fresh fruits and vegetables before eating them.*

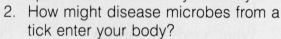

SECTION 3 Your Body Can Fight Communicable Diseases

Brandon, Heather, and Carter are classmates. They are friends, too. They play together after school and on most weekends. One day Carter was not at school. Mr. Thomas, their teacher, told the class that Carter was ill with chicken pox. "Chicken pox is a communicable disease caused by a virus," Mr. Thomas said.

Two weeks later, Heather became ill with chicken pox. As more weeks passed, other children in Mr. Thomas's class became ill, too. Brandon, however, did not get chicken pox. Why, do you think, did Brandon not become ill?

KEY WORDS

immunity
antibodies
vaccines
resistance

How Does Your Body Defend Itself Against Disease?

Your body has ways to defend itself against disease microbes. If these microbes enter your blood, your body's inner defenses go to work. **Immunity** is your body's ability to defend itself against certain kinds of microbes. You become immune to one disease at a time.

immunity (ihm YOO nuht ee), your body's ability to defend itself against certain kinds of diseases.

■ A disease such as chicken pox can affect many students in the same class.

163

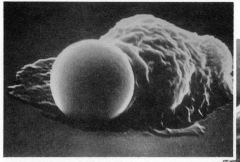

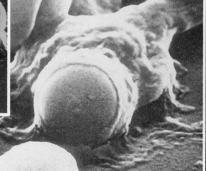

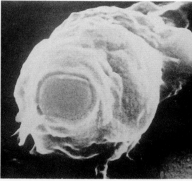

■ *This white blood cell is fighting disease by destroying a disease microbe.*

Your body's immunity depends partly on your white blood cells. White blood cells are always present in your blood. They work to destroy disease microbes before the microbes can make you ill. If you get an infection, your body makes more white blood cells. They move in your blood to the part of your body that is infected.

Sometimes disease microbes enter your body, and your white blood cells, working alone, cannot destroy them. When this happens, your body uses another defense against disease microbes. This defense uses antibodies. **Antibodies** are chemicals that help defend the body against certain diseases.

Antibodies work with one kind of white blood cell to destroy disease microbes. The antibodies cling to the disease microbes. Then the antibodies send out signals to a certain kind of white blood cell. Those white blood cells then surround and destroy the disease microbes.

Each antibody acts against only one kind of disease microbe. It cannot act against any other kind. For example, if you have chicken pox, your white blood cells will make antibodies just for the chicken-pox virus. These antibodies can cling only to the chicken-pox virus. They can also protect you from the chicken-pox virus for the rest of your life.

After you are well, some of the antibodies stay in your blood. Months or years later, disease microbes of the same kind may enter your body again. This time your body will be prepared. It already has the antibodies needed to stop an infection. You will have immunity to the disease caused by those microbes.

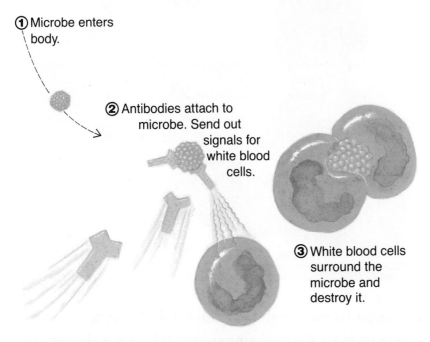

① Microbe enters body.

② Antibodies attach to microbe. Send out signals for white blood cells.

③ White blood cells surround the microbe and destroy it.

■ *Antibodies are always at work destroying harmful microbes that enter your body.*

What Can You Do to Build Up Your Body's Defenses Against Disease?

Substances called **vaccines** can help you form immunity to some communicable diseases without your having the disease itself. The vaccine against polio is swallowed. Other vaccines are given as *injections*, or "shots."

Each vaccine will protect you from only one disease. For example, you need one kind of vaccine for polio, another kind for measles, and still another kind for mumps. However, two or three kinds of vaccines may be given together in one injection. There are no vaccines yet for some diseases, such as AIDS or colds. A chicken-pox vaccine has been made, but it is not yet widely used.

vaccines (vak SEENZ), substances made to help you form immunity to some communicable diseases.

165

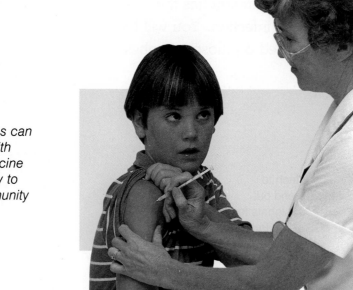

■ *Some diseases can be prevented with vaccines. A vaccine causes the body to produce an immunity to the disease.*

resistance (rih ZIHS tuhns), the ability of your body to fight disease microbes by itself.

Some vaccines can give you immunity to a disease all your life. Others give you immunity for a shorter time. You will need a *booster* of those vaccines. That is, your physician will have to give you the vaccine again in a few years. More vaccine will be needed to boost your immunity, which may have become weak by that time.

Vaccines have been made only for certain diseases. But your body can fight against all diseases better if it has resistance. **Resistance** is the ability of your body to fight disease microbes by itself.

Good health habits can help you build your resistance. You need a balanced diet and plenty of water each day. You also need exercise and enough sleep to feel healthy every day. If you have good health habits, you may avoid getting some diseases. You are taking responsibility for staying healthy.

REMEMBER?

1. What is immunity?
2. How do antibodies protect your health?
3. How do vaccines protect your health?

THINK!

4. Why did you need to receive certain vaccines before you could start school for the first time?
5. How can good health habits help protect you from disease?

Thinking About Your Health

Are You Doing All You Can to Stop the Spread of Colds?

At the top of a sheet of paper, write the title "How I Can Help Stop the Spread of Colds." Divide the page into four columns, and write the following headings at the tops of the columns. Under each heading, follow the instructions given.

1. ACTIONS I MUST TAKE. List the actions you need to take to meet your goal of stopping the spread of colds.
2. PROBLEMS I MAY FACE. List the things that might interfere with each action you plan to take.
3. HOW TO HANDLE PROBLEMS. List the ways you might handle the problems you may face in each action you plan to take.

4. WHO CAN HELP ME. List people who might help you handle the problems you may face in each action you plan to take.

Try the ideas you have listed to meet your goal of helping stop the spread of communicable disease.

How I Can Help Stop the Spread of Colds			
ACTIONS I MUST TAKE	PROBLEMS I MAY FACE	HOW TO HANDLE PROBLEMS	WHO CAN HELP ME

167

4 Some Noncommunicable Diseases and Disorders

disorders (dihs AWRD uhrz), noncommunicable health problems that may appear at birth or later in life.

There are many kinds of noncommunicable diseases. There are also noncommunicable health problems that are not diseases. They are called **disorders.** Some disorders, such as being blind, may appear at birth. Other disorders may not affect people until sometime later in their lives. Noncommunicable health problems do not spread from one person to another.

What Are the Dangers of Heart Diseases and Disorders?

Heart diseases kill more adults in the United States than any other noncommunicable disease. Some people are more likely than others to have heart diseases. High blood pressure and too much fat in the blood may lead to one kind of heart disease. Scientists believe that certain poor health habits also lead to other heart diseases.

■ *This heart has a normal artery. If the artery were blocked, however, a heart disease might develop. Learning how diet and exercise affect your heart can help you stay healthy.*

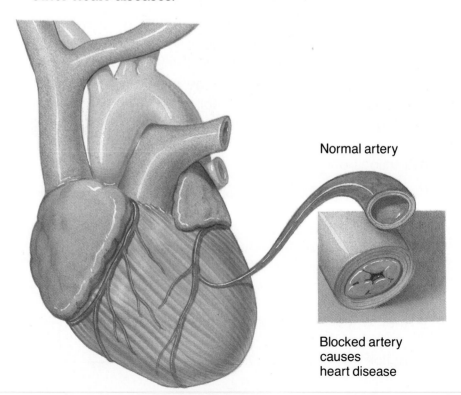

Normal artery

Blocked artery causes heart disease

Heart diseases often take a long time to appear. Sometimes these diseases appear sooner because of poor health habits. Certain health habits also add to the chances of getting a heart disease. People who smoke cigarettes, for example, are more likely to get a heart disease than those who do not smoke. People who eat a high-fat diet or do not exercise enough are also more likely to get a heart disease.

Some people are born with heart disorders. A heart murmur may be a sign of a heart disorder. A *heart murmur* is a sound that is not usually made by a healthy heart. The sound may be made by a heart valve that does not close tightly. Many heart murmurs in children are just normal sounds for a young heart.

What Is Cancer?

Cancer is a kind of noncommunicable disease that can damage any part of the body. Nearly half a million people in the United States die from cancer each year. Many people who have cancer can be treated for it. If cancer is treated early, the person may get well again.

There are about two hundred different kinds of cancer. All kinds of cancer begin with one harmful cell. Scientists are not sure why cancer cells start to grow. Cancer cells grow faster and divide sooner than healthy cells. Cancer cells form lumps. These lumps then grow in place of other healthy cells. Cancer cells keep a healthy cell from working. Not all body lumps are signs of cancer. All lumps need to be checked by a physician.

Cancer can grow in people of any age. But some people are more likely to get cancer than other people. Sometimes several members of one family will get a certain cancer. People who use tobacco products are much more likely to get cancer of the mouth, throat, or lungs than people who do not. People who work with certain chemicals risk getting certain kinds of cancer.

cancer (KAN suhr), a kind of noncommunicable disease caused by one kind of cell growing out of control.

■ *Special clothing can protect workers from cancer-causing materials.*

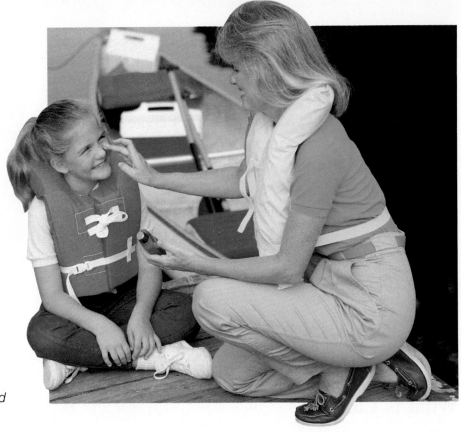

■ *Using a sunscreen protects your skin and may prevent certain kinds of skin cancer.*

Some kinds of cancer are easy to prevent. Skin cancer, for example, is caused by getting too much sun. Being responsible for your health by protecting your skin from the sun may help you prevent skin cancer.

What Are Allergies?

allergy (AL uhr jee), a noncommunicable disorder in which a person has a negative reaction to a certain thing.

One kind of disorder many people have is an allergy. An **allergy** is a noncommunicable disorder in which a person is bothered by a certain thing, such as dust, tiny parts of plants, insect stings, animal hair, or certain foods or chemicals. Something that causes an allergic reaction in a person may not bother most other people. An allergy can come about at any age. The symptoms of an allergy may happen at any time.

Hay fever is really an allergy. Some people are allergic to tiny parts of plants. The parts float in the air. A person with hay fever will have symptoms after

170

 Some people are allergic to certain foods or certain kinds of cloth.

 Poison ivy is a plant that causes allergy symptoms in most people.

breathing in those tiny parts. Some symptoms are sneezing, red eyes, and a runny nose. People with hay fever or other allergies can be treated by a physician. A physician can order medicines to help ease the symptoms of hay fever.

A rash from poison ivy is really an allergy symptom. It is not poisoning. A person who has an allergy to the poison ivy plant can have a rash. A physician may need to help the person if the rash does not go away in a few days.

STOP ## REVIEW
SECTION 4

REMEMBER?

1. What are two possible causes of heart diseases?
2. How does cancer begin?
3. What kinds of things may cause reactions in people with allergies?

THINK!

4. What are some good health habits you can follow to help prevent heart disease?
5. Why do cancer and heart diseases cause so many deaths?

People in Health

An Interview with a Cancer Researcher

Philip A. Pizzo helps children who are ill with cancer. He is a cancer researcher at the National Cancer Institute in Bethesda, Maryland.

What does a cancer researcher do?

A cancer researcher tries to understand cancer. He or she studies why cancer happens and what can be done to prevent it and treat it.

■ *Dr. Pizzo helps young people who have cancer.*

How have cancer researchers helped children?

They have helped save the lives of many children. The cancer most often seen in children is called *leukemia*. Leukemia is cancer of the blood cells. Not long ago, most children who had leukemia died as a result of it. Some died as soon as three months after becoming ill. Today, more than half of the children with leukemia are cured. They go on to lead normal lives. This change came about because of cancer research.

How have cancer researchers saved lives?

Cancer researchers have made many different medicines that fight cancer cells. They have also learned how to treat people with these medicines. This kind of treatment is called drug therapy, or *chemotherapy*.

When did you know you wanted to study cancer?

I decided to go into cancer research when I was a young physician. While I worked in a hospital, I was learning about noncommunicable diseases that affect children. I saw children who had cancer. I saw that there was a lot of work to be done. I believed that if I became a cancer researcher, I could help children. I felt I wanted to make things better. I wanted to learn new ways of helping children and bring new ideas to the treatment of cancer.

Besides medicine, did you need to know other things to be a researcher?

Cancer treatment and research call for a lot of knowledge and experience. A researcher needs to know about cancer cells and how they grow. But a researcher needs to know much more than that. I had to learn how to help people face cancer. That means helping not only patients but also their parents, other family members, and friends.

Researchers work in laboratories. What does research have to do with caring for patients?

There are two kinds of research. One is called *basic research*. It is done in laboratories. There researchers look at how cancer cells behave. The second kind of research is called *clinical research*. It is about better ways to treat patients. Both kinds of research really have to do with treating people. For example, it is important to know the effects that different cancer drugs have on children with cancer.

What do you like best about your work?

I feel a great deal of satisfaction when I see a child get better. One of the things I like best is seeing a child get well because of a treatment I helped develop. I have always been excited by the challenge to help children get well.

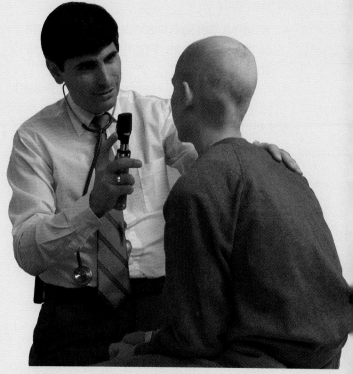

■ *New information from cancer research is important to Dr. Pizzo. He studies cancer research reports so he can help his patients. He helps his patients understand what cancer is and how they can be treated.*

Learn more about people who work as cancer researchers. Interview a researcher. Or write for information to the American Cancer Society, 1599 Clifton Road, N.E., Atlanta, GA 30329-4251.

Main Ideas

- When a person becomes ill, some part of the body has stopped working as it should.
- Communicable diseases are spread to people in many ways.
- Healthful living habits help people avoid many kinds of diseases.
- Several kinds of microbes cause communicable diseases.
- The body's inner defenses help fight disease microbes that can cause infection.
- Some communicable diseases can be prevented by vaccines.
- Some noncommunicable diseases can be prevented by having good health habits.
- Disorders may appear at birth or later in life.

Key Words

Write the numbers 1 to 10 in your health notebook or on a separate sheet of paper. After each number, copy the sentence and fill in the missing term. Page numbers in ( ) tell you where to look in the chapter if you need help.

disease (152)   prevent (154)
symptoms (153)   chronic (155)
treatment (153)   microbes (156)
communicable   infection (156)
   disease (154)   fever (158)
noncommunicable
   disease (154)

1. A __?__ is an illness that spreads from person to person.

2. To stop a disease from happening is to __?__ it.

3. Germs, or disease __?__ , can make you ill.

4. An illness or health problem that cannot be spread from one person to another is said to be a __?__ .

5. The discomfort you feel and other signs of a disease are called its __?__ .

6. Any disease that continues for a long time is said to be __?__ .

7. An __?__ is the growth of disease microbes in some part of the body.

8. When you have symptoms of a disease, you may need __?__ , or care.

9. When your body temperature is higher than normal, you have a __?__ .

10. A breakdown in the way the body works is a __?__ .

Write the numbers 11 to 21 on your paper. After each number, write a sentence that defines the term. Page numbers in ( ) tell you where to look in the chapter if you need help.

11. acute (155)
12. viruses (157)
13. bacteria (158)
14. fungi (159)
15. immunity (163)
16. antibodies (164)
17. vaccines (165)
18. resistance (166)
19. disorders (168)
20. cancer (169)
21. allergy (170)

Remembering What You Learned

Page numbers in ( ) tell you where to look in the chapter if you need help.

1. How do people get communicable diseases? (154)

2. How can a person avoid getting some noncommunicable diseases? (154)

3. What is meant by a chronic disease? (155)

4. What causes a communicable disease? (156)

5. What are three kinds of microbes? (156)

6. How does a virus cause an infection? (157)

7. Name four things you can do to avoid spreading disease microbes to others. (160–161)

8. Why should you wash your hands after covering a cough? (160–161)

9. What inner defense goes to work as soon as disease microbes enter your body? (164)

10. How do antibodies act against disease microbes? (164–165)

11. What are two ways you can form immunity to some diseases? (165)

12. What healthful habits can help your body build up strong resistance? (166)

13. How does cancer usually start in a person's body? (169)

Thinking About What You Learned

1. Why is flu a disease?

2. Why are some kinds of diseases not spread from one person to another?

3. Microbes are everywhere. Why is it that people are not ill all the time?

4. Why might it be unwise to drink from the same glass your best friend used?

5. How have vaccines helped keep you healthy?

Writing About What You Learned

1. Pretend you are in charge of caring for the health of all students in your school. Your job is to prepare a list of health tips to help students and teachers reduce their chances of getting a communicable disease. From your list, choose one health tip. Write a paragraph explaining why the tip is important for good health.

2. Write a how-to paragraph. Explain how to avoid spreading a cold at school or at home.

Applying What You Learned

SOCIAL STUDIES

Sometimes schools or businesses close when too many students or workers become ill. What kinds of problems might occur from this?

Modified True or False

Write the numbers 1 to 15 in your health notebook or on a separate sheet of paper. After each number, write *true* or *false* to describe the sentence. If the sentence is false, also write a term that replaces the underlined term and makes the sentence true.

1. A <u>microbe</u> is any breakdown in the way the body works.

2. A cough may be a <u>symptom</u> of a disease.

3. Chicken pox is a <u>noncommunicable</u> disease.

4. The smallest kind of microbe is a <u>bacterium</u>.

5. Your body has <u>resistance</u> if it is able to fight disease microbes by itself.

6. Taking medicine for a disease is a <u>treatment</u>.

7. Eating a balanced diet and exercising daily are two ways to <u>prevent</u> illness.

8. <u>Fungi</u> are chemicals that help defend the body against disease.

9. AIDS is caused by a <u>bacterium</u>.

10. A <u>fever</u> is a body temperature that is higher than normal.

11. If you get an infection, your body makes more <u>vaccines</u>.

12. <u>Cancer</u> kills more adults in the United States than any other noncommunicable disease.

13. A cold is a <u>chronic</u> disease.

14. Chemicals in the body that help fight disease are <u>antibodies</u>.

15. Blindness is one example of a <u>disease</u> that may appear at birth.

Short Answer

Write the numbers 16 to 23 on your paper. Write a complete sentence to answer each question.

16. How are communicable diseases spread?

17. What are the three main groups of disease microbes?

18. What does a fever mean?

19. When is a booster shot needed?

20. List three health habits that will help prevent some diseases.

21. Why should you cover a sneeze?

22. How do cancer cells harm the body?

23. How do vaccines help your body fight disease?

Essay

Write the numbers 24 and 25 on your paper. Write paragraphs with complete sentences to answer each question.

24. Joan seems to get many infections. She does not get much exercise. She likes to eat snacks and sodas for breakfast and lunch, and she often skips dinner. What should Joan do to help herself build resistance?

25. Explain how the three main kinds of disease microbes are similar and how they are different.

ACTIVITIES FOR HOME OR SCHOOL

Projects to Do

1. Play "disease detective" for a day. Watch for ways you might be spreading disease microbes to others. Have your family watch, too. At the end of the day, make a list with your family of all the ways you could have spread disease to one another. Then decide what you can do to prevent disease microbes from speading to others.

2. To see how microbes can grow in foods, try this activity. Find three empty containers that have tight lids. Or cover bowls with plastic or foil wrap. In one, put a small piece of bread with a few drops of water. In the second, put a spoonful of cottage cheese. In the third, put a slice of orange. Cover each container or bowl tightly. Leave them at room temperature. After 24 hours, check each one. Has the food changed in any way? Cover the containers again. Leave them for two more days. How has the food changed? What could you do to prevent the food from changing?

Information to Find

1. When a communicable disease spreads to many people, the result is called an *epidemic*. Find out about five communicable diseases that have caused epidemics in the past. Use an encyclopedia or other sources to do research.

2. In 1954 Dr. Jonas Salk invented a vaccine against a disease called *polio*. In 1960 Dr. Albert Sabin invented another polio vaccine. Find out about polio and the first polio vaccines. Use library books about vaccines or an encyclopedia.

■ *Dr. Sabin, left, and Dr. Salk*

3. Skin cancer is one of the most common kinds of cancer. Find out more about its causes and symptoms and learn how to prevent it. Your school librarian can help you find books or magazines on the subject.

Books to Read

Here are some books you can look for in your school library or the public library to find more information about the prevention and treatment of diseases.

Berger, Melvin. *Germs Make Me Sick*. T. Y. Crowell.

Cobb, Vicki. *Inspector Bodyguard Patrols the Land of U.* Simon & Schuster.

Swenson, Judy Harris. *Cancer: The Whispered Word*. Dillon.

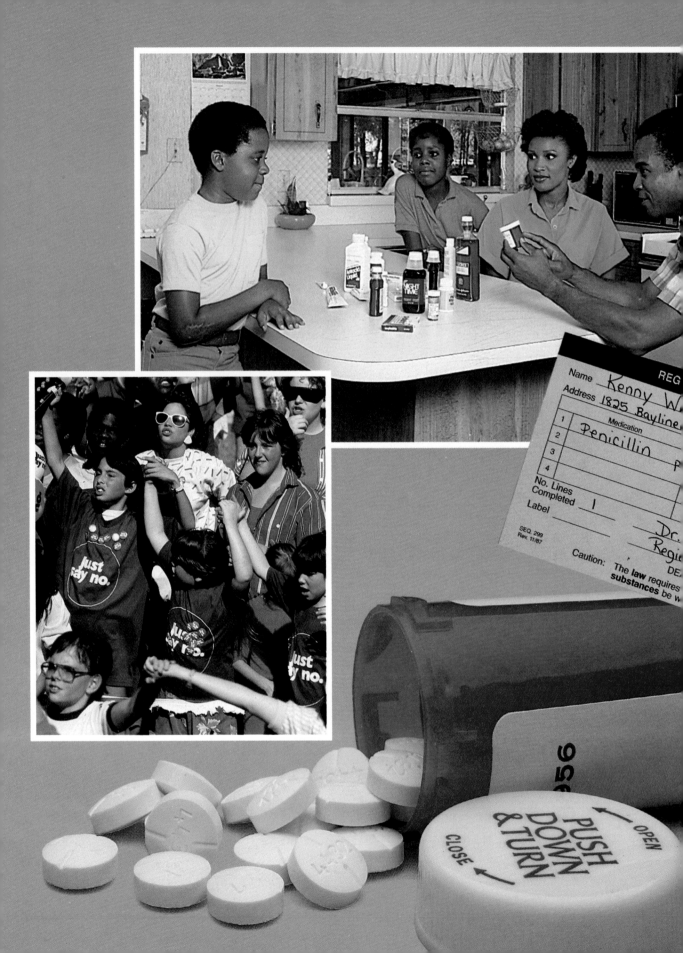

REG

Name Kenny W.

Address 1825 Bayline

1	Medication
2	Penicillin
3	
4	

No. Lines
Completed   1

Label

SEQ. 299
Rev. 11/87

Dr.
Regie

DE

Caution: The **law** requires
substances be w

just
say no.

KNOWING ABOUT MEDICINES AND DRUGS

You hear many confusing messages about medicines and drugs. Medicines and drugs often seem to be the same. But you hear in advertising that medicines can be good for people to use. You also hear that drugs are bad. It is easy to get confused, so it is important to know how medicines and drugs are different and how they are alike.

Knowing about medicines and drugs can help you make some important choices. Many of those choices can affect your health all through your life.

GETTING READY TO LEARN

Key Questions

- Why is it important to learn about medicines and drugs?
- Why is it important to know how you feel about the use of medicines and drugs?
- How can you learn to turn down drugs?
- How can you learn to be safe with medicines?
- How can you take more responsibility for your health when it comes to medicines and drugs?

Main Chapter Sections

1 How Medicines Affect the Body
2 Common Substances That Can Be Harmful
3 Illegal Drugs
4 Acting Against Using Illegal Drugs
  and Harmful Substances

1 How Medicines Affect the Body

medicine (MEHD uh suhn), a drug used to treat or cure a health problem.

drug (DRUHG), any substance, other than food, that causes changes in the body.

Kenny had a very sore throat and a fever. His father thought that Kenny's body might not be able to get rid of the infection by itself. So Kenny's father took him to see a physician. The physician decided that bacteria were causing Kenny's health problem. The physician ordered a medicine to help kill the bacteria. Kenny followed the physician's orders and took the medicine. He felt well sooner than he thought he would. Kenny's father helped him remember to finish the medicine as the physician had ordered.

A **medicine** is a drug used to treat or cure a health problem. A **drug** is any substance, other than food, that causes changes in the body. All medicines are drugs. Not all drugs are medicines!

■ When you are ill, a parent may take you to see a physician. If you have an infection, the physician may order a medicine for you.

There are many kinds of medicines. Each kind of medicine causes changes in the body. For example, allergy pills and cough syrup are medicines taken for exact reasons. Some medicines do not help get rid of an illness. But they can make a person who has an illness feel better. They can lessen the symptoms for a while.

Some medicines can be bought only when a physician orders them. Other medicines can be bought without a physician's order. When medicines are used wisely, they often help the body work as it should. When medicines are not used the right way, they can harm a person's health. Knowing about medicines can help you make important choices about your health and safety.

■ *A physician's order for certain medicines is called a prescription. Prescription medicines are prepared by a pharmacist and need to be taken exactly as directed on the label.*

What Are Prescription Medicines?

Physicians, dentists, and certain other doctors are the only ones who can decide when some medicines should be used. Such medicines are called prescription medicines. They can be bought only with an order, or **prescription.** The order for medicine is most often written, but a prescription can be given over the telephone, too.

prescription (prih SKRIHP shuhn), an order for a certain medicine.

JOHNSON PHARMACY
131 THIRD STREET
ORLANDO, FL 32821
555-6787
JOHNSON R
Rx# 870595   QTY. 40 CAPSUL   0 Refills

WILSON, KENNY
111 PARADISE LANE
TAKE ONE CAPSULE FOUR TIMES
A DAY FOR 10 DAYS.
AMPICILLIN TR 500MG CAP   DR. SMITH

181

A prescription is ordered for only one person. No other person should take the medicine bought with that prescription. The medicine is for only one certain illness and for only one person.

When Kenny had a sore throat, his physician gave him a prescription. Kenny and his father took the prescription to a pharmacy. They gave the prescription to the pharmacist. A **pharmacist** is a person trained to prepare medicines.

The pharmacist prepared the medicine for Kenny. She made a prescription label for it that had Kenny's name on it. Kenny's name on the label meant that only Kenny should use the medicine. The label also told how much of the medicine Kenny needed and when he should take it. The label warned Kenny's father to stop giving the medicine if Kenny got a skin rash.

What Are Over-the-Counter Medicines?

Adults can buy some medicines without a prescription. Such medicines are called over-the-counter, or OTC, medicines. **OTC medicines** can be bought without a prescription in pharmacies and in most food stores.

OTC medicines are easier to buy because they are thought to be safer than prescription medicines. But they can still cause harm if they are used in the wrong way. The labels on all OTC medicines have directions for using the medicines. People need to read the directions carefully before using OTC medicines.

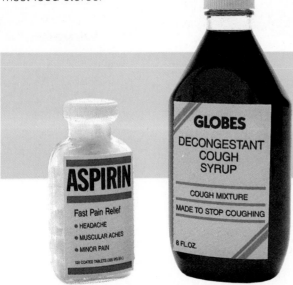

■ OTC medicines can be bought without a prescription. They should also be used exactly as the label directs.

182

The nurse at your school can help you when you feel ill.

Labels and advertising on most OTC medicines tell what health problems the medicines are supposed to help. The directions on a label also tell how to use the medicine, how much of the medicine to take, and how often to take the medicine. Label directions warn about the changes that the medicine may cause in the body. Directions also warn when the medicine may no longer be safe to use. They tell when to check with a physician instead of taking the medicine. When people use any OTC medicine, they need to follow the directions exactly.

Though adults can buy OTC medicines directly, such medicines are not to be used for every ache or discomfort. Medicines are not to take the place of good health habits such as eating a balanced diet, exercising daily, resting, and getting enough sleep. It is wise to talk to a parent, a school nurse, or a physician about aches and discomfort. These adults can help you figure out your problem. Finding the cause is more healthful than asking for medicine to change the feeling.

REAL-LIFE
SKILL

Comparing and Contrasting

Look at two different packages of medicine. One should be a prescription medicine. The other should be an OTC medicine. What kind of information on the labels is alike? What kind of information is different?

Aches are important body signals that show you might have a health problem. Many times the problem can be helped without the use of OTC medicines.

How Can People Take Medicines Safely?

When using a medicine is the best choice for a health problem, the medicine must always be taken with great care. Young people need to talk to a parent or another trusted adult before taking any medicine. A medicine may cause many changes in the body all at once. One of those changes may help if you are ill. But others may be unwanted changes. These are called **side effects.**

Most cold medicines have side effects. They dry up a runny nose. But they may also make a person very sleepy. People need to read the label to find out the possible side effects of a medicine before using it. They can also ask a pharmacist.

■ You should only take medicines that a parent or guardian gives you.

Some medicines should never be taken by certain people for certain illnesses. For example, aspirin should never be taken by young people who have an illness caused by a virus. Aspirin taken for influenza or chicken pox may lead to an illness much more dangerous than the one caused by the virus.

Medicines can do great harm when people use them in the wrong way. Sometimes people take too much of a medicine. They may take it too often. Or they may take the wrong medicine. For example, aspirin is a medicine that is very useful for some problems. But aspirin can hurt people if used too often or for problems it cannot help. Although aspirin helps a headache, it will not help a stomachache. It burns the stomach wall, making a stomachache worse.

The following good health habits can help you and your family use medicines safely:

- Use a medicine only with a responsible adult's help.
- Read all labels on a medicine package *before* using the medicine.
- Never buy an OTC medicine in an opened package.
- Never take a medicine bought with a prescription for someone else.
- If a medicine makes you feel ill or if it has any other side effects, tell your parents.

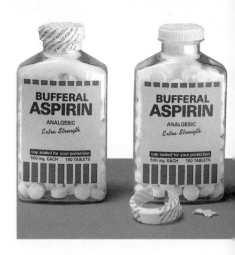

■ *A medicine bottle with a broken seal, right, is not safe to buy.*

 **REVIEW**
SECTION 1

REMEMBER?

1. What is a drug called that is taken to treat or cure a health problem?
2. What do people need from a physician or dentist to buy a medicine that cannot be bought directly?
3. What safety rule should people follow before taking any medicine?

THINK!

4. Describe how a medicine can be both helpful and harmful.
5. Why should people never buy an OTC medicine in an opened package?

Health Close-up

Making Medicines Safer

Last winter Val had an illness. It made her ears ache. Val's mother gave her some medicine that her physician had ordered. The medicine was in the form of a pill. When Val swallowed the pill, the medicine went into her stomach. The pill was digested, and the medicine went into her circulatory system. Her blood then carried the medicine to all parts of her body—not just the parts that needed it.

Scientists today think that this way of taking medicines can sometimes be wasteful. The medicines do not go only to the parts of the body that need them. Medicines taken by mouth more often than not spread to all parts of the body. Scientists are looking for better ways for people to use medicines. Scientists want to put smaller amounts of medicine close

■ *This medical device holds a medicine. It is placed inside the body near the organ that needs the medicine.*

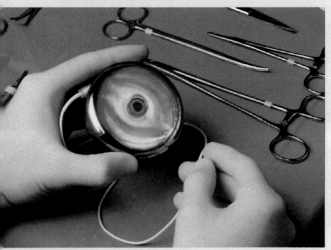

to the part of the body that has a problem. They want to keep the medicine away from other parts of the body. Doing so can be very important for people who need medicines for a long time for certain diseases.

Some people with asthma are now being treated with medicines in nose sprays or inhalers. A nose spray or inhaler has measured supplies of medicine to be breathed in through the nose or mouth, just where it is needed. The medicine goes directly to the part of the body that needs it, and most of it stays there. The medicine also goes to the body part just when it is needed.

Medicines used just where they are needed are not wasted. Also, side effects that happen when a medicine is swallowed are reduced. When a medicine is swallowed, it can cause side effects because it goes to all body systems. Medicine sprays and inhalers are only two ways that scientists have developed for people who need strong medicines for a long time.

Thinking Beyond

1. Why might medicine sprays or inhalers be helpful to people with certain illnesses but not helpful to other people?
2. How else could medicines be made safer?

2 Common Substances That Can Be Harmful

Though medicines are drugs used for health reasons, not all drugs are medicines. Some drugs are found in foods. They are not meant to treat illness. But they can cause changes in the body that are not healthful.

Some household products can actually harm people. Such products have druglike substances in them that can cause dangerous changes in the body if the products are used unsafely.

What Does Caffeine in Food Do to the Body?

Mr. Ortega often has a cup of coffee with breakfast. He says coffee helps him wake up in the morning. Coffee makes Mr. Ortega's heart beat faster. It causes his blood vessels to become narrower. Coffee also affects his nervous system. The part of coffee that causes changes in a person's body is caffeine. **Caffeine** is a natural chemical that is a drug. It is found in coffee and most cola drinks. Chocolate and tea also have caffeine.

Most people can drink small amounts of coffee without damaging their health. However, drinking a lot of coffee puts too much caffeine into the body at one time. Too much caffeine can make people jittery. It can keep people awake when they want to fall asleep. It can cause a sense of burning in the stomach.

KEY WORDS

caffeine
illegal

caffeine (ka FEEN), a natural drug found in coffee and most cola drinks.

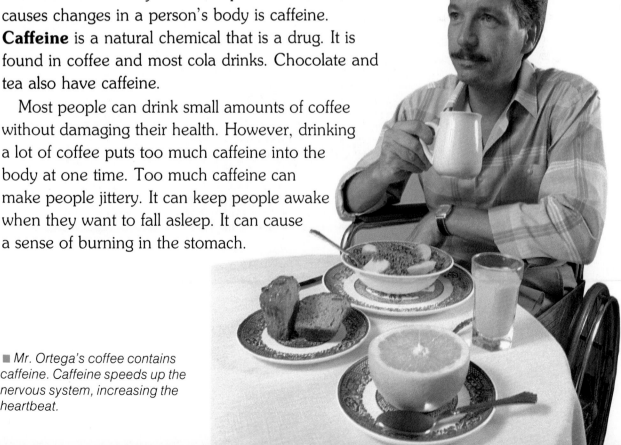

■ *Mr. Ortega's coffee contains caffeine. Caffeine speeds up the nervous system, increasing the heartbeat.*

■ *These beverages contain no caffeine.*

■ *Products such as these are found in most homes. They can be harmful if they are not used properly.*

What caffeine does to the body is not healthful for young people. Caffeine can keep you from getting to sleep when your body needs to sleep. Adults who drink a lot of caffeine daily may get painful headaches if they stop. Their bodies get used to having caffeine. They feel discomfort when they decide not to have any more.

Many companies that make coffee, cola drinks, and tea now sell no-caffeine products. Have you seen the term "caffeine-free" on labels? People can choose between drinks with caffeine and the same drinks without caffeine. However, milk and fruit juice are more healthful drinks that naturally have no caffeine.

How Can Common Substances Be Harmful?

Harmful substances may be found in products in many homes. Those substances can act as drugs. If used in the wrong way, they can cause changes that

188

harm a person's body. Spray paints, paint thinners, and some kinds of glue contain such chemicals. The labels often warn people to keep those products off their skin because the chemicals can burn and injure skin cells. The chemicals can also harm the body through the respiratory system.

A person who breathes in gases from those products might become dizzy or ill. People who breathe the gases on purpose take the chance of being harmed. Sniffing those substances can damage the brain and other parts of the nervous system. It can also damage other organs, such as the liver and lungs. Sometimes sniffing those substances causes death by stopping the heart or blocking the lungs.

Because those harmful substances are so dangerous, there are laws about their purchase. In some communities, young people are not allowed to buy them.

■ *Some kinds of glue should be used only where there is a good supply of fresh air. Be sure to read the label for cautions before using any glue.*

illegal (ihl EE guhl), against the law.

It is **illegal,** or against the law, for young people to buy them. Making laws is one way a community shows it cares for young people—for example, by protecting them from harmful substances. Such laws help keep you safe as you learn how to use certain products only in responsible ways.

STOP REVIEW
SECTION 2

REMEMBER?

1. What effects can too much caffeine have on a person?
2. How can glue be a harmful product?
3. What are three body parts changed by inhaling gases from paint?

THINK!

4. Why might you recommend that a friend use certain glues and spray paints outside?
5. Why are some substances illegal for young people to buy?

Making Wellness Choices

It is a warm summer evening, and it will be dark in another hour. Mark and Larry are playing near Larry's house when Larry pulls a tube from his pocket. He tells Mark that the stuff in the tube really smells good. Larry takes the cap off the tube, puts the tube to his nose, and breathes in deeply. He gives the tube to Mark. Mark puts it to his nose and takes a quick sniff. Mark says, "This is glue!"

 What should Mark do? Explain your wellness choice.

190

3 Illegal Drugs

Some drugs are so dangerous that they are illegal for everyone. Illegal drugs are harmful to the body. Using any illegal drug is **drug abuse.** Using a medicine in the wrong way is also drug abuse. **Drug abusers** are people who abuse drugs. They take the chance of harming their bodies and getting into trouble.

Drugs work on the nervous system. They change the way a person thinks and acts. Drug abusers often take a drug on purpose to change how they feel. After a time, they come to need the drug. Or they come to believe they need it to feel all right. That need or belief is called **drug dependence.** Drug dependence makes it very hard for a drug abuser to stop taking the drug without the help of health workers.

KEY WORDS

drug abuse
drug abusers
drug dependence
marijuana
controlled
    substance
cocaine

drug abuse (DRUHG • uh BYOOS), the use of any harmful and illegal drug; the use of a medicine in the wrong way.

drug abusers (DRUHG • uh BYOOZ uhrz), people who abuse drugs.

drug dependence (DRUHG • dih PEHN duhns), a condition in which a person needs a drug in order to feel all right.

■ *There are special places a person with a drug dependence can go for help.*

191

What Can Marijuana Do to the Body?

marijuana (mair uh WAHN uh), an illegal drug that is made from a certain plant and then usually smoked.

Marijuana is an illegal drug that is usually smoked. Like tobacco, marijuana is made from the leaves of a certain plant. But the harmful substances in marijuana are different from those in tobacco. The harmful substances in marijuana can damage the nervous system more than those in tobacco. They can change cells deep inside the brain. Drug abusers who smoke marijuana often forget things. They cannot remember facts. They also feel mixed up. They have trouble judging time and distance correctly, so they can accidentally get hurt or hurt others.

It is not easy for the body to get rid of the harmful substances in marijuana smoke. Some substances stay in the brain cells for a long time. After a while, a person who uses marijuana can have long-lasting harm to the brain. He or she may have trouble learning.

■ *Scientists have discovered that marijuana harms the body in many ways.*

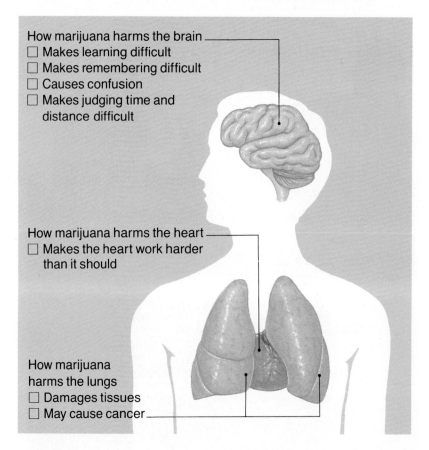

How marijuana harms the brain
☐ Makes learning difficult
☐ Makes remembering difficult
☐ Causes confusion
☐ Makes judging time and distance difficult

How marijuana harms the heart
☐ Makes the heart work harder than it should

How marijuana harms the lungs
☐ Damages tissues
☐ May cause cancer

People who use marijuana seem to become ill more easily than people who have never smoked marijuana. The substances in marijuana can harm a person's immunity. They can destroy the white blood cells that protect people from illness.

Marijuana smoke can cause great harm to the heart and lungs. In fact, scientists have shown that people who smoke marijuana may harm their heart and lungs more than people who smoke cigarettes. Marijuana makes the heart beat very fast. One chemical in marijuana, carbon monoxide, takes the place of oxygen in the blood. Also, the tars in marijuana smoke can settle in the lungs and destroy the lung tissue.

In many states, marijuana is put in a category of drugs called controlled substances. A **controlled substance** is a drug that is illegal to produce, possess, sell, or use in any amount. A person arrested for growing, having, selling, or using marijuana may be fined or put in jail. Sometimes the penalty is both a fine and a jail term.

controlled substance (kuhn TROHLD • SUHB stuhns), a drug that is illegal to produce, possess, sell, or use in any amount.

cocaine (koh KAYN), an illegal drug that dangerously speeds up the working of the body.

What Can Cocaine Do to the Body?

Some illegal drugs dangerously speed up the working of the body. **Cocaine** is an illegal drug that acts this way. Like marijuana, cocaine makes the heart beat very fast. It can damage the nervous system. Drug abusers who use cocaine feel that they have a lot of energy. However, they cannot rest or sleep well, so they cannot do their work well.

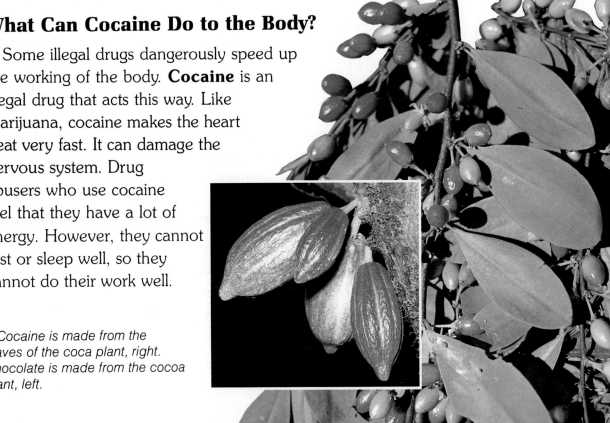

■ Cocaine is made from the leaves of the coca plant, right. Chocolate is made from the cocoa plant, left.

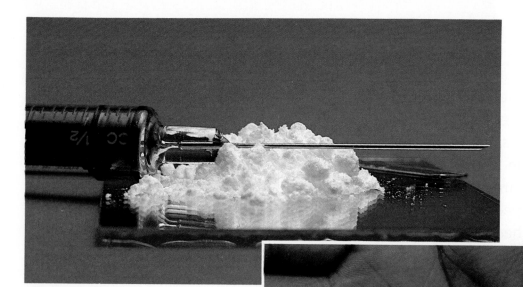

■ *Cocaine is sold as a white powder. Crack, a powerful form of cocaine, is sold as lumps called rocks.*

FOR THE
CURIOUS

Crack cocaine is the number one illegal drug problem in the United States.

Cocaine is made from the leaves of the coca plant. The coca plant is not the same as the cocoa plant, from which chocolate is made. Cocaine most often looks like a white powder. A powerful form of cocaine called "crack" looks like a block of white powder.

Besides damaging the heart and the nervous system, cocaine changes how the body's immunity works. People who use cocaine often get infections that their bodies cannot fight. Cocaine users form a drug dependence on cocaine. This dependence happens quickly. When they stop using cocaine, even for a short time, they feel very ill.

Cocaine, like marijuana, is a controlled substance in the United States. People caught with cocaine are arrested. They may be sent to jail. They may also be sent to special health care centers. In those centers, people help the drug abusers overcome their drug dependence.

REMEMBER?

1. Why do some people abuse drugs?
2. What are three body organs harmed by using marijuana?
3. How does cocaine harm the body?

THINK!

4. How might someone's personality change if he or she abuses drugs?
5. Why might using drugs to try to solve a problem cause more problems?

Thinking About Your Health

Do You Know How to Turn Down Illegal Drugs?

Fold a piece of paper in half. On the front, write the title "My Choose to Refuse Journal." A journal is a book in which people write their experiences. In this journal, you might describe ways you think of to turn down someone's offer to use a harmful substance or an illegal drug. Or you might describe ways to turn down a suggestion to do something you know is wrong. Each time you try one of your ideas, write what happens. For example, finish the sentence "I said no and . . ."

How well do your ways of refusing work? How do you feel about yourself when you say no? Whenever you think of new ideas for refusing to use illegal drugs, add them to your journal.

Acting Against Using Illegal Drugs and Harmful Substances

Communities make laws to try to help people stay healthy and safe. They make laws about having, giving, using, and selling harmful substances. These substances include illegal drugs. Still, many harmful illegal substances are present in communities. You must take responsibility for helping yourself stay healthy even when such substances are in the community.

Sometimes young people try to talk each other into taking drugs. The following steps can help you in planning to refuse drugs. By refusing drugs, you act against pressures from others that can harm you.

■ *Stay healthy and safe. Say no to drugs!*

REFUSE DRUGS SAY NO!

1. If someone offers you a harmful substance or illegal drug, you do not have to accept. You need to refuse.

2. Remember what you have learned about the harm illegal drugs and other substances can do. They can cause brain damage. They can damage the heart, the lungs, and other organs. They can change a person's personality. They could get you into trouble with your family, your school, and the police. People who care about you would be angry or sad if you harmed yourself. You would be angry or disappointed with yourself, too.

3. Think of the good consequences of refusing drugs. (A **consequence** is what happens because of your behavior.) Your health is important to you. When you choose to protect your health, you can feel good about yourself. You can make your family proud of you, too.

consequence (KAHN suh kwehns), what happens because of a behavior.

Refusing something that can harm you shows that you care about yourself and have responsibility for your own health. People will admire you for taking charge of your own health. They will know you did the wise thing, even if they are not ready to tell you so. Refusing illegal drugs may be one of the best health choices you ever make.

STOP REVIEW
SECTION 4

REMEMBER?

1. Why are drug laws made?
2. Why is refusing illegal drugs a positive health choice?

THINK!

3. How can self-esteem help you refuse illegal drugs?
4. Why do some people try to pressure others into taking drugs?

People in Health

An Interview with a Pharmacist

Sharlea Blessing knows about medicines and other drugs. She is a pharmacist who works in Kansas City, Missouri.

■ *A pharmacist knows about all medicines.*

What is it like to be a pharmacist?

I prepare the medicines that physicians order for people. People most often bring their prescriptions to me in the pharmacy. If a person comes into the store for the first time, I need to find out about him or her before I fill the prescription. I ask several questions. I try to find out if the person has an allergy to the medicine. If I think a person will have a problem or if I have other questions, I call the physician. I keep a file on each person who gets a prescription filled at my pharmacy. Along with filling prescriptions, I give advice.

What kinds of advice do you give?

I talk to people about the medicines they will be taking. I tell them what side effects they might expect from their medicines. I tell them exactly how and when to take their medicines. For example, a medicine might need to be taken with food or on an empty stomach. I answer any questions the people might have. I give advice over the telephone. I receive a lot of calls from people who are not feeling well but who do not feel sick enough to visit a physician. I tell them about the over-the-counter medicines they can take. I also tell them to see a physician if they are not feeling better soon.

How is the advice that a pharmacist gives different from the advice that a physician gives?

Pharmacists cannot tell people what is wrong with them or what illnesses they have. Treating illness and ordering medicines are physicians' jobs. Pharmacists can suggest only over-the-counter medicines and products to treat the symptoms. They can also explain how to take these medicines safely.

What are some of the other things most pharmacists do?

Today pharmacists also help with home health care. Sometimes a family has a child who is ill at home and cannot pick up a medicine. Pharmacists can have the medicine sent to the home.

198

They can also supply bandages, braces, and hospital furniture. They can even help measure people for such things as leg braces.

What are some unusual ways pharmacists help people?

People can walk into a pharmacy at any time and receive free advice from a pharmacist. That is unusual, if you think about it. People cannot do that with most other health workers. They almost always have to pay for advice. Pharmacists have a lot of training and knowledge about medicine that is helpful in many ways. Pharmacists can also answer questions from people who want to know about preventing drug abuse.

■ *Pharmacists also give advice about other health products.*

What skills do pharmacists need at work?

It is very important for pharmacists to keep their work areas clean and in good order. Many of the products they work with go into people's bodies. Since a pharmacy often has more than 1,500 medicines, pharmacists must make sure they have them in alphabetical order. Many medicines and drugs have similar names and could be mixed up if they were out of order. Also, pharmacists must be able to work with many people at one time without making mistakes or mixing up prescription orders.

When did you know you wanted to become a pharmacist?

Before I went to college, I knew I wanted some kind of career in science. I liked chemistry and studied that subject. At first, I thought I wanted to become a teacher. Then I became more and more interested in medicine and health. A pharmacist uses chemistry, medicine, and health, so pharmacy seemed just right for me.

> *Learn more about people who work as pharmacists. Interview a pharmacist. Or write for information to the American Pharmaceutical Association, 2215 Constitution Avenue, N.W., Washington, DC 20037.*

Main Ideas

- Medicines must be used wisely because they can cause changes in the body.
- Prescription medicines and over-the-counter medicines can be helpful when people follow the directions on the labels.
- Some products found in the home contain substances that may harm a person's health if used unwisely.
- Illegal drugs are dangerous to the health of all people.
- Choosing to refuse harmful or illegal drugs is your responsibility.
- When people refuse to use harmful drugs, they build self-esteem.

Key Words

Write the numbers 1 to 15 in your health notebook or on a separate sheet of paper. After each number, copy the sentence and fill in the missing term. Page numbers in ( ) tell you where to look in the chapter if you need help.

medicine (180)
drug (180)
prescription (181)
pharmacist (182)
OTC medicines (182)
side effects (184)
caffeine (187)
illegal (190)
drug abuse (191)

drug abusers (191)
drug dependence (191)
marijuana (192)
controlled substance (193)
cocaine (193)
consequence (197)

1. A ___?___ is a drug used to treat or cure health problems.

2. A ___?___ is any substance, other than food, that causes changes in the body.

3. A ___?___ is a result of a behavior.

4. Some medicines cannot be bought without an order, or ___?___, from a physician.

5. A ___?___ is a trained health worker who can prepare medicines.

6. ___?___ can be bought in pharmacies and in most food stores.

7. Unwanted changes in the body that are caused by medicines are called ___?___.

8. A drug found in coffee, most cola drinks, chocolate, and tea is called ___?___.

9. It is ___?___ for young people to buy harmful substances.

10. Using a drug that is harmful and illegal is known as ___?___.

11. If a person needs a drug, he or she has a ___?___.

12. One kind of illegal drug that is usually smoked is ___?___.

13. Any substance that is against the law for anyone to have, sell, or use is a ___?___.

14. One illegal drug that dangerously speeds up the activities of the body is ___?___.

15. People who use harmful drugs are called ___?___.

Remembering What You Learned

Page numbers in ( ) tell you where to look in the chapter if you need help.

1. What is the difference between a medicine and a drug? (180)

2. Name two health workers who can order prescription medicines for someone. (181)

3. What kind of health worker is trained to prepare medicines? (182)

4. What information should appear on a prescription medicine label? (182)

5. What is the difference between OTC and prescription medicines? (182)

6. Who should help you take a medicine when you are ill? (185)

7. List five rules to follow for using medicines safely. (185)

8. What is caffeine? What does it do to the body? (187–188)

9. Describe how sniffing glue can be dangerous. (189)

10. What is marijuana? What does it do to the body? (192–193)

11. What is cocaine? What does it do to the body? (193–194)

Thinking About What You Learned

1. Why is it necessary for any medicine to have directions on its label?

2. Why should you take a medicine only when your parent or another trusted adult is present?

3. Some people take illegal drugs because their friends want them to do so. Tell why a friend who would want you to take illegal drugs might not be a friend at all.

4. What does it mean to abuse something, such as a medicine?

Writing About What You Learned

1. Interview four adults to get definitions of *proper drug use, drug misuse,* and *drug abuse.* Ask each person to give you an example of each. In a paragraph or two, write what you learn from those interviews.

2. Write a short story or a play about someone who is deciding whether to use illegal drugs. Before you begin writing, you might want to make a list of reasons for turning down illegal drugs. Select one or two of your reasons, and develop your story or play around them.

Applying What You Learned

SOCIAL STUDIES

Tell how drug abusers might affect life in a community.

LANGUAGE ARTS

Take part in group discussions about different activities people can do instead of using drugs. Prepare a list of the other things to do.

Modified True or False

Write the numbers 1 to 15 in your health notebook or on a separate sheet of paper. After each number, write *true* or *false* to describe the sentence. If the sentence is false, also write a term that replaces the underlined term and makes the sentence true.

1. The use of medicine in the wrong way is one example of <u>drug abuse</u>.
2. <u>Cocaine</u> is found in coffee.
3. Medicines used just where they are needed can reduce the chances of <u>side effects</u>.
4. A <u>medicine</u> is any substance other than food that causes changes in the body.
5. Caffeine is a <u>drug</u>.
6. Marijuana is a <u>legal medicine</u>.
7. Aspirin is an <u>OTC</u> medicine.
8. People who use illegal drugs must accept the <u>consequences</u>.
9. Drug abusers who smoke marijuana have <u>good</u> memories.
10. Sniffing glue is an example of <u>drug abuse</u>.
11. Caffeine causes your heart rate to <u>increase</u>.
12. A <u>physician</u> is a person who is trained to prepare medicines.
13. Medicines <u>can</u> take the place of good health habits.
14. <u>Crack</u> is one kind of cocaine.
15. Feeling sleepy after taking medicine for a cold may be a <u>side effect</u>.

Short Answer

Write the numbers 16 to 23 on your paper. Write a complete sentence to answer each question.

16. Why is it important to read the label on a medicine before taking it?
17. What is the difference between a medicine and a drug?
18. What is the difference between a pharmacist and a physician?
19. Name two controlled substances.
20. Explain how drug abuse is different from drug dependence.
21. How does caffeine affect the body?
22. Explain why people who use cocaine may get ill often.
23. What are the consequences of getting caught with a controlled substance?

Essay

Write the numbers 24 and 25 on your paper. Write paragraphs with complete sentences to answer each question.

24. Your physician has just given you a prescription to help you fight an infection. Explain what steps you would follow before taking the medicine.
25. Explain how you would convince a friend that he or she should not smoke marijuana.

ACTIVITIES FOR HOME OR SCHOOL

Projects to Do

1. Ask to have a health meeting with your family. Suggest a time when you can meet to talk about safety and medicines in your home. Here are some important questions to answer:
   - Are all medicines labeled clearly?
   - Are any medicines out of date (more than one year old)?
   - Do you have an emergency number by your telephone in case someone takes too much medicine or the wrong medicine?

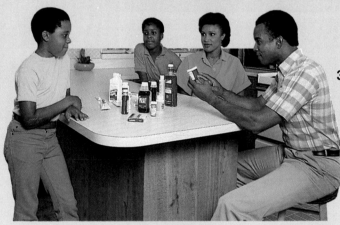

■ *Talk with your family about medicine safety.*

2. Make a poster using the theme that some drugs are harmful to your health. Do not write a slogan on your poster. When your poster is complete, show it to your classmates. Have them think of slogans for your poster. Decide which slogan you like best, and write it on your poster. Do the same thing with a poster to show how medicines can be important to your health.

Information to Find

1. Many kinds of illegal drugs come into the United States from other countries. One way that the U.S. government prevents drugs from entering is by using specially trained dogs. Find out more about how the dogs help prevent drugs from entering the United States. You might ask your librarian for magazine and newspaper articles about this topic.

2. Find out your state's laws against illegal drugs. Find out the penalties for breaking those laws. Ask a police officer in your community for more information.

3. Many health workers are trying to let people know how to control some health problems without using medicines. Ask your school nurse or a pharmacist about methods of solving health problems without using medicines. How can headaches, for example, be helped without medicines?

Books to Read

Here are some books you can look for in your school library or the public library to find more information about medicines and illegal drugs.

Ardley, Neil. *Health and Medicine.* Franklin Watts.

Hughes, Barbara. *Drug-Related Diseases.* Franklin Watts.

Woods, Geraldine. *Drug Use and Drug Abuse.* Franklin Watts.

ALCOHOL AND TOBACCO

Many people in the United States drink beverages that have alcohol in them. Some people smoke or chew tobacco. But did you know that using alcohol and tobacco can harm people's health and safety? Alcohol and tobacco have chemicals in them. Many of the chemicals are drugs.

Communities make laws to protect young people from alcohol and tobacco. When people reach the age of 21, they are allowed to make their own choices. Choosing not to use alcohol and tobacco can help a person stay healthy. It could be one of the most important choices you will make to protect your wellness.

GETTING READY TO LEARN

Key Questions

- Why is it important to learn about the dangers of alcohol and tobacco?
- Why is it important to know how you feel about the use of alcohol and tobacco?
- How can you learn to turn down alcohol and tobacco?
- How can you take responsibility for your health when it comes to alcohol and tobacco?

Main Chapter Sections

1 About Alcohol
2 About Tobacco
3 Acting Against Using Alcohol and Tobacco

1 About Alcohol

KEY WORDS

alcohol
peer pressure
problem drinkers

Tom, Denise, and Julia were playing a game with their friend Mike at Mike's home. In the family room, there were many games. There was also a shelf that had bottles of wine and whiskey on it.

Mike thought it might be fun to make-believe having an adult party. "Let's open one of the bottles and try it," Mike said.

Tom, Denise, and Julia said, "No, thank you."

Tom told Mike his family did not want him to try any drink with alcohol in it.

"It is against the law for children to drink alcohol," Denise quickly added. "Let's play another game instead." They decided to play a board game.

■ *People can have a good time without drinking alcohol.*

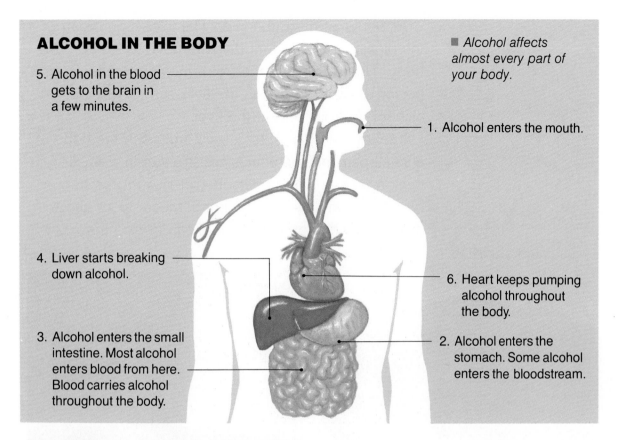

ALCOHOL IN THE BODY

■ *Alcohol affects almost every part of your body.*

5. Alcohol in the blood gets to the brain in a few minutes.

1. Alcohol enters the mouth.

4. Liver starts breaking down alcohol.

6. Heart keeps pumping alcohol throughout the body.

3. Alcohol enters the small intestine. Most alcohol enters blood from here. Blood carries alcohol throughout the body.

2. Alcohol enters the stomach. Some alcohol enters the bloodstream.

How Does Alcohol Affect the Body?

Alcohol is a drug found in such drinks as beer, wine, and whiskey. Because alcohol is a drug, it causes changes in someone who drinks it.

When swallowed, alcohol quickly passes from the stomach into the blood. The blood then carries the drug to all parts of the body.

The brain is the organ that alcohol affects most quickly. Alcohol slows down the brain's ability to control the body's nervous system. The nervous system controls the whole body.

Drinking two or more beverages that contain alcohol in a short time can change the way people act and think. It can make their speech unclear. They may talk very loudly because they cannot tell they are being too loud. They may do things they would not do if they were not drinking. Some people start fights or fall asleep if they drink.

alcohol (AL kuh hawl), a drug found in such drinks as beer, wine, and whiskey.

Alcohol can harm the liver. The liver is an organ of the digestive system that helps remove waste from the body. The liver has the job of removing alcohol from a person's blood. Although the liver can do this job, alcohol destroys cells in the liver.

It takes less alcohol to cause changes in the body of a small person. The effects are stronger in a small person than in a large person. Yet alcohol can be harmful at any age or size. For someone your age, even a small amount of alcohol can cause harm.

 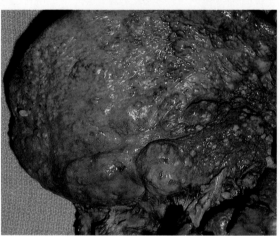

■ *A healthy liver, left, removes waste from the body. A liver damaged by alcohol, right, cannot work properly.*

Why Do Some People Start Using Alcohol?

Young people see some adults drinking beer, wine, or whiskey. The young people may not know much about alcohol. Or they may not know that alcohol can harm them.

The first time many young people taste alcohol is with their families, as part of either a big party or a religious service. Young people may think that alcohol must be safe because their families let them taste it.

In other families, young people may start to wonder what alcohol tastes like. They may think that drinking alcohol is a grown-up thing to do. For these and other reasons, some young people try drinking alcohol.

Most young people like to do the things their friends do. They want other young people to like them and to admire the things they do. Because of those feelings, their friends have a strong influence on them. That influence is called **peer pressure.**

Sometimes young people try to talk each other into drinking alcohol outside the family. They may say that it is fun. Young people may dare their friends to drink. They may tease them if they refuse. Sometimes friends give in to peer pressure and take a drink. Other times, the friends know about alcohol. They refuse to drink.

Why Do Some People Use or Not Use Alcohol?

State laws do not allow young people to buy, drink, or sell alcohol. Most families have rules against the drinking of alcohol by children. Protecting your health and safety and staying in control of your body are good reasons not to drink alcohol.

Many people, young and old, know about the health problems caused by drinking alcohol. Some people follow family or religious rules never to use alcohol. They believe those are good rules. They refuse to drink.

■ *Saying no to alcohol shows that you care about yourself.*

peer pressure (PIHR · PREHSH uhr), the influence on a person by a group of people about the same age.

■ *Selling alcohol to someone younger than 21 is illegal.*

209

Some people do drink alcohol. They give many reasons. Some people drink alcohol because they think it helps them rest. Some people drink to be part of a group—at a party, for example.

What Happens When People Drink Too Much Alcohol?

Some people form a habit of drinking too much alcohol. When they try to stop, they become uneasy. They say they need alcohol to feel normal. These people have a drinking disorder and are called **problem drinkers.** You may also hear them called *alcoholics.* Their disorder is *alcoholism.*

Anyone who drinks a lot might be a problem drinker. The person can be young or old. Young people who drink alcohol face a greater chance of becoming problem drinkers. Their smaller size and incomplete emotional growth make it hard for young people to handle the effects of alcohol. Alcohol has very strong effects on all people. It harms the body and may change a person's personality and lower his or her self-esteem.

problem drinkers, people who have a habit of drinking or a drinking disorder; they say they need alcohol to feel normal.

210

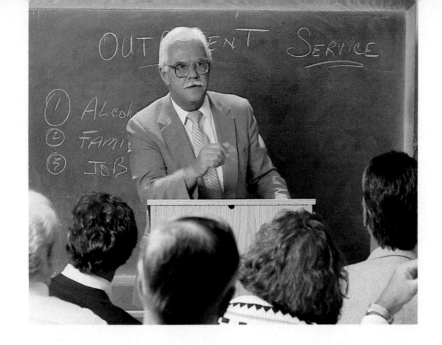

■ *This is a group of people who are alcoholics. They are helping each other stop drinking alcohol.*

Alcohol keeps problem drinkers from doing many things very well. Problem drinkers may do things that cause problems at work or school. They may hurt the feelings of people who love them. They do not mean to hurt people. The alcohol affects the way they think and act. Problem drinkers can become healthy again only if they stop drinking. They often need help to stop. Most communities have groups or centers to help.

STOP REVIEW
SECTION 1

REMEMBER?

1. Why is alcohol a drug?
2. What does alcohol do to the brain?
3. Why do some people start using alcohol?

THINK!

4. How might drinking a lot of alcohol at one time affect a person's safety?
5. What might happen if a young person drinks alcohol outside a family special event or religious ceremony?

Health Close-up

Alcohol Is No Laughing Matter

Franz was watching a Western movie on television. One actor in the movie drank a lot of whiskey. Whiskey is a kind of alcohol. When the man tried to stand up, he fell over. He could not walk or talk properly. He tried to get on a horse but tripped and fell. Everyone laughed.

After the movie, Franz watched a news story on television. It was a sad story. An automobile accident had killed the driver and her passenger. The car had gone off the road and hit a tree. The accident happened because the driver had been drinking alcohol. The alcohol made her unable to steer the car properly.

Alcohol has many effects on the body. Often a person who has been drinking does not have good coordination. The person may trip and fall like the actor in the Western movie. The person may be unable to drive a car properly, like the driver in the news story.

Movies, television programs, and advertising often show people enjoying alcohol. Some young people see them and want to try alcohol. Sometimes movies show people drinking to be funny or to be part of a group. What can happen to a real person who thinks alcohol is a joke? Why?

Thinking Beyond

1. Why do people laugh when someone in a movie drinks too much?
2. Why is drinking alcohol no laughing matter?

■ *In the United States, over half of all fatal traffic accidents involve alcohol.*

212

2 About Tobacco

Connie and Rosa went out to eat with their parents. When they got to the restaurant, their mother asked for seating in a no-smoking area. On the way to their table, however, the family walked by the smoking area. After they reached their table, Connie, Rosa, and their parents talked about how the air looked and smelled in the smoking area.

KEY WORDS

smokeless
   tobacco
nicotine
tar
carbon monoxide
tumors
sidestream smoke

■ *Many people choose to eat where they do not have to smell smoke.*

■ *All forms of tobacco are harmful.*

The smoke they saw and smelled came from burning tobacco. Tobacco is a plant whose leaves are dried to make tobacco products. Most people who use tobacco smoke it in cigarettes. Others smoke it in cigars and pipes. Some tobacco is put directly into the mouth and left there for a while. It is called **smokeless tobacco.** Snuff and chewing tobacco are two kinds of smokeless tobacco.

All tobacco products have drugs and other substances in them. The substances enter the body when smoke is breathed into the lungs. Substances in smokeless tobacco enter the body through blood vessels in the mouth or nose. Because of the chemicals in them, all tobacco products can harm your health.

smokeless tobacco
(SMOH kluhs • tuh BAK oh), tobacco that can be put directly into the mouth and left there for a while.

213

What Is in Tobacco?

nicotine (NIHK uh teen), a drug in all tobacco products that makes the heart beat faster.

tar, a sticky, dark brown substance formed by the particles in tobacco smoke.

carbon monoxide (KAHR buhn • muh NAHK syd), one of many poisonous gases made by burning tobacco.

■ *Healthy lungs, left, provide the body with plenty of oxygen. Lungs damaged by cigarette smoke, right, cannot provide all the oxygen an active body needs.*

One drug in all tobacco products is **nicotine.** Nicotine makes the heart beat faster. Nicotine also makes the openings of blood vessels smaller than they should be. This makes it hard for blood to flow easily. When the blood vessels become smaller, the heart must pump much harder to move blood throughout the body. The blood pressure rises. High blood pressure can harm the circulatory system.

The smoke of burning tobacco contains a sticky, dark brown substance called **tar.** Sometimes you can see tar spots on windows and walls in rooms where people smoke. Inside a smoker's body, tar coats the tubes leading to the lungs, as well as the lungs. Tar that builds up in the lungs makes it hard for oxygen to pass into the smoker's blood. Because of this, a smoker's body cells get less oxygen than they need for good health.

Smokers also get less oxygen because they breathe the carbon monoxide in tobacco smoke. **Carbon monoxide** is one of many poisonous gases made by burning tobacco. Carbon monoxide takes the place of oxygen in the blood when a smoker breathes it. The result is that a smoker's body cells get less oxygen. Cells need oxygen to stay healthy and grow.

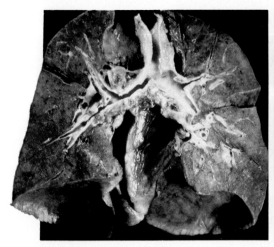
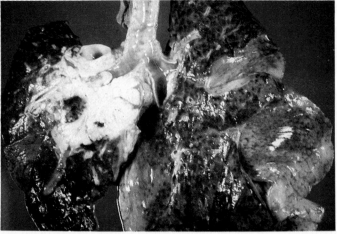

How Can Tobacco Harm People Who Use It?

Substances in tobacco cause many immediate and harmful changes in the body. Nicotine makes the heart beat faster. The faster heartbeat might cause a smoker to feel nervous. At the same time, carbon monoxide might make a smoker feel tired, because the body gets less oxygen. Smoke from one cigarette can also make a person cough and feel ill.

Using tobacco of any kind has other bad effects. It gives a person bad breath. Tobacco can also cause the color of teeth to change to a darker yellow color.

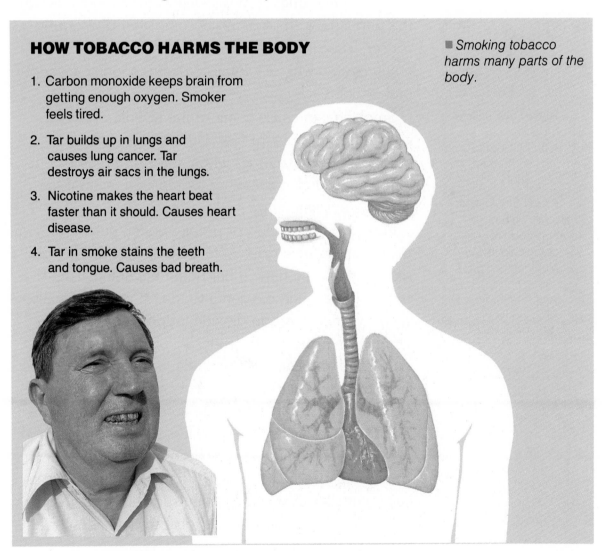

HOW TOBACCO HARMS THE BODY

1. Carbon monoxide keeps brain from getting enough oxygen. Smoker feels tired.

2. Tar builds up in lungs and causes lung cancer. Tar destroys air sacs in the lungs.

3. Nicotine makes the heart beat faster than it should. Causes heart disease.

4. Tar in smoke stains the teeth and tongue. Causes bad breath.

■ Smoking tobacco harms many parts of the body.

There is a large amount of sugar in smokeless tobacco. It can cause cavities in teeth. Tobacco can also cause a person to be less able to taste food.

Certain substances in smokeless tobacco can change the way cells grow in the mouth. Those substances can harm the inside of the mouth and the gums. Harmful cells might grow on the cheeks, gums, lips, and tongue. These cells form white patches. The patches in the mouth can become a noncommunicable disease called *oral cancer*.

The tar in tobacco smoke may cause harmful lumps called **tumors** to grow in a smoker's lungs. Tumors can make the lungs stop working as they should. When this happens, a smoker can become very ill with *lung cancer*. The American Cancer Society reports that many people who use tobacco die from lung cancer or oral cancer each year.

Smoking can cause some of the alveoli, or air sacs, in the lungs to burst or tear. Burst or torn alveoli prevent the release of air when a person breathes out. The damaged alveoli cannot be repaired, even if the person stops smoking.

People with this kind of problem often get a noncommunicable disease called *emphysema*. People with emphysema have a hard time breathing. They cannot get enough oxygen into their bodies. They also keep too much carbon dioxide inside their bodies. Emphysema can cause death.

Nicotine and carbon monoxide in tobacco can cause heart disease. Over many years of using tobacco, nicotine and carbon monoxide harm the heart muscle. Heart disease makes the heart less able to pump blood.

Not all people who use tobacco get cancer, emphysema, or heart disease. However, tobacco users have a greater chance of getting such diseases. People who smoke or use smokeless tobacco have less healthy lives than people who do not use tobacco.

tumors (TOO muhrz), lumps that grow in the body and that can become cancers.

MYTH AND FACT

Myth: Smokeless tobacco is a natural product with no harmful chemicals.

Fact: Smokeless tobacco has hundreds of chemicals in it. Many of them can cause harm to your health.

How Can Tobacco Harm Nonsmokers?

Tobacco can harm the health of a person who does not smoke, too. When tobacco burns, a smoker breathes in some of the smoke. The rest of the smoke floats off into the air. Smoke breathed in by a person other than the smoker is called **sidestream smoke.** It is a form of air pollution.

Sidestream smoke can cause the eyes of people who do not smoke to burn. Sidestream smoke can make nonsmokers' hair and clothing smell like smokers' hair and clothing. Drugs and other substances in tobacco smoke can enter the lungs of nonsmokers who breathe sidestream smoke. Many nonsmokers cough because of the smoke. Some have an allergy to the smoke.

Nonsmokers who breathe sidestream smoke take a chance of having many of the same health problems as smokers. Because of this, some communities do not allow smoking in certain public places, such as schools.

sidestream smoke (SYD streem • SMOHK), smoke from burning tobacco that is breathed in by a person other than the smoker.

■ Breathing in other people's smoke can be harmful. It is illegal to smoke in many places, including elevators.

217

Why Do Some People Start Using and Keep Using Tobacco?

Many people know the dangers of tobacco. But some still use it. People start using tobacco for many different reasons. Some young people try it just to see what it is like. Others use it because their parents, older brothers or sisters, or friends do. Some young people try tobacco to show off. They think using tobacco makes them look and feel grown-up.

Many adults who smoke did not know the health risks of tobacco when they were young. They saw advertising by attractive actors and sports heroes. Smoking was thought to be safe. Some adults have a hard time if they try to stop smoking. Most of them do not want their own children ever to start smoking.

Nicotine in tobacco causes drug dependence. Nicotine makes a person feel a need to have this drug in the blood all the time. To get nicotine, the person uses more tobacco. A person with a nicotine dependence may not feel able to go without tobacco for even a few hours.

MYTH AND FACT

Myth: Smoking tobacco will relax a person who is upset.

Fact: Tobacco contains nicotine. Nicotine is a drug that speeds up the heartbeat. A faster heartbeat makes a person more excited. It can make a person feel more irritable.

■ *Many people smoke even though they know it harms their health.*

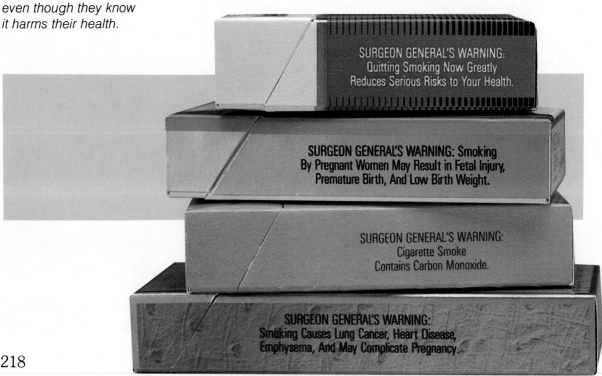

SURGEON GENERAL'S WARNING: Quitting Smoking Now Greatly Reduces Serious Risks to Your Health.

SURGEON GENERAL'S WARNING: Smoking By Pregnant Women May Result in Fetal Injury, Premature Birth, And Low Birth Weight.

SURGEON GENERAL'S WARNING: Cigarette Smoke Contains Carbon Monoxide.

SURGEON GENERAL'S WARNING: Smoking Causes Lung Cancer, Heart Disease, Emphysema, And May Complicate Pregnancy.

Breaking the tobacco habit can be very hard. People who want to stop may need help. Many health centers and communities have classes to help people break the tobacco habit. A supportive family also can help a person stop smoking. People who do not start using tobacco never have to face the problem of stopping. They are taking responsibility for their health.

■ It is much harder to stop smoking than it is to never start.

STOP REVIEW SECTION 2

REMEMBER?

1. What is the difference between nicotine and tar?
2. Describe how tar affects the air sacs in the lungs.
3. How does sidestream smoke affect a nonsmoker?

THINK!

4. How is using tobacco harmful to people's health?
5. Why are laws made to keep young people from buying tobacco?
6. Why is refusing to take even the first puff from a cigarette a healthful choice?

219

3 Acting Against Using Alcohol and Tobacco

Sometimes peer pressure causes some young people to begin using alcohol or tobacco. You can feel very good about yourself when you refuse what you know can harm you.

How Can a Person Say No to Peer Pressure?

John was walking home from school with Tony and Clark. They are John's friends in his fourth-grade class. Along the way, Clark pulled out a pack of cigarettes from his coat pocket.

"Take one," said Clark. "It's for you."

John looked at Clark and said, "No, thank you."

Clark wanted his two friends to smoke a cigarette with him. He kept asking his friends to take one. Tony had never smoked a cigarette and gave in to the pressure to try one.

"Smoking is not good for your health. It's a bad habit," said John. He continued, "It is also against the

Making Wellness Choices

It is a warm fall morning, and school will be starting in a few minutes. Antonio walks across the playground and then around to the other end of the school building. There he sees Sharon and Kim, two fifth-graders, smoking cigarettes. Sharon and Kim look up and see Antonio watching them. Antonio turns quickly and starts running. Mrs. Alvarez, the principal, sees him and calls out, "What's wrong, Antonio?"

 What should Antonio do? Explain your wellness choice.

law. It is against my family rules. Why don't we go to my house and play a game?''

Clark kept trying to change John's mind. He told John, ''I have the cigarettes. Don't be a chicken.''

John said, ''No!'' He then began walking away and added, ''If you change your mind and want to play a game, I'll be at my house.''

What Are the Steps for Acting Against Peer Pressure?

Read the story again about how John refused a cigarette. Follow the steps John took to refuse a cigarette. Knowing those steps helped him decide right away not to smoke a cigarette with his friends.

The first step John took was to *know that he did not have to accept the offer.* He said, ''No, thank you.''

■ *No one can make you smoke. The first step in refusing is saying "No, thank you."*

■ *Choosing not to smoke has a good effect on your health. It also shows that you can make responsible decisions.*

The second step John took was to *remember what he had learned about harmful substances*. John knew about the health problems that tobacco can cause. John knew that smoking can harm his health. John also knew that smoking could get him into trouble. He said, "It's against the law and our family rules." State laws do not allow the sale of tobacco products to young people.

The third step John took was to *know what was important to him*. He knew that his family and good health were important to him. He did not want to do anything to make his family feel angry or sad. He also did not want to be angry or disappointed with himself.

The fourth step John took was to *walk away* from what he knew would harm him. But he left in a good way. He invited his friends to join him at his house if they chose not to smoke. Not using tobacco and not drinking alcohol will also have a good effect on your health. Refusing harmful substances is a responsible health decision.

REMEMBER?

1. What was John's first step in refusing to smoke?
2. What are three reasons not to smoke?
3. Why did John turn down Clark's offer to smoke?

THINK!

4. In what way would John be abusing drugs if he finally decided to smoke?
5. Tell why John's decision not to smoke was a wise choice.

Thinking About Your Health

How Do You Feel About the Use of Tobacco?

Below are seven situations. Each one has to do with tobacco use in some way. Read about each situation. How does each one make you feel? Think of a word or phrase to describe your feeling. How do your feelings about tobacco affect your health decisions?

1. You see a person smoking a cigarette in an area clearly marked No Smoking.

2. A relative who is a heavy smoker gives you a hug.

3. You are riding in a car with the windows up because it is cold outside. The driver is smoking.

4. You see an ashtray full of used cigarettes near food.

5. Your clothes smell like smoke after you have been in a room where people were smoking.

6. Someone that you care about is a heavy smoker.

7. You see someone sneak cigarettes from a parent. That person wants you to smoke with him or her.

223

People in Health

An Interview with a Police Officer

James L. Byrd helps students stay away from harmful substances. He is a police officer in Houston, Texas.

How do you help students stay away from harmful substances?

I am one of three police officers who teach Houston students about the dangers of illegal drugs and other harmful substances. I am part of a special project sponsored by Houston's police department and the public schools.

The name of the project is DARE. The letters in DARE stand for *d*rug *a*buse *r*esistance *e*ducation. DARE is aimed at preventing substance abuse among school students.

How does DARE work?

In the DARE project, police officers are assigned to different schools. I work in five schools. I go to each school one day a week for 17 weeks. Each week, I spend 45 minutes to an hour with each class. My main message to students is to say no to illegal drugs and other substances that might harm students.

What else do you discuss in your classes?

I teach students ways to solve their problems without using harmful substances. I teach students what to do when gangs and peers try to pressure them into taking illegal drugs or other substances. In one class, we discuss how television and movies sometimes influence students to put things in their bodies that might harm them. Other subjects I present are building self-esteem, or pride, and making decisions. I also explain different ways to say no to harmful substances.

■ *Officer Byrd tells about the many ways to refuse drugs.*

■ *Police officers have special training to teach children about the dangers of drug abuse.*

How do you teach about alcohol and tobacco?

I call alcohol and tobacco "gateway drugs." That is how some young people begin using illegal drugs. They see others around them smoking and drinking. Of course, alcohol and tobacco are bad for all people.

What do you do to direct young people away from harmful substances such as alcohol and tobacco?

I help students understand that their bodies are very important. They do not need to put anything harmful into their bodies. I teach young people that they are in control of their own bodies. They must take care of their bodies in order to lead healthy lives.

What is the most important thing you teach young people?

The most important thing I teach young people is to do anything they can to stay away from the use of any harmful substance. I want students to understand that they are our country's future. If they are not going to be healthy, then the country is not going to be healthy. That is one of the main points that I try to get across. I tell them not to take any risk that might ruin their lives.

Has the DARE project been a success?

Overall, I think things are getting better because of DARE. I have noticed that young people have much more knowledge about the dangers of harmful substances, especially alcohol and tobacco. They are better prepared to make good choices about their health.

Learn more about police officers who teach children about the dangers of alcohol, tobacco, and illegal drugs. Interview a police officer in your community. Or write for information to DARE America, P. O. Box 2090, Los Angeles, CA 90051-0090.

Main Ideas

- Because alcohol is a drug, it causes changes in someone who drinks it.
- Drinking alcohol can cause physical, emotional, and social problems.
- Some people, young and old, keep drinking alcohol even though they know it is harmful to their health.
- Concern for your health and a desire to stay in control of your body are reasons to avoid drinking alcohol.
- All tobacco products have drugs and other substances in them.
- Substances in tobacco cause harmful changes in a smoker's body.
- Using tobacco over time can cause deadly noncommunicable diseases.
- Refusing alcohol and tobacco can help you feel good about yourself and can protect your health.

Key Words

Write the numbers 1 to 9 in your health notebook or on a separate sheet of paper. After each number, copy the sentence and fill in the missing term. Page numbers in ( ) tell you where to look in the chapter if you need help.

alcohol (207)
peer pressure
  (209)
problem drinkers
  (210)
smokeless
  tobacco (213)

nicotine (214)
tar (214)
carbon monoxide
  (214)
tumors (216)
sidestream smoke
  (217)

1. Tobacco that can be put directly into the mouth and left there for a while is called ___?___ .

2. A drug in tobacco called ___?___ makes the openings of blood vessels smaller than they should be.

3. The drug found in drinks like beer, wine, and whiskey is called ___?___ .

4. People who need alcohol to feel normal are called ___?___ .

5. Harmful cells caused by the tar in tobacco form lumps called ___?___ .

6. The smoke of burning tobacco contains a sticky, dark brown substance called ___?___ .

7. Burning tobacco forms the gas ___?___ .

8. Smoke breathed by a nonsmoker is called ___?___ .

9. When young people try to talk other young people into doing something, the other young people may feel ___?___ .

Remembering What You Learned

Page numbers in ( ) tell you where to look in the chapter if you need help.

1. What organ is most quickly affected by drinking alcohol? (207)

2. What are two ways that some young people pressure others into drinking alcohol? (209)

3. What is one reason that some people do not drink alcohol? (209)

4. Who can become a problem drinker? (210)

5. What are two problems that a problem drinker might have? (211)

6. How is carbon monoxide from tobacco smoke harmful to the body? (214)

7. How do the drugs in tobacco get to cells in a smoker's body? (213–214)

8. What body parts are often harmed by smokeless tobacco? (216)

9. Why are smokers more likely to develop certain kinds of tumors than nonsmokers? (216)

10. What are two diseases that smoking cigarettes can cause? (216)

11. What are two reasons that some people start smoking? (218)

12. What four steps can you take to turn down an offer to use tobacco? (221–222)

Thinking About What You Learned

1. Why might a person who has drunk too much alcohol be dangerous to others?

2. How might a problem drinker cause problems for his or her family and friends?

3. What are some polite statements a parent might make to someone whose smoking is bothering you?

4. How might refusing to take a first puff from a cigarette make you feel about yourself?

5. How might trying to act grown-up by smoking be a bad health choice?

6. Why are there laws against selling tobacco products to young people?

Writing About What You Learned

1. Why do alcohol and tobacco sellers use actors and sports people to advertise their products? Write a letter to a celebrity who is seen in alcohol or tobacco advertising. Ask why he or she helps sell harmful products.

2. Prepare five "Did you know . . . ?" questions about tobacco. Your questions should stress the dangers of using tobacco. When you finish your questions, work in small groups to make a larger list. Share your lists with your classmates, parents, and friends.

3. Suppose a friend asked you to try some smokeless tobacco. In a paragraph or two, tell what you would say and do to refuse.

Applying What You Learned

ART

Draw a poster that shows you, at some time in the future, having fun without using alcohol or tobacco.

SOCIAL STUDIES

Tell why communities make laws against smoking in some public places.

Modified True or False

Write the numbers 1 to 15 in your health notebook or on a separate sheet of paper. After each number, write *true* or *false* to describe the sentence. If the sentence is false, also write a term that replaces the underlined term and makes the sentence true.

1. <u>Tobacco</u> can harm the liver.
2. If you drink to make your friends like you, you are giving in to <u>peer pressure</u>.
3. All tobacco products contain the drug <u>caffeine</u>.
4. Burning tobacco produces a harmful gas called <u>carbon monoxide</u>.
5. Wine contains <u>alcohol</u>.
6. Smoke breathed in by a person other than the smoker is <u>sidestream smoke</u>.
7. Lung cancer is caused by <u>alcohol</u>.
8. The tar in tobacco smoke can cause the <u>alveoli</u> in the lungs to burst.
9. People who need to drink alcohol to feel good may be <u>problem drinkers</u>.
10. <u>Tumors</u> are lumps that grow in the body and can become cancer.
11. People who smoke can get a <u>communicable</u> disease called emphysema.
12. Alcohol destroys the brain's ability to control the <u>circulatory</u> system.
13. Alcohol may change a person's personality and lower <u>self-esteem</u>.
14. <u>Tar</u> is a sticky, dark brown substance formed by tobacco smoke.
15. Substances in smokeless tobacco enter the body through blood vessels in the nose or <u>lungs</u>.

Short Answer

Write the numbers 16 to 23 on your paper. Write a complete sentence to answer each question.

16. Why is alcohol considered a drug?
17. How can peer pressure be used in a good way?
18. Why is alcohol more harmful for a person who is small?
19. How is smokeless tobacco different from cigarettes?
20. What are four things to remember that can help you say no to harmful substances?
21. How does nicotine affect the body?
22. Why do some people have difficulty when they try to stop smoking?
23. What are some unattractive things about people who use tobacco?

Essay

Write the numbers 24 and 25 on your paper. Write paragraphs with complete sentences to answer each question.

24. Explain why starting to smoke tobacco at a young age is an unwise choice.
25. Describe how you think a family would be affected if one of the members were a problem drinker.

ACTIVITIES FOR HOME OR SCHOOL

Projects to Do

1. This project will help you understand the effects of alcohol on bodies of different sizes. Find two glasses that are the same size. Fill one glass halfway with water. Fill the other glass completely with water. Put one drop of food coloring in each glass. In which glass is the color darker? Why? How does this effect relate to the effects of alcohol?

2. Cut out advertisements for tobacco products in magazines. What are the people in the ads doing, besides using tobacco? How do they look? How do they seem to feel? What do advertisers want you to think about tobacco use? Use the advertisements as models for making your own posters with slogans for *not* smoking. Ask to display your no-smoking posters in your school.

Information to Find

1. All states have laws against the use of alcohol and tobacco by young people. Find out about the laws in your state. Call the local police department to find out about state and local laws concerning the sale and use of alcohol and tobacco.

2. About how many of the people who get lung cancer each year are smokers? The American Cancer Society or the American Lung Association will have helpful information. Look in a telephone book

■ *Think of a slogan and share it with your family and classmates.*

for the address and telephone number of a local branch.

3. Many people realize the dangers of problem drinking. Special health workers often work with people who are problem drinkers to help them become nondrinkers. Find out the places in your community where problem drinkers and their families may find help.

Books to Read

Here are some books you can look for in your school library or the public library to find more information about alcohol and tobacco.

Be Smart! Don't Start! Just Say No! U.S. Department of Health and Human Services.

Stepney, Rob. *Alcohol.* Franklin Watts.

Stepney, Rob. *Tobacco.* Franklin Watts.

CHAPTER 9

KEEPING SAFE

Accidents can happen at any time and at any place. They can happen when you are playing. They can happen at home or at school. Sometimes they seem to happen for no reason. Other times they happen because someone was not careful.

Accidents are one of the greatest dangers to your health. Knowing what causes accidents may help you keep many of them from happening. Knowing what to do when accidents occur can help you and others. You can plan ahead for safety. Being careful is the best self-defense against accidents. Your safety is your responsibility.

GETTING READY TO LEARN

Key Questions
- Why is it important to learn about safety and first aid?
- What choices can you make to keep yourself safe?
- What can you do to become more responsible for your own safety and the safety of others?

Main Chapter Sections
1 Planning Ahead for Your Safety
2 Safety at Home
3 Safety at Play
4 Safety on the Road
5 Safety near Water

1 Planning Ahead for Your Safety

accident (AK suhd uhnt), an unexpected event.

Think about some of the things you do each day to keep yourself healthy. Your daily health habits are sometimes not enough. Your health could be harmed by an unexpected event. This kind of event is called an **accident.** If you know what to do when an accident happens, you can keep yourself and others safe. Knowing what to do when an accident happens will make you feel good about yourself. It will help you become a confident person!

■ *Even when you are careful, you or a friend could be hurt in an accident. You need to know what to do when an accident happens.*

What Can You Do When an Accident Happens?

Sometimes an accident causes harm, and help is needed right away. This is called an **emergency.** Car accidents and fires are emergencies that sometimes happen. If you see an emergency, you should first try to stay calm. Staying calm can help you remember the best actions to take.

emergency (ih MUR juhn see), a situation in which help is needed right away, as in a serious accident.

232

In an emergency, take time to check the scene and the victim. You may need an adult to help you. If you cannot find an adult, you may need to act on your own. If you are near a telephone, you can get help by calling 911 or 0 (zero). **911** is an emergency telephone number in many places. You can use it to get help from the police, the sheriff, the fire department, an ambulance service, or the emergency medical services (EMS). You can use it when there is a fire or an injury from an accident or when you are in danger.

911, a special telephone number for emergencies.

If you call 911 or 0 (zero), tell the operator that you are making an emergency call. Clearly state where the emergency is. If you do not know the address, describe or name the nearest buildings. Tell the operator what kind of accident you are reporting and how many people you think are hurt.

■ *In an emergency, you can call 911 or 0 (zero). Tell the operator that you need help. This is a free call; you do not need a coin.*

The operator needs to know your first and last name and the telephone number from which you are calling. Someone may need to call you back for more facts. The telephone number should be on the telephone you are using. The operator will tell you if you have given enough facts about the emergency. Wait for the operator to tell you to hang up. The operator will send help right away.

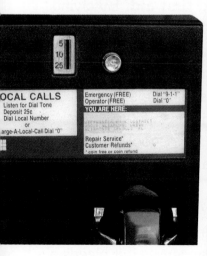

■ *Volunteers of the American Red Cross can teach you and your classmates first aid for helping someone who is hurt.*

What Can You Do to Help Someone Who Is Hurt?

You may have to act on your own in an emergency until trained medical help arrives. The help you give before trained help arrives is called **first aid.** By giving first aid, you could stop an injury from getting worse and help it heal faster. This is because your actions could keep another injury or an infection from happening. You might even save someone's life!

first aid, emergency help given before trained help arrives.

First aid for many kinds of injuries is taught by the American Red Cross. Your teacher or school nurse can also teach you ways to help in many kinds of accidents.

wound (WOOND), a break or cut in the skin.

One kind of injury is a wound. A **wound** is a break or cut in the skin. Small scrapes and cuts are not dangerous wounds. A wound is dangerous if it bleeds a lot and does not stop bleeding in a few minutes.

If you give first aid, do not touch the hurt person's wound or blood. Microbes on your hands could pass an infection or disease to the person you want to help. Some diseases can be passed through the blood from one person to another. By not touching another person's wound or blood, you may avoid giving a disease to someone else. You may also avoid getting a disease yourself.

Here are some steps to follow when giving first aid for a small wound:

- Stay calm.
- Use a clean cloth to wash the wound with soap and cool, running tap water.
- Put a bandage over the wound to keep it clean. A bandage can be a specially made cloth pad with sticky tape. Or you can make one with clean cloth. Then you need to hold it in place with another piece of clean cloth.

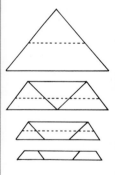

Making a Bandage

Take a clean cloth and fold it into the shape of a triangle. Fold the top point of the triangle down to the middle of the base. Then keep folding the cloth in half until the width is the size you need. (See diagram.) This kind of bandage can be used for many different injuries. It can be used to bandage almost any part of the body.

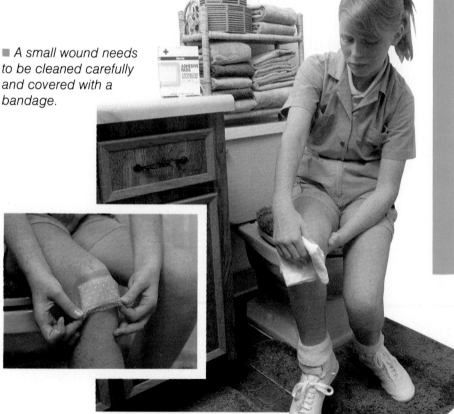

■ *A small wound needs to be cleaned carefully and covered with a bandage.*

235

■ *You can help someone who has a serious wound. Stay calm. Try to stop the bleeding with a clean cloth. Call for help.*

Here is what you can do to give first aid for a serious wound:

■ Stay calm and get help or send for help.
■ Put a clean cloth over the wound to keep the wound clean.
■ If the wound is bleeding, use the person's hand to push down on the cloth to put pressure on the wound. This will slow down or stop the flow of blood.
■ If possible, raise the wounded part of the body above the level of the heart. This will slow the blood going to the wound, so it will bleed less.

REVIEW SECTION 1

REMEMBER?

1. What are two emergencies that happen often?
2. What are two telephone numbers you can call to get help during an emergency?
3. How can you help someone who has a wound?

THINK!

4. Why might you cause a problem if you are not calm during an emergency?
5. Why is it very important to tell an emergency operator where you are?

2 Safety at Home

You can plan for safety by learning how to keep accidents from happening. You can practice accident prevention. **Accident prevention** means acting in ways that do not cause hazards. **Hazards** are unsafe conditions that can cause accidents. Think about ways you can prevent accidents at home.

accident prevention (AK suhd uhnt • prih VEHN chuhn), keeping accidents from happening.

hazards (HAZ uhrdz), conditions that are not safe.

■ *There are many hazards around you. You can prevent some accidents by looking for hazards and removing them.*

People of all ages do a lot of things at home. Cooking, bathing, and using cleaning products present special hazards. You and your family can check for hazards in and around your home. Look for hazards that could lead to injuries such as falls, burns, wounds, poisoning, and electric shock. You need to become more aware of the hazards in your home.

How Can You Prevent Home Accidents?

Terry and her father talked about some hazards in their home. Falls often happen where floors are wet or when things are left where someone can trip over them. Bathtubs and bathroom floors should have mats or towels for people to step on when they have wet feet. Terry's father praised her for keeping her toys off the stairs and away from doorways.

Terry's mother pointed out that she always unplugs appliances when they are not in use. She showed Terry the locations of all the smoke detectors. Terry and her mother reviewed a family rule that no matches or lighters are to be used unless an adult is watching.

■ *It is dangerous to light a candle when an adult is not watching. The candle might be tipped over, causing a fire.*

Look around your house. Check for things that could cause someone to fall or be burned. Offer to help remove or change these hazards. The things you do to keep yourself safe are called **safety measures.**

safety measures (SAYF tee • MEHZH uhrz), the things you do to keep safe.

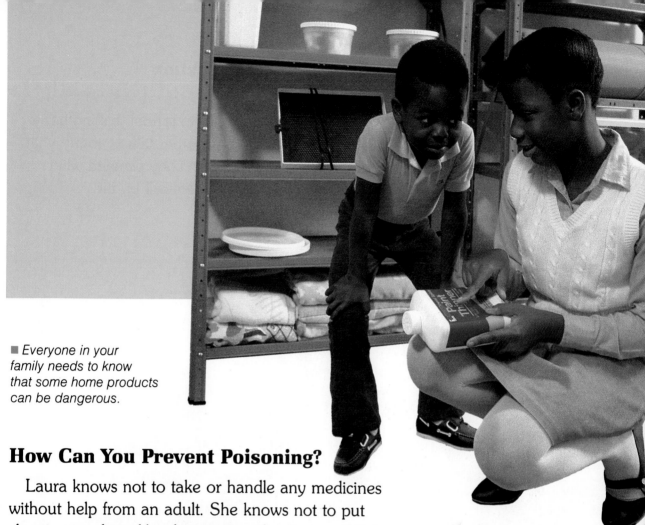

■ Everyone in your family needs to know that some home products can be dangerous.

How Can You Prevent Poisoning?

Laura knows not to take or handle any medicines without help from an adult. She knows not to put cleaning products like detergent or furniture polish in or near her mouth. She helps keep her little brother away from paint thinner and bug sprays in the garage. Such products are poisonous. They can cause illness or even death. These things must be kept out of the reach of all children.

Laura wants to know how to help if someone swallows poison. Here are some helpful hints:

- Stay calm and get help right away.
- If you see the poison container, take it with you to the phone. There may be directions on it that tell what kind of treatment is needed in an emergency.
- If an adult is not near, call 911 or 0 (zero) on the telephone to get help. Or call the Poison Control Center. The telephone number is in your phone book.

How Can You Be Safe When You Are Home Alone?

When Michael gets home from school, his mother is still at work. Michael and his mother talked about what he should do when he is alone. They planned what Michael should do when strangers call on the telephone or come to the door.

■ Michael calls his mother as soon as he gets home from school to let her know that he is safe. Michael also tells his mother what he will be doing until she comes home.

If a stranger calls on the telephone, Michael will not let the person know that he is alone. The caller may ask for Michael's mother. Michael will say that his mother is busy and cannot come to the telephone. He will offer to take a message.

If a stranger comes to the door, Michael will not open the door or talk to the stranger. If the stranger does not go away, Michael will call for help. Michael's mother has put her work number, the neighbors' telephone numbers, and emergency numbers next to the telephone. The emergency telephone numbers are those of the police, fire station, and hospital. The 911 emergency number is also near the telephone. These are good emergency numbers for everyone to keep handy. Like Michael, you should talk to your family about how to stay safe when you are home alone.

STOP REVIEW SECTION 2

REMEMBER?

1. What three steps should you follow if someone has swallowed a poison?
2. What are three common accidents that occur in homes?
3. When should you call 911?

THINK!

4. How might having emergency telephone numbers next to the telephone in your home be helpful for everyone?
5. What is the best way for you to stay safe at home when you are alone?

3 Safety at Play

KEY WORD

sunscreen

Play and sports are more fun for everyone if games are played safely. Safe play means choosing or making a safe place to play. When you play outdoors, safe play also means dressing for the weather to protect your body from being too hot or cold. Before you go out, make sure you have permission from a parent or guardian. Your family should know where you plan to play. This is just as important as knowing how to reach your family when you are home alone.

What Can You Do to Be Safe at Play?

School grounds and parks are usually safe. But you and your friends need to look around the area for hazards before you start to play. Stay away from places where there are motor vehicles, too. Report hazards such as broken play equipment to an adult.

■ *Let your family know where you will be at all times.*

■ *Reporting broken equipment helps keep your play area safe.*

242

Even when you choose a safe place to play, accidents might happen. A dog or cat might come into your play area. Stay away from any animal, even if it looks friendly. When an animal is frightened, it may scratch or bite you. Animal scratches can cause infection. Get help from an adult if an animal does scratch or bite you. Tell the adult what kind of animal bit you. Describe what it looked like.

Staying away from strangers is another way to be safe. It is never safe to get into a car or to go anywhere with a stranger. Sometimes strangers act friendly but tell lies. They may say they need help to find a lost pet. They may say that your family asked them to take you home.

■ *Never go with a stranger, even if he or she asks for your help.*

If a stranger tries to make you go with him or her or tries to make you do something that you know is not right, there is something you can do. Yell "No!" as loudly as you can, and scream for help. This may scare the stranger away.

If a stranger comes near you and your friends, try to notice what the person looks like. If the stranger is in a car, notice its color and license plate number. Write down the number, even if you have to scratch it in the dirt with a stick or on a sidewalk with a rock. Then get help from an adult you know or from a police officer.

How Can You Be Safe When Playing in the Sun?

When playing outside in the summer, Chris and her friends choose ways to protect themselves from the sun. Being in the sun too long can give you a sunburn. A sunburn can be painful and can also damage the skin. Chris and her friends protect their skin by covering most of it with light-colored, loose-fitting clothes. Where their skin is not covered, they wear a sunscreen. A **sunscreen** is a substance that blocks the sun's strong rays and protects you against a sunburn. The label on a sunscreen product gives important directions about how often to use it.

Like Chris and her friends, you need to know about the hazard of getting too much sun. The sun is strongest from about 11 A.M. to 3 P.M. During this time, you have a greater chance of getting a sunburn. You need to protect your skin.

sunscreen (SUHN skreen), a substance that blocks the sun's harmful rays and protects against sunburn.

■ *Zinc oxide ointment blocks out the sun's rays. It protects your skin from sunburn.*

244

How Can You Be Safe When Playing in Cold Weather?

During the winter, Carlota plays outdoors. She likes to ice-skate and go sledding. She skates only on ponds or lakes where places are marked for safe skating. When Carlota goes sledding, she chooses a hill without trees. She also stays away from roads. That way, she will not slide into a car's path.

Carlota dresses in layers of winter clothes to stay warm and dry when she goes outdoors in cold weather. Loose-fitting clothes are warmer than tight-fitting clothes. Hats, gloves, and boots or shoes that can keep feet dry and warm will help you protect the parts of your body that get cold easily. If you do not cover your skin in cold weather, your body will lose much of its warmth. By dressing properly for cold weather play, you can stay warm and dry and have fun, too.

■ *Dressing to stay warm and dry and sledding only where it is safe can add to the fun of winter play.*

STOP

**REVIEW
SECTION 3**

REMEMBER?

1. What should you do if an animal scratches or bites you?
2. What is a sunscreen?
3. What safety steps should you take when playing in cold weather?

THINK!

4. What makes a place safe for play?
5. How might playing alone on a playground be a risk to your safety?

245

Health Close-up

Playing on Holidays

Playing on holidays can be fun. But there are special dangers that can cause serious accidents.

Ben and his family went on a Fourth-of-July picnic. Many people in the park were using firecrackers. Ben's family knew that people could be badly hurt by firecrackers. Ben's family stayed away from the people who were using them.

On Halloween Jonathan made a scary costume. It was brightly colored so that people could see him. He did not wear a mask because masks are hard to see through. Instead, he made up his face to look scary.

Jonathan and Rita went trick-or-treating together. They stayed in their own neighborhood. Then they went to Rita's house for cider. They made sure their treats would be safe. Before eating any of their treats, they let Rita's mother look at them.

Some special days bring extra danger. Christmas and Hanukkah candles are beautiful parts of many holiday activities. Candles, however, can cause fires. To have a good time without being hurt on a holiday, you should think about dangers ahead of time. Knowing the dangers will help you avoid accidents and have fun.

Thinking Beyond

1. What special holiday dangers, other than those mentioned, should you watch out for?
2. How would you design a safe Halloween costume?

■ *Face painting is safer than wearing a mask at Halloween. Many masks limit vision and breathing.*

246

4 Safety on the Road

Think about how you get from your home to where you play. Sometimes, you may ride your bicycle or skateboard. At other times, you may walk or ride in a car. Your actions while walking, riding a bicycle, or riding in a motor vehicle are important for your safety and the safety of others. You have to choose the right safety habits and rules for each kind of travel.

How Can You Be a Safe Pedestrian?

When Jorge walks home after playing, he is a **pedestrian.** This means Jorge is walking to get from one place to another. He remembers that he has a responsibility to walk safely, just as a car driver has a responsibility to drive safely. Jorge walks on the sidewalk. If there are no sidewalks, he walks on the left side of the road facing oncoming traffic. He walks on the ground away from the edge of the road, if possible. When Jorge and his friends walk along the road, they walk single file. They watch and listen for motor vehicles. They stay alert!

KEY WORDS

pedestrian
crosswalks

pedestrian (puh DEHS tree uhn), a person who walks to get from one place to another.

■ Where there is no sidewalk, walk along the edge of the road, facing traffic. In a group, walk single file.

When crossing streets, Jorge and his friends use crosswalks. **Crosswalks** are marked places where people can cross a street safely. Even in crosswalks, Jorge and his friends stay alert for motor vehicles. If there is no crosswalk, they cross only at street corners. They look for traffic lights or crossing guards to help them keep safe. They cross only when there is a green light or Walk sign. They follow the directions of the crossing guards and school safety patrol.

At night Jorge never walks alone. As safe pedestrians, he and his friends always wear light-colored clothing at night. That way, drivers passing by can see them better. Jorge tries to walk where there are streetlights. Lights help him to be seen. They also help him see where he is going. If Jorge must walk where there are no lights, he uses a flashlight.

Thinking About Your Health

Do You Act Safely?

Some people act in ways that are dangerous. Read the following descriptions of people who act in unsafe ways. Each way of acting could lead to an accident. Do you sometimes act like any of these people?

- Samantha Showoff takes a lot of chances. She will do anything to call attention to herself.
- Dan Daydreamer forgets where he puts things. Sometimes it seems he does not think about what he is doing.
- Denise Daredoer will take a dare to do anything. She is afraid her classmates might not accept her if she does not take a dare.
- Robby Robot walks and moves at a steady, slow pace. He usually does not see what goes on around him.

From time to time, everyone is like Samantha, Dan, Denise, or Robby. Which one are you like most often? In your health notebook or on a separate sheet of paper, describe something you once did when you were like one of these people. Also describe what happened as a result.

light

horn

reflectors

chain guard

reflector

Right turn

Left turn

Stop

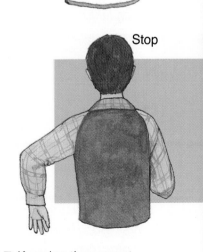

How Can You Be Safe When Riding?

Riding on bicycles, skateboards, or roller skates can be fun. But riding also means you are responsible for your safety and the safety of other people. Even though you are having fun, there are safety habits and rules to follow. To be a safe rider, you must first learn the necessary skills by practicing. You also need to know the rules, wear a helmet, and use equipment that can keep you from getting an injury while riding.

Cora rides her bicycle on the right side of the road. She stays close to the edge of the road so she can keep out of the way of traffic. At corners she walks her bicycle across the road. Cora uses the proper hand signals. This lets car drivers know when she is turning, slowing, or stopping. She knows that drivers count on her to obey traffic signs and signals. Cora rides extra carefully when roads are slippery or wet.

■ Knowing the correct arm signals can help make you a safe rider.

249

At dusk and at night, Cora wears light-colored clothing so drivers can see her. Her bicycle also can be seen because it has the proper equipment. Every bicycle should have reflectors and a light. These things make bicycles easier for drivers to see.

Proper safety gear is important no matter what you are riding. Knee pads and elbow pads are important to wear when you ride a skateboard or go roller-skating. Wearing a helmet is a way to help prevent a head injury.

How Can You Be Safe in Motor Vehicles?

Arlon acts responsibly while riding in a car. He wears a seat belt. Arlon helps the driver of a car or bus by being a polite passenger. He sits quietly in his seat.

■ *Wearing a seatbelt is one of the most important safety steps you can take.*

Making Wellness Choices

After school one day, William and Edward have an argument. Edward asks to ride William's new bicycle. William says no. Edward walks away from William feeling angry at his friend.

Before school starts the next day, Edward is walking around the school building. He sees some older students doing something to William's new bicycle. He sees that they are loosening the safety nuts on the wheels.

 What should Edward do? Explain your wellness choice.

He speaks softly to other passengers. He does not distract the driver. Arlon never bothers drivers in other vehicles. He knows that when he is in his school bus, these actions set a good example for younger students.

Many school-bus accidents happen when students cross the street in front of their bus. You need to walk far enough in front of your bus so that the bus driver can see you. Before you cross in front of the bus, look at the bus driver and get a hand signal that he or she sees you. Make sure that the red lights on the bus are flashing. Even when the lights are flashing, look both ways before you cross the street. Sometimes drivers forget that they must stop for a school bus.

Being safe on the road is everyone's responsibility. Obeying the street signs and safety rules will help keep riders and pedestrians safe. Passengers in cars and school buses can work with drivers to prevent accidents.

■ *When approaching or leaving a school bus, be sure to cross in front of the bus. Look both ways before crossing traffic.*

STOP REVIEW SECTION 4

REMEMBER?

1. Where is it most safe for pedestrians to cross a street?
2. What kind of clothing can help you be safe when you are outside at night?
3. What safety gear can help keep a bicycle rider or skateboard rider safe?

THINK!

4. When there is no sidewalk, why should you walk facing oncoming traffic?
5. How might yelling or fooling around inside a moving motor vehicle be a hazard?

5 Safety near Water

Swimming in a pool is good exercise. Going to the beach can be great fun. Some people, however, forget about their safety at these places. When you have fun around water, there are two things you need to think about—fun *and* safety. They work well together.

How Can You Be Safe When Swimming?

Betty Ann and Steve took swimming lessons to be safe and to have fun in the water. They learned the survival float. They learned the buddy system, too. This is a way they can help protect themselves in the water. They swim together, as "buddies," never alone. Betty Ann and Steve also learned that even good swimmers can get tired while swimming. When Betty Ann and Steve get tired, they get out of the water to rest. They know how to use the survival float if they suddenly feel tired in deep water.

■ *The survival float is easy to learn and do.*

Betty Ann and Steve swim only in places where there is a lifeguard or an adult who swims well. Many places have rules for people who swim. These rules are made to protect the people in or near the water.

Knowing what to do in bad weather is a safety measure, too. When a storm is coming, Betty Ann and Steve quickly get out of the water. They know that lightning can hit a person in the water or can hit the water nearby. If this happens, a person could be injured or even killed.

How Can You Be Safe When Boating?

Betty Ann, Steve, and their families camped near a lake last summer. Betty Ann's father took them out in a boat. Before getting into the boat, everyone put on a life jacket. Betty Ann's father knew that if their boat were to sink or tip over, the life jackets would help them float.

Betty Ann and Steve sat still. If someone moves around too much or stands up in a boat, it might turn over. A boat that turns over can float upside down.

SURVIVAL FLOATING

If you get into trouble while you are in the water, follow these rules for survival floating.

- Stay calm. Do not thrash about or try to hold your head above water all the time.
- Take a deep breath. Relax. Let yourself sink. Move your arms and legs slowly. You will stay near the surface of the water.
- When you let out the air, lift your head above water. Take a deep breath. Relax. Repeat these steps until help arrives.

■ Staying in your seat and wearing a life jacket can make boating fun and safe.

Holding on to it can help you float. Holding on to the boat also makes it easier for someone to see you and to rescue you.

What Can You Do When Someone in the Water Needs Help?

If you see someone in trouble in the water, call loudly for help. Do not jump into the water to save the person. Instead, reach out with any long object that can reach the person. It can be a towel, a pole, or a tree branch. If the person is far away, throw a life preserver tied to a rope. Hold on to something or lie on your stomach so that you will not be pulled into the water. When the person grabs what you have held out or thrown, pull him or her to safety.

If you do not have a life preserver, throw anything that floats, such as an empty Styrofoam cooler or a boat cushion. Then the person can hold on to it and keep floating until help arrives.

■ *Use a pole or life preserver to help someone who is having trouble in deep water.*

STOP REVIEW
SECTION 5

REMEMBER?

1. What should you do if you get tired while swimming?
2. What can you do to keep safe while boating?
3. How can you help a swimmer in trouble and still keep yourself safe?

THINK!

4. Why should you always have a buddy when you go swimming?
5. What are three swimming safety rules you might find on a sign near a public pool?

255

People in Health

An Interview with a School Crossing Guard

Richard Kamal is a school crossing guard in Bradford, Massachusetts. He knows a lot about pedestrian safety.

What does it mean to be a school crossing guard?

I help students cross busy streets. During the school week, I am at my crossing when students are on their way to and from school. There is often a lot of traffic at my crossing. My job is to signal the traffic to stop so that students can cross the street safely. The students cross only when I tell them it is safe. After they are safely across the street, I walk back to the sidewalk. Then I signal the traffic to start moving again.

■ *Students cross the street only when Mr. Kamal tells them it is safe.*

What are some ways to help students learn pedestrian safety?

I do not let the students take chances with their safety. For example, I do not let them cross the street riding bicycles. For their safety, I ask them to get off their bicycles and walk the bicycles across the street. I also do not let students bounce balls while they are crossing the street. A safe pedestrian needs to give full attention to watching for traffic. I remind students that I am there to help them. The safety habits we learn will help us stay safe for a lifetime.

How did you learn to be a crossing guard?

In my area, the police department directs the crossing-guard program. I work for the police department.

■ *Stopping busy traffic can be dangerous. Some drivers are in a hurry and do not want to obey a signal to stop.*

I understand that this might be different in other places. Police officers meet with all the crossing guards regularly. We discuss ways to make crossing streets safer for the students. At one meeting, for example, we talked about what to do when drivers do not drive safely. If a driver does not obey my signal to stop, I write down the car's license-plate number. I give the number to the police. They contact the driver.

Do you wear special gear for your job?

The police department gave me a badge and a belt that I wear across my chest. I also wear a brightly colored safety vest. That way, drivers can see me easily when I signal them to stop.

What is the hardest part of your job?

Stopping busy traffic is dangerous. Many drivers are in a hurry. They do not always see me. Sometimes even when they do see me, they do not obey my signal to stop. This can be scary and dangerous. Also, I sometimes see students trying to cross without my help farther up the street. It is safer to cross with a crossing guard.

What do you like about being a school crossing guard?

It makes me feel good about myself. I am helping students travel safely to and from school. I like helping them think about good pedestrian safety. Many of the students are glad I am there to help. It is nice to hear them say thank you. I really enjoy my work because I think it is important. I even received an award for my work as a crossing guard.

Learn more about people who work as crossing guards. Interview a crossing guard. Or write for information to the International Association of Chiefs of Police, 1101 North Glebe Road, Suite 200, Arlington, VA 22201.

Main Ideas

- Staying calm during an emergency can help you remember what you need to do.
- Knowing first-aid skills could prevent further injury or even death.
- Safety at home means knowing what accidents happen at home, and it means working to prevent them.
- Talk with your family about how to stay safe when you are home alone.
- Selecting a safe play area will help prevent injuries while playing.
- Following guidelines about weather and about strangers can help protect your health and safety.
- Following safety rules while walking, riding, or being a passenger can prevent accidents.
- Following the rules for swimming and boating safety and never swimming alone could prevent an accident.

Key Words

Write the numbers 1 to 11 in your health notebook or on a separate sheet of paper. After each number, copy the sentence and fill in the missing term. Page numbers in ( ) tell you where to look in the chapter if you need help.

accident (232)
emergency (232)
911 (233)
first aid (234)
wound (234)
accident
  prevention (237)

hazards (237)
safety measures
  (238)
sunscreen (244)
pedestrian (247)
crosswalks (248)

1. Keeping accidents from happening is called ____?____ .

2. Unsafe conditions that should be avoided are called ____?____ .

3. In an ____?____, help is needed right away.

4. The help you give to an injured person is called ____?____ .

5. A special emergency telephone number in many communities is ____?____ .

6. The things you do to remove a hazard or to prevent an accident are called ____?____ .

7. A person who is walking is called a ____?____ .

8. A ____?____ is a lotion that blocks the sun's harmful rays and protects against sunburn.

9. A break or cut in the skin is a ____?____ .

10. An unexpected event that can cause harm is an ____?____ .

11. Marked places where people can safely cross a street are ____?____ .

Remembering What You Learned

Page numbers in ( ) tell you where to look in the chapter if you need help.

1. What is the first thing you should do in any emergency? (232)

2. What can you do to get help for someone who is hurt? (233)

3. Why should you be careful not to touch a wound or blood? (235)

4. What are the steps for giving first aid for a serious wound? (236)

5. What steps can you take if someone swallows poison? (239)

6. What can you do to be safe in your home when you are alone? (240–241)

7. What can you do to stay safe in a play area? (242–243)

8. What are some important safety rules for playing in the sun? (244) For playing in cold weather? (245)

9. What can a pedestrian do to walk safely at night? (248)

10. What two safety items need to be on a bicycle? (250)

11. List four safety rules to follow when you are in a motor vehicle. (250–251)

12. Name two safety measures for swimmers. (252–253)

13. What safety rules should boaters follow? (253–254)

Thinking About What You Learned

1. If you are talking to an operator about an emergency, why should you wait until the operator tells you to hang up?

2. How might your family's safety be affected if no one followed safety measures in your home?

3. Why is staying away from strangers a way to keep safe?

4. Why might walking in the same direction as traffic be a risk to your safety?

5. When a swimmer needs help, why should you throw the person an object that floats rather than swim to the person?

Writing About What You Learned

1. Write an accident report. Think of an accident you heard about recently. Describe who was in the accident and how, when, where, and why it happened. Tell what safety measures could have been followed to prevent the accident.

2. Suppose you are in a crowded shopping mall and you meet a young child who is lost. The child does not talk to strangers. Describe in a paragraph how you would help the child find his or her parent or guardian.

Applying What You Learned

SCIENCE

Summer is the season of the year when most people need protection from the sun. Explain why the sun is most harmful between 11 A.M. and 3 P.M.

LANGUAGE ARTS

Write about two decisions you made today that helped protect your safety.

259

Modified True or False

Write the numbers 1 to 15 in your health notebook or on a separate sheet of paper. After each number, write *true* or *false* to describe the sentence. If the sentence is false, also write a term that replaces the underlined term and makes the sentence true.

1. Remember in an emergency to stay <u>calm</u>.

2. A <u>wound</u> is a condition that is not safe.

3. To protect yourself from sunburn, use a <u>sunscreen</u>.

4. Dial <u>901</u> for help in an emergency.

5. Because there are <u>microbes</u> on your hands, do not touch a wound.

6. Putting your toys away every day is a good <u>safety measure</u>.

7. A pedestrian is a person who <u>rides</u> from one place to another.

8. Bug sprays and paint thinner can be <u>poisonous</u> if swallowed.

9. Always cross a street at a <u>crosswalk</u>.

10. A fire is an example of a <u>hazard</u>.

11. If you put a bandage on a wound, you are giving <u>first aid</u>.

12. For a serious wound, place that part of the body <u>below</u> heart level.

13. If a <u>stranger</u> calls, do not let the person know you are alone.

14. It is a good idea to put all emergency phone numbers <u>in a drawer</u>.

15. Wearing <u>dark-colored</u> clothing can protect your skin from the sun.

Short Answer

Write the numbers 16 to 23 on your paper. Write a complete sentence to answer each question.

16. What is the difference between an emergency and an accident?

17. Why is it important to stay calm in an emergency?

18. When should you call an adult for help in an emergency?

19. What should you do if you see someone in the water who needs help?

20. Why should you walk far in front of your school bus when crossing the street?

21. How can you keep warm while playing outside in cold weather?

22. What are some accidents that can happen at home?

23. Why should you try to find the container if someone has swallowed poison?

Essay

Write the numbers 24 and 25 on your paper. Write paragraphs with complete sentences to answer each question.

24. Describe what you should do to determine if a play area is safe.

25. Describe what you would do if you and a friend had to walk to another friend's house in the dark. In your essay, include how you would dress.

ACTIVITIES FOR HOME OR SCHOOL

Projects to Do

1. The class can make a first-aid kit to use in the classroom and to take on field trips. Your teacher may use American Red Cross Basic Aid Training or first-aid films to help you learn how to use the supplies. Your school nurse or principal can help you by supplying a heavy zippered bag or small kit box to store the supplies. Always keep the kit stocked.

2. Look at or draw a map of your community. Locate your home, your play areas, and your school or school bus stop. Trace the routes you take to get from one place to another. Identify each possible safety hazard on your map with an *H*. Put an *A* where there is usually an adult to help in an emergency. Put a *T* where there is a telephone that can be used to call for help in an emergency. Make a list of several places on your map where accidents could happen. Then make a list of ways you can prevent those accidents from happening.

Information to Find

1. What kinds of accidents happen most often to people your age? With a few other students, ask the school nurse, a local physician, and other people who help with local emergencies. List four to six of the most common accidents, and discuss with your classmates how they could be prevented.

■ *These are some products to include in a first-aid kit.*

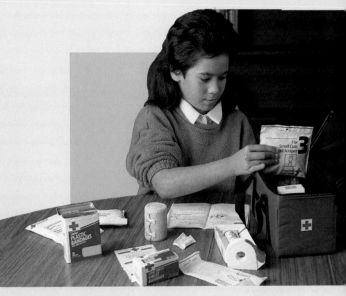

2. What swimming courses are given in your city or town? Contact your local American Red Cross, YMCA, or YWCA about these courses. Ask where and when the courses are given. Ask about the cost of each course. Create a chart with information for your class.

Books to Read

Here are some books you can look for in your school library or the public library to find more information about safety and first aid.

Cole, Joanna. *Cuts, Breaks, Bruises, and Burns.* T. Y. Crowell.

Kyte, Kathy S. *In Charge: A Complete Handbook for Kids with Working Parents.* Random House.

Ward, Brian. *First Aid.* Franklin Watts.

LIVING IN A
HEALTHFUL PLACE

Everyone needs a clean and safe place in which to live. States and towns have laws to tell people of ways to keep their communities clean. Some people where you live have jobs in which they help protect your health and safety.

Dirty air and dirty water are two problems that many communities have. Some community problems can be solved by people working together. Your community needs your help. You have a responsibility to protect your own health and not harm the community. You can help yourself reach wellness by making your community a healthful place in which to live.

GETTING READY TO LEARN

Key Questions

- Why is it important to know how your community can help you stay healthy?
- Why is it important to know how you and your family could harm or help protect your community's environment?
- How can you learn to make healthful choices about protecting your environment?
- How can you take responsibility for protecting the environment of your home and community?

Main Chapter Sections

1 Your Community Helps You Stay Healthy and Safe
2 Protecting the Environment
3 Guarding Community Resources

1 Your Community Helps You Stay Healthy and Safe

community (kuh MYOO nuht ee), a group of people who live in the same area.

Think how busy you and your family would be if you had to meet all your own health needs. You would have to plan for getting rid of all the trash from your home. You would have to make sure your food, milk, and water had no disease microbes.

You and your family depend on a lot of other people to meet some of your health needs. Your family and those other people make up the community in which you live. A **community** is made up of people who live in one area.

Some people in your community do jobs for you that take care of services. For example, some people deliver newspapers. Community workers operate libraries. Some people in your community, such as physicians, the police, and fire fighters, offer services that help you stay healthy and safe.

■ *Delivering the newspaper is a service other people do for you and your family.*

In most communities, government agencies take care of many kinds of health and safety services. Each **agency** is made up of people who work on one part of community health and safety. Some agencies make sure that food and water are clean and safe for people to use. Some agencies work to keep people safe. Some keep community parks safe and in good condition. Other community agencies give health care.

agency (AY juhn see), a group of government workers who are responsible for one kind of service.

What Kinds of Workers Help Keep Your Community Clean?

Miss Saito is one of many food inspectors in her community. She visits restaurants and the factories and stores where food is prepared and sold. Miss Saito checks to see that each restaurant kitchen, factory, or store is clean. She checks food that is going to be cooked or packaged. She checks food sold in markets.

■ Inspectors make sure food is safe to eat.

sanitary (SAN uh tehr ee), clean.

Miss Saito makes sure food is **sanitary,** or clean. Food that is not sanitary can cause illness among people who eat it.

A community also needs other sanitary services to help prevent communicable disease. Mr. Garcia's job is to check the water in his community. He takes samples of drinking water from public places and wells. Then the water is tested for disease microbes and harmful chemicals. If Mr. Garcia finds anything harmful in the water, he tells workers in the community's water department. The department treats the water or keeps people from drinking it until the water is safe.

Almost every community has sanitary services. Local governments may pay for many of the services, such as collecting garbage and inspecting food and water. Governments pay for the services with tax money from the people living in the community. What other sanitary services in your community can you name?

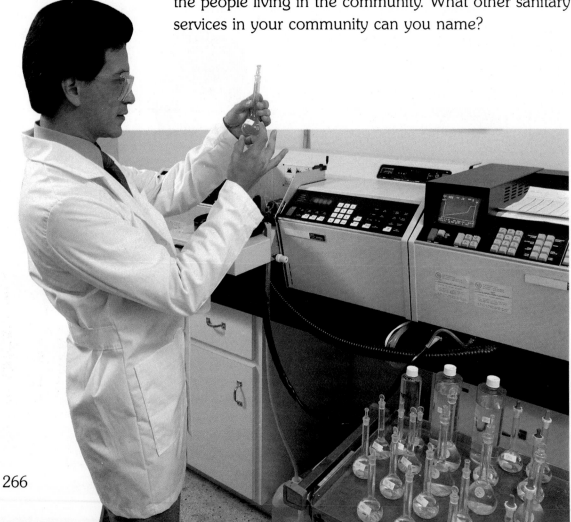

■ The water supply of a community must be checked regularly to make sure that it is clean and safe to drink.

What Kinds of Workers Help Keep Your Community Safe?

People often need community agencies for **public safety,** or community protection. Public safety is a shared responsibility of people and communities. Public safety workers help keep accidents from happening. They also help people in emergencies. Two important public safety agencies in your community are the fire and police departments.

Mr. Lesko is a fire fighter with the community fire department. He helps put out fires and saves people from fires. He also helps people in other emergencies. For example, he might be called to help save a person who has been trapped in a car after an accident.

Fire fighters also work to help keep fire emergencies from happening. They inspect schools and other public places for fire hazards. They make sure the buildings have safe escape routes. Sometimes Mr. Lesko explains fire safety rules to people.

■ *Public safety in your community includes fighting fires and saving people.*

public safety (PUHB lihk • SAYF tee), the protection of people in a community.

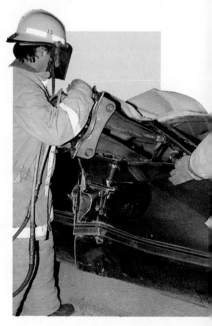

267

By following fire safety rules, people can keep many fires from starting. Mr. Lesko recommends

- putting smoke detectors in homes.
- making sure that a match is out and that its tip is cold before throwing it away.
- keeping matches away from young children.
- keeping furniture, clothing, rugs, and paper away from gas and electric heaters.
- designing and practicing a fire drill plan for home.

■ *The job of police officers includes helping pedestrians. Following a police officer's directions will help you safely cross busy streets.*

Mrs. Asher is a police officer. She reminds people to obey community laws. Communities make laws to help people live together safely in the community.

Officer Asher is talking with Geraldo and Sheila. She is reminding them that they should cross the street only at crosswalks and only when the light is green. If they cross at any other place or time, they may be hit by a car. Or they may surprise a driver and cause an accident in which other people are hurt.

Officer Asher talks to young people. She shows them how to be safe pedestrians. She shows them how to ride their bicycles safely.

Officer Asher teaches adults how to drive their cars safely. She tells people to use their seat belts in cars. She also shows people ways to make their homes safe from robbers. Every community has public safety workers like Officer Asher to help keep the people safe.

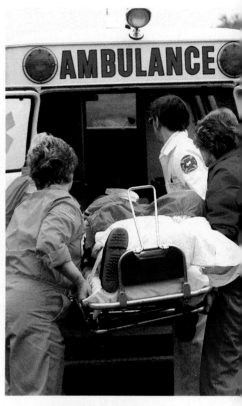

■ Both this nurse and these emergency medical workers are health workers in your community. They help you to stay healthy and well.

What Community Workers Help Keep You Healthy?

Some health workers in your community work directly with people. They help people meet their needs for physical care. Your school nurse, for example, is a community health worker. He or she may test hearing and vision. The nurse helps students and their parents learn how to take care of health problems. Your school nurse may talk to your class about preventing illness and injuries.

Other kinds of community health workers help when people become ill or injured. Health workers for an emergency medical service (EMS) are trained to handle serious illness and injuries. When someone is in an accident, EMS workers drive the ambulance and take care of the person on the way to the hospital.

hospital (HAHS piht uhl), a place where people receive health care they cannot get at home.

clinic (KLIHN ihk), a place where people receive medical services.

volunteer (vahl uhn TIHR), a person who offers to do something without being paid.

Many communities have a hospital. A **hospital** is a place where people can receive health care they cannot get at home. Some communities also have other places where people might find health services.

Physicians, nurses, and other health workers at a community **clinic** offer medical services. They work to find the causes of illnesses and to treat and prevent illnesses. Health workers at clinics test people for certain diseases. They give vaccines to prevent certain diseases. They teach people good health habits. At some clinics, people do not have to pay for health services. At others, they pay what they can. People who are very ill do not stay at a clinic. They go to a hospital.

Community health centers, like hospitals and clinics, also help people meet a variety of physical and emotional health needs. One person might need help for family troubles. Another person might need help for problems connected with the use of drugs, including alcohol. Community health centers have workers who can help people with their health needs. Some workers at community clinics and health centers are volunteers. A **volunteer** is a person who offers to do something without being paid.

■ *There are many ways that people can help with health care in their communities. Some are volunteers at hospitals.*

REMEMBER?

1. How does a food inspector help keep people healthy?
2. What do public safety workers do?
3. Name three different kinds of health care workers found in most communities.

THINK!

4. Describe how a community would be different without public safety workers.
5. How might being a community health volunteer help you when you are a teenager?

Thinking About Your Health

Who Do You Ask for Help?

Imagine you are in each of the situations listed below. In each case, you would most likely ask a parent or guardian for help first. Think of other people you might go to for help if a parent or guardian were not available. You may think of a number of different people or agencies for each situation. If you cannot think of any, you might want to talk with a parent, your guardian, the school nurse, or a teacher for help in these situations.

- You want to make sure a playground water fountain is safe.
- You want to design a fire-drill plan for your home.
- You want to learn more about taking care of your vision.
- You want to know who to call in an emergency.
- You want to know who to call if you become ill.
- You want to know where to get help if someone puts you in danger.

2 Protecting the Environment

KEY WORDS

environment
resource
pollution
solid waste

environment (ihn VY ruhn muhnt), everything found in and around you.

Your community depends on its environment for meeting people's needs. The **environment** is everything found in and around you. It includes all the nonliving things, such as air, water, and soil. It also includes all the living things, such as people, animals, and plants.

■ *Planting a garden is one way to learn about growing food and about protecting the environment.*

Everyone needs clean water and air. Everyone depends on the soil that grows food. Everyone also depends on plants and animals for clothing and shelter. All these parts of the environment are resources. A **resource** is something people use to meet their needs.

resource (REE sohrs), something people use to meet their needs.

272

What Causes Changes in the Physical Environment?

People change their environment by using it. Water, air, and food from the environment are used by people. They take trees for wood to make homes and other buildings. They take oil and coal for fuel.

At times people change the environment by adding to it. Sometimes they make it better, by building dams for flood control or by planting trees. Other times people harm the environment by adding to it.

People can harm the environment by adding matter to it that is not healthful. Unhealthful matter in the environment is **pollution.** When people pollute their environment, or make it dirty, they harm its water, air, and land.

Harmful matter in oceans, lakes, rivers, and streams is called *water pollution*. Garbage thrown into water causes water pollution. Chemicals from factories and oil from ships also pollute water. Wastes from people and animals can cause pollution, too.

pollution (puh LOO shuhn), unhealthful matter in the environment.

■ *By getting rid of pollution, it is possible to return polluted beaches and waterways to a natural state.*

solid waste (SAHL uhd • WAYST), garbage and litter.

Dirt and harmful matter in the air are *air pollution*. You can see smoke and dust that pollute the air. Some gases and chemicals pollute the air, too, but you cannot see them. Some air pollution is caused by cars and factories. Small bits of a building material called *asbestos* found in the air are dangerous to people. People pollute the air when they smoke tobacco. Smokers pollute the air not only for themselves but also for other people around them. Therefore, smoke from tobacco is a kind of "personal" air pollution.

When **solid waste**—garbage and litter—is tossed at the edge of a road or piled up in open spaces, it causes *land pollution*. This kind of pollution makes the environment not only unhealthful but also ugly.

■ *Every member of the community should share in the responsibility of keeping the environment clean.*

What Health Problems Does Pollution Cause?

Pollution is a harmful change in your environment. Pollution can also cause harmful changes in your body. If you drink polluted water, for example, it can make you ill. Swimming in polluted water can be dangerous. Disease microbes living in polluted water can get into your body through your skin, ears, and nose. You may also swallow some of the water by accident. When this happens, you can become ill.

■ *Drinking, swimming in, or even playing near polluted water can be dangerous to your health. Many disease microbes live in polluted water.*

Land pollution can also cause illness. Disease microbes can grow in garbage dumped in the open. Rats and insects eat the garbage. They can spread many kinds of communicable diseases.

Making Wellness Choices

One day Pamela sees her neighbor Mr. Wilson changing the oil in his car. He puts the old oil in a bucket. When Mr. Wilson has finished, he does some other chores. Later Pamela sees Mr. Wilson with the bucket of oil. He goes to the curb and dumps the oil down the drain. By doing so, Mr. Wilson is polluting the community water supply.

 What could Pamela do? Explain your wellness choice.

■ *Some factories still pollute the air with dangerous chemicals. However, many factories have installed special equipment that greatly reduces air pollution.*

Air pollution can harm people's health in many ways. It can make people's eyes sting or water. Air pollution can cause some people to have trouble breathing. This kind of pollution is believed to be a cause of noncommunicable diseases, such as heart and lung diseases. Noncommunicable diseases that come from breathing polluted air may take many years to develop.

You need to breathe oxygen to stay alive. Gases that pollute the air, such as carbon monoxide, can harm the tissues of the heart over time. The damage can cause the heart to beat unevenly. It may even cause the heart to weaken or stop beating. Polluted air can also cause damage to the lungs. Lung diseases from air pollution can cause a person to have poor health for many years. These diseases can even cause death.

Air pollution seriously harms very old and very young people. Older people who already have heart and lung diseases can become more ill by breathing polluted air. Air pollution can harm young people, whose hearts and lungs are still growing.

REVIEW
SECTION 2

REMEMBER?

1. What are three ways in which people can change their environment by using it?
2. What are three parts of your environment that are harmed by pollution?
3. How are people affected by air pollution?

THINK!

4. How might picking up litter help improve your community's environment?
5. Why is it risky to drink water directly from a stream or body of water?

Noise Can Be Pollution, Too

When there is too much noise in the environment, there is *noise pollution*. Noise pollution has many causes. It can be caused by car horns, loud sirens, or the roar of airplanes. Lawn mowers, weed trimmers, and power tools create noise problems for families at home. Television sets, radios, or tape players turned up loud can cause noise pollution at home, too. Noisy machinery in factories can cause noise pollution where people work.

Noise can harm people's health. It can make them nervous, cause them to have trouble sleeping, or make them get tired easily. Sudden noise can make a person's heart beat faster than it should. Being in a loud, noisy place can cause people to lose their hearing for a short time or even for a lifetime.

Listening to loud music is one cause of hearing loss in young people. Many times people turn the sound up too loud. Stereo headphones can cause even more hearing loss by bringing loud sounds too close to a person's ears. Loud music from headphones can damage parts of the inner ear.

Some communities try to cut down on noise pollution by passing certain laws to control it. Some laws keep car drivers from honking their horns, except in an emergency. Other laws keep airplanes from landing or taking off during certain hours of the day.

You can help prevent noise pollution in your environment. You can keep the

■ *Loud noise, such as from a crowded gym or an airplane, is a form of pollution.*

sound of your television, radio, or tape player turned down low. You can wear ear protection while using mowers or power tools. Doing these things will help make your environment less noisy and more healthful. You can ask family members to do the same things.

Thinking Beyond

1. What are some causes of noise pollution in your community?
2. Name five things that often cause noise pollution in your school.

People have learned about the health problems that pollution can cause. People have also taken responsibility for guarding community resources from pollution. They have become worried about their environment. Because of their worry, many people have begun to take action in their communities and at home. They are acting to cut down on the amount of pollution in their environment. They are working to keep new kinds of pollution from happening.

How Can Communities Protect Resources?

water treatment plant
(WAWT uhr • TREET muhnt • PLANT), a place in the community where water is made safe.

■ *A water treatment plant makes water safe for human use.*

The water that comes out of the faucets in your home needs to be safe to use. If you get water from a community water system, the water you bathe in, drink, wash clothes in, and cook with has been cleaned. The place in your community where water is made safe is called a **water treatment plant.** At the water treatment plant, disease microbes and wastes are removed from water. Then the water is safe for people in the community to use.

Many communities also have treatment plants for wastewater that comes from people's homes. At these wastewater treatment plants, solid materials are removed from the water. Any disease microbes left in the water are then killed. The treated water can be sent more safely into lakes, rivers, or streams.

Communities work to prevent air pollution by making pollution laws that must be followed by people in factories and homes. For example, laws require factory owners to remove harmful matter from factory waste. Factories are not allowed to dump their waste in the open.

■ *Some people take steps for reducing air pollution.*

The companies that make cars, trucks, and buses are working to improve engines. Then cars, trucks, and buses will put less pollution into the air. People who own vehicles are responsible for making sure the engines work the way they are supposed to work. Keeping a vehicle running properly cuts down on the amount of new air pollution. Some communities ask people to use buses and trains instead of driving cars. Use of buses and trains reduces the pollution because there is less traffic on the roads.

Some communities are working to cut down on land pollution by burying solid waste. First, community sanitary service workers pick up the garbage from people's homes. Then they take the waste to a dumping ground. Land that is built up by dumping solid waste in it is called a **landfill.**

After a landfill has been built up and covered properly, the land can be used in different ways. The land can be used as a park. Or houses or office buildings can be built on the land.

landfill, land that is built up by dumping solid waste.

■ *Waste is covered in a landfill so the land can be used again.*

■ *Recycling keeps the environment clean, saves resources, and provides a community service. It even earns money for people.*

Some communities reduce land pollution by making some waste useful. They **recycle,** or use again, the materials in many kinds of solid waste. Metal cans can be melted down and made into new cans. Newspapers can be cut up and made into new paper. Glass bottles and jars can be melted down. The melted glass can be made into new glass containers.

Recycling cuts down on land pollution. It also helps the environment in another way. It saves resources. When people recycle old materials, they use up fewer new resources.

recycle (ree SY kuhl), to use again.

What Can You Do to Prevent Pollution?

Communities can act to protect their resources. Individuals and families also can make choices that protect resources. There are many ways you can cut down on pollution. You can help by

- not littering.
- using cans and bottles that can be recycled.
- not bathing or washing in lakes, rivers, or streams when camping. Soap may harm plants and animals living in or around the water.
- recycling paper bags and newspapers.
- obeying community laws meant to reduce water, air, and land pollution.

■ Everyone can do something, such as picking up litter, to help keep the environment clean.

All people deserve clean and safe resources in their environments. You need such resources to meet your needs. Your environment has an effect on your health. Fighting pollution needs to be important to you all your life. It is your responsibility.

STOP REVIEW SECTION 3

REMEMBER?

1. Where is a community's water made safe to use?
2. How do communities work to prevent air pollution?
3. What is one purpose of a landfill?

THINK!

4. What are some things in your home that could be recycled?
5. Why is it important for you to take responsibility for helping to protect your environment?

People in Health

An Interview with a Fire Fighter

Mike Spath knows about keeping his community safe from fire. He is a fire fighter in the city of Charlotte, North Carolina.

As a fire fighter, what do you do every day?

When I am not fighting fires, I have other duties. I help keep the fire station and the trucks clean. I check fire-alarm boxes and fire hydrants in the neighborhood to make sure they work properly. I check buildings for fire hazards. I put in smoke detectors and give talks on fire safety. Fire fighters in Charlotte are also trained to help in all kinds of emergencies. So I must be ready to help in any kind of emergency.

What would you say is the hardest part of your job?

Fighting fires is very dangerous. In a building full of smoke, it is easy to get confused and lost. Many fire fighters are injured when they cannot find their way out of burning buildings.

What did you have to do to become a fire fighter?

I had to take many kinds of tests given by the city government. Some of the tests were written. They tested my ability to think. Others tested my physical strength. I also had to be able to talk about fire fighting and fire safety. After I passed all those tests, I took a training program given by the city fire department. The training lasted 16 weeks. I learned the best ways to put out fires and to keep fires from happening. I learned emergency first aid, too. The tests and the training were not easy to pass.

■ *Mike Spath wears special equipment when he puts out fires.*

■ *Part of a fire fighter's job is teaching people how to prevent fires.*

What special qualities does a fire fighter need besides knowing how to fight and prevent fires?

A fire fighter needs to be able to make smart decisions and to make them quickly. I never know what kinds of emergency calls I will get. Fire fighters must stay physically fit through a regular exercise program for endurance and strength.

What is the cause of most fires?

I would say that most fires are caused by people who act in careless ways. Smoking cigarettes and letting children play with matches cause many fires. Fires caused by careless people are the fires that can be prevented.

When you talk to young people about fire prevention, what do you say?

I teach children about using the telephone to report an emergency. I also teach them how important smoke detectors are. I tell them what to do if there is a fire. Their families need to have a home fire drill plan. I always try hard to make sure young people know they play an important part in community fire safety. Fire fighters put out many fires. Only the people in the community can keep fires from happening in the first place.

Learn more about people who work as fire fighters. Interview a fire fighter. Or write for information to the International Association of Fire Fighters, 1750 New York Avenue, N.W., Washington, DC 20006.

Main Ideas

- You depend on a lot of other people to meet some of your needs.
- A community uses many kinds of health workers to protect the health of its people.
- Workers such as fire fighters and police officers protect your safety.
- There are several kinds of health workers in your community who help when people become ill or are injured.
- Your community depends on its environment for meeting people's basic needs.
- Each person in a community has responsibility for protecting the community's resources from pollution.
- Pollution can have harmful effects on people's health.
- Each person can help protect resources needed for good health.

Key Words

Write the numbers 1 to 14 in your health notebook or on a separate sheet of paper. After each number, copy the sentence and fill in the missing term. Page numbers in ( ) tell you where to look in the chapter if you need help.

community (264)
agency (265)
sanitary (266)
public safety (267)
hospital (270)
clinic (270)
volunteer (270)
environment (272)

resource (272)
pollution (273)
solid waste (274)
water treatment
    plant (278)
landfill (280)
recycle (281)

1. People who __?__ materials reuse many kinds of old metal or paper.

2. A __?__ has garbage and other solid waste in it.

3. A __?__ is something people use in meeting their needs.

4. Unhealthful matter found in the environment is __?__ .

5. A special __?__ in your community might work to keep the food you buy safe and clean.

6. If food is __?__ , it is free of disease germs.

7. Police officers and fire fighters are examples of __?__ workers who protect the people in your community.

8. A __?__ is a place where people in a community can get health care they cannot get at home.

9. At a community __?__ , people can often get free medical help.

10. A __?__ in a hospital or clinic works without asking for pay.

11. Litter is an example of a __?__ that can cause land pollution.

12. The place in your community where water is made safe for home use is called a __?__ .

13. The people who live and work close to you make up your __?__ .

14. Your __?__ is everything found in and around you.

Remembering What You Learned

Page numbers in ( ) tell you where to look in the chapter if you need help.

1. Name two kinds of sanitary service workers. (265–266)

2. What kinds of safety workers help prevent accidents from happening? How? (267–269)

3. Name five fire safety rules. (268)

4. Name three places where people can get health services in a community. (270)

5. What parts of the environment are harmed by pollution? (273)

6. What are three causes of water pollution? (273)

7. How can swimming in polluted water be harmful to your health? (275)

8. What are three ways air pollution can harm a person's health? (276)

9. In what way does a water treatment plant make water safe to use in the home? (278)

10. How does recycling benefit the environment? (281)

11. What are three actions you can take to cut down on pollution? (282)

Thinking About What You Learned

1. How might your health be affected if your community did not have sanitary services?

2. Why should your family know where a hospital is located in your community?

3. What are some ways in which you have changed your environment today by using it?

4. Why do people need to work together to protect their environment?

5. How can you help protect your environment?

Writing About What You Learned

1. Imagine you are in a place with a lot of litter. You might be at the playground or walking along a street. Write a paragraph about what you feel and what you can do to make the place less polluted.

2. Signs in the community remind people to follow health and safety rules. Think about signs you have seen. Write the words for a sign reminding people to protect community resources.

3. "Every litter bit hurts." This is a slogan once used to get people to think about pollution. What does this slogan remind you to do about your environment? Write a paragraph or two about what the slogan means to you.

Applying What You Learned

MATHEMATICS

Do you know how much solid waste your family throws away each week? Weigh the bags of trash to be thrown away each week. Find out the total for a month.

Modified True or False

Write the numbers 1 to 15 in your health notebook or on a separate sheet of paper. After each number, write *true* or *false* to describe the sentence. If the sentence is false, also write a term that replaces the underlined term and makes the sentence true.

1. If something is sanitary, it is <u>dirty</u>.

2. Pollution can harm people's <u>health</u>.

3. Putting smoke detectors in homes is a good <u>safety measure</u>.

4. If you are very ill and need special health care, you could go to a <u>clinic</u>.

5. Land that is built up by dumping waste in it is a <u>landfill</u>.

6. If you offer to work without being paid, then you are a <u>resource</u>.

7. Asbestos can be a form of <u>land</u> pollution.

8. Air pollution can harm young people whose hearts and <u>lungs</u> are still growing.

9. Water that has not gone through a water treatment plant may have <u>disease microbes</u> in it.

10. Not littering is one way you can <u>increase</u> pollution.

11. All living things and nonliving things are part of the <u>environment</u>.

12. A <u>dam for flood control</u> changes the environment to make it better.

13. A fire fighter helps <u>public safety</u>.

14. Glass bottles left at a campsite are an example of <u>air</u> pollution.

15. Police officers belong to an <u>agency</u>.

Short Answer

Write the numbers 16 to 23 on your paper. Write a complete sentence to answer each question.

16. What is the difference between a clinic and a hospital?

17. Name three ways air pollution can harm your health.

18. What happens to water when it goes through a water treatment plant?

19. What are four things you can do to cut down on pollution?

20. What are two good things about living in a community?

21. How can having a fire drill plan protect you from fires?

22. How do fire fighters protect you from fires?

23. What are four different causes of air pollution?

Essay

Write the numbers 24 and 25 on your paper. Write paragraphs with complete sentences to answer each question.

24. Explain what you, as a member of a community, can do to help make it a better place in which to live.

25. Describe what you think might happen to the community if people did not take care of the environment.

ACTIVITIES FOR HOME OR SCHOOL

Projects to Do

1. Show how you and your family can help prevent pollution in your community. Use a sheet of poster board to make a "Pollution Prevention" chart. Make four columns on the poster. Write *Air, Water, Land,* and *Noise* at the top, in separate columns. Discuss with your family how you can prevent each kind of pollution. Then write down the ideas you all agree on. Put your chart where your family can see it. Use it as a reminder to help keep your community free of pollution.

2. Draw a map of your neighborhood. On your map, label all the fire-alarm boxes and fire hydrants. If there is a fire station in your neighborhood, label it on your map, too.

3. Plan and put on a skit for your class with a partner. The subject of the skit should be how to turn down a dare. The dare should be to do something that could make your school or neighborhood environment unclean or unsafe. One partner should encourage the other to take the dare. The other partner should explain why neither person should do anything to hurt the environment.

Information to Find

1. What is acid rain? What causes it? Does acid rain happen as often as air pollution? How can acid rain harm living things in rivers and lakes? Use library books to find out about this kind of pollution.

2. Certain stores take clothing or household goods that people no longer want. They often fix the goods and then sell them for a low price. Find out whether your community has such stores. How are such stores like recycling centers?

Books to Read

Here are some books you can look for in your school library or the public library to find more information about your environment.

Lambert, Mark. *The Future for the Environment*. Franklin Watts.

Woods, Geraldine, and Harold Woods. *Pollution*. Franklin Watts.

Pollution Prevention			
AIR	**WATER**	**LAND**	**NOISE**
Walk to the store	Don't put oil into sewer	Don't litter	Don't use the car horn unnecessarily

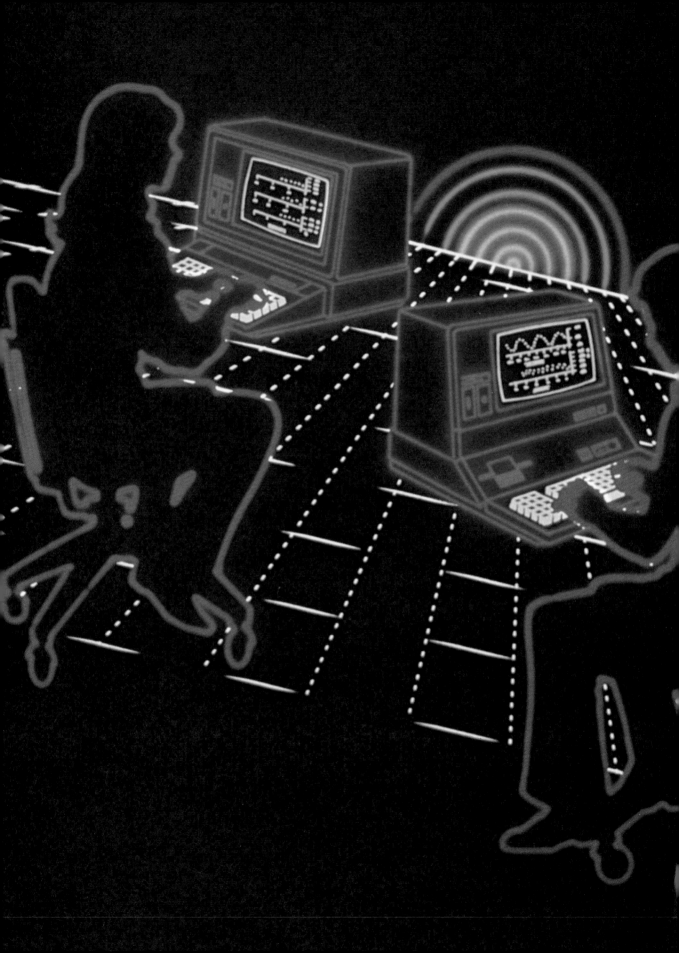

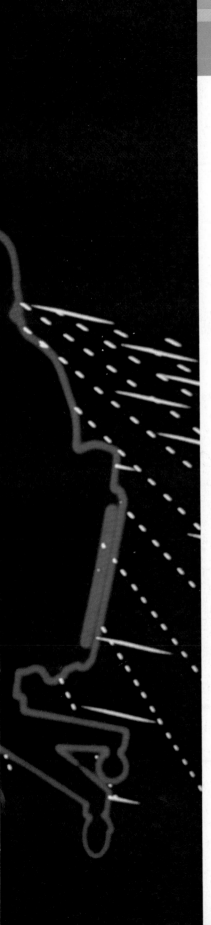

For Your Reference

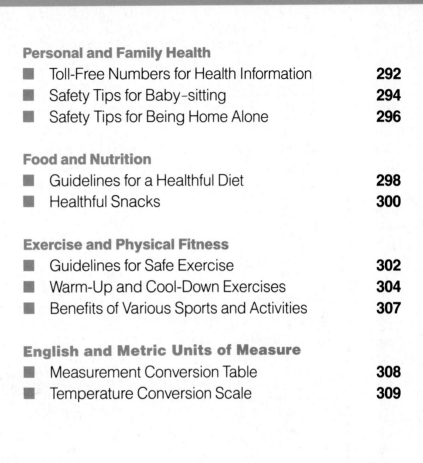

REFERENCE

Toll-Free Numbers for Health Information

The following toll-free numbers can provide you with immediate information about health problems or concerns. To call any of these numbers, simply dial 1 and then the number that is listed. Your call will be received by a qualified person who may be able to provide you with the information you need or refer you to someone who can. Do not hesitate to call if you have a question or concern.

General Health	(800) 336-4797		**Headache**	(800) 843-2256
In Maryland	(301) 565-4167			
			Hearing	(800) 222-EARS
AIDS and HIV Infection	(800) 342-AIDS			
In Washington, D.C.	(202) 332-2437		**Learning Disabilities**	(800) ABCD-123
Information in Spanish	(800) 344-SIDA		**(Dyslexia)**	
Auto Safety	(800) 424-9393		**Missing Children**	(800) 843-5678
In Washington, D.C.	(202) 366-0123		**English and Spanish**	
Cancer	(800) 525-3777			
English and Spanish	(800) 4-CANCER		**Pregnancy**	(800) 238-4269
In Alaska	(800) 638-6070			
			Runaway Hotline	(800) 231-6946
Child Abuse	(800) 422-4453			
	(800) 421-0353		**Runaway Switchboard**	(800) 621-4000
Cocaine	(800) COCAINE		**Sexually Transmitted**	(800) 227-8922
			Diseases	
Consumer Product Safety	(800) 638-CPSC			
			Sports and Fitness	(800) 227-3988
Diabetes	(800) 223-1138			
	(800) ADA-DISC		**Teen Crisis (Suicide)**	(800) 621-4000
Drug Abuse	(800) 662-HELP		**Vision Problems**	(800) 232-5463
			In New York	(212) 620-2147
Eating Disorders	(800) 334-8415			

Telephone Etiquette

The following tips will help you communicate effectively when calling any of the numbers listed or when making any other important telephone calls:

■ Before placing a call, spend a few minutes thinking about what you want to say and what you are interested in finding out. You may want to write down your questions on a notepad for ready reference. It is also a good idea to have a notepad and pencil or pen handy for taking notes during the conversation.

■ Select a telephone in a quiet location where you are sure you will not be disturbed.

■ When the party you are calling answers the telephone, give your name immediately: "Hello, my name is Alicia."

■ State the reason you are calling: "I am calling because I would like more information about...."

■ Ask your question or questions. If necessary, refer to your notepad. After asking a question, be sure to give the person time to answer. Give him or her your undivided attention. If necessary, take notes so you will remember the answer.

■ Upon completing the conversation, thank the person for his or her time and say good-bye in a polite manner.

■ While the information is still fresh in your mind, add to your notes as necessary.

Safety Tips for Baby-sitting

Baby-sitting can be a very rewarding and enjoyable activity. When accepting a job as a baby-sitter, discuss with the parents

- when they expect you to arrive.
- how long they will be away.
- what your responsibilities will be.
- the amount of pay you will receive.
- what arrangements will be made for your transportation to and from the home.

When baby-sitting, your primary concern is for the safety of the children. You are responsible for them, and they depend on you to make safe decisions. The following tips will help you be a successful and safe baby-sitter:

- Arrive for baby-sitting several minutes early so there will be time for the parents to give you important information about the care of their children.
- Write down where the parents can be reached.

- Know where emergency telephone numbers, such as those for the fire and police departments and for the children's physician, are located.

- Ask where first-aid supplies and any special medications the children must take are located. Note: You should not give any medications, even children's aspirin or cough syrup, unless specifically directed to do so by either the parents or a physician.

- Ask what and when the children should eat and how the food should be prepared.

- Ask what activities are allowed and preferred before bedtime.

- Ask when the children should go to bed and what the normal routine is for preparing for bed.

Additional Safety Tips

- Never leave an infant alone on a changing table, sofa, or bed.
- Never leave a child at home alone, even for a short time.
- Check children often while they are playing and while they are sleeping.
- Never leave a young child alone in a bathtub.
- Never leave children alone near or in a swimming pool.
- Never let a child play with a plastic bag.
- Keep breakable and dangerous items out of reach of children.
- Know where all the outside doors are, and keep them locked.
- Unless the parents have personally given you other instructions, do not unlock the doors for anyone except the parents.
- If the phone rings, take a message in a brief and businesslike manner. Do not tell the caller that you are the baby-sitter or that the parents are out. Simply say that the person asked for is busy now and that you will give him or her the message.
- In case of an accident or illness, depend on parents, neighbors, or emergency personnel instead of trying to handle the situation yourself.

REFERENCE

- Keep the outside doors and windows of your home locked.
- If someone you do not expect comes to the door, keep the door closed and locked. Ask, "Who is it?" through the closed door. Do not tell the person you are alone. The most you should do is offer to give your parents a message. If the person is selling something, you can simply say, "We're not interested," and nothing more.

- If someone calls on the telephone, be polite but do not offer any information. Do not tell the person that you are alone. Say that your parents are busy but you would be glad to take a message.
- If someone calls who is nasty or mean, hang up immediately. Tell your parents about the call when they get home.

- If you suddenly see or smell smoke that has an unknown source, leave the house or apartment immediately. If you live in an apartment, do not take the elevator. Go to a neighbor's house, and call the fire department right away.

- If you have a medical emergency, call 911 or 0 (zero) for the operator. Describe the problem, and give your full name, address, and telephone number. Wait for instructions. Hang up only when told to do so.

- Avoid being bored when you are home alone. Work on a hobby, read books or magazines, do your homework, or clean your room.

- Avoid spending your time alone watching television, unless there is a specific program you and your parents agree you should watch. Do not waste time watching just any program that happens to be on.

Guidelines for a Healthful Diet

- Eat a variety of healthful foods from the following food groups:
  - Bread, Cereal, Rice, and Pasta Group
  - Vegetable Group
  - Fruit Group
  - Milk, Yogurt, and Cheese Group
  - Meat, Poultry, Fish, Dry Beans, Eggs, and Nuts Group
- Eat few foods that are high in fat content, such as deep-fried foods, butter and other fat-rich dairy products, and red meat.

- Eat whole-grain products, vegetables, and fruits. Foods such as whole-grain breads, cereals, potatoes, and fresh vegetables and fruits are high in complex carbohydrates and fiber. Carbohydrates should represent about one-half of your daily calories.
- Achieve and maintain your ideal body weight. You may become overweight by eating more calories than your body uses. You can reduce your weight by eating fewer calories and less fat and by exercising more.
- Limit the amount of sweets that you eat. These foods are high in calories but provide very few nutrients.
- Avoid using additional salt, or sodium, in your diet. Limit your use of the saltshaker, and reduce your intake of foods such as pretzels, salted crackers, dill pickles, and cured or smoked meats.
- Drink plenty of water. Your body needs a ready supply of water to help transport nutrients, eliminate wastes, and regulate body temperature.

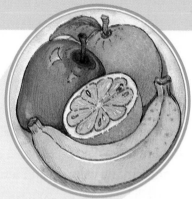

Food Needs of Young People 9 to 12 Years of Age

Food Group	Recommended Daily Amounts	Average Serving
Bread, Cereal, Rice, and Pasta	6– 11 servings	1 slice bread 1 ounce dry cereal 1/2 cup cooked cereal, rice or pasta
Vegetable	3– 5 servings	1 cup raw, leafy vegetables 1/2 cup cooked or chopped raw vegetables 3/4 cup vegetable juice
Fruit	2– 4 servings	1 medium-sized apple, banana, or orange 1/2 cup chopped, cooked, or canned fruit 3/4 cup fruit juice
Milk, Yogurt, and Cheese	2– 3 servings	1 cup milk or yogurt 1 1/2 ounce natural cheese 2 ounces processed cheese
Meat, Poultry, Fish, Dry Beans, Eggs, and Nuts	2– 3 servings	2–3 ounces cooked lean meat, poultry, or fish 1/2 cup cooked dry beans, 1 egg, or 2 tablespoons peanut butter count as 1 ounce lean meat

Healthful Snacks

Your health and growth depend greatly on the foods you eat. Therefore, you should try to eat the most nutritious and healthful foods that you can. This applies whether you are eating a formal meal or just having a snack. Unfortunately, many of the foods that are often eaten as snacks are not very healthful. They contain many calories and few or no nutrients. The foods listed here will help you to "snack smart." These foods are easy to find, nutritious, and taste great!

Crunchies
Apples and pears
Broccoli spears
Carrot and celery sticks
Cauliflower chunks
Green–pepper sticks
Radishes
Unsalted rice cakes
Zucchini slices

Hot Stuff
Soups: clear soups, homemade vegetable or tomato soups
Cocoa made with nonfat milk
Tortillas topped with green chilies and a little
   grated mozzarella

Munchies

Almonds and walnuts

Bagels

Bread sticks

Popcorn (prepared without butter, margarine, oil, or salt)

Mixture of 2 cups soy nuts, 2 cups raw peanuts roasted in oven, and 1 cup raisins or other dried fruit

Mozzarella (made from part-skim milk)

Unsalted sunflower seeds

Whole-grain breads

Thirst Quenchers

Nonfat milk or buttermilk

Unsweetened juices

Unsweetened fruit juice concentrate mixed with club soda

Sweet Stuff

Baked apple (plain—without sugar or pastry)

Dried fruit

Fresh fruit

Raisins

Thin slice of angel food cake

Unsweetened canned fruit

Guidelines for Safe Exercise

Exercise is a necessary part of a healthful life-style. Exercise can help you tone your muscles and improve your cardiovascular system. Exercise can also help you look and feel your best.

- Start each workout by doing warm-up exercises. First, spend a few minutes stretching your muscles as shown on pages 304 to 306. These exercises will improve your flexibility. Then spend a few minutes gradually working into the main activity of your workout. By taking it slowly, you gradually increase your heart rate and prepare yourself for vigorous exercise. An adequate warm-up will reduce your chances of injury during the workout and will make the workout less of a strain and more enjoyable.

- Set realistic goals for the workout. Do not try to do too much too fast.

- Stop exercising if pain occurs. Continuing to exercise while in pain may lead to serious injuries.

- Avoid exercising in high-heat situations. If you are not used to the heat, exercise less than your normal amount.

- Drink plenty of fluids, particularly water.

- In cold weather, wear layers of clothing when exercising. That way you can take off a layer at a time as you get warm. Wear a hat when exercising outdoors in cold weather.

- Do not do vigorous exercises immediately before or after a meal. It is best to exercise at least one hour before or two hours after eating.

- Avoid exercising on extremely hard surfaces, such as concrete. Surfaces with more "give," such as grass, dirt, and wooden floors, are easier on the joints of your body. Also avoid exercising on an uneven surface, which may cause you to fall and injure yourself.

- Wear shoes that are comfortable and suited to the type of exercise you are doing. The shoes should provide necessary cushioning and support.

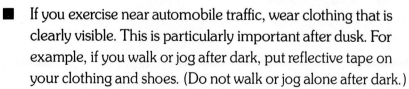

- If you exercise near automobile traffic, wear clothing that is clearly visible. This is particularly important after dusk. For example, if you walk or jog after dark, put reflective tape on your clothing and shoes. (Do not walk or jog alone after dark.)

- At the end of your exercise routine, spend a few minutes doing cool-down exercises. Your cool-down should be the opposite of your warm-up. Gradually decrease the vigor of your workout to slowly decrease your heart rate. Then finish with at least two minutes of flexibility exercises.

- Get plenty of rest and sleep between workouts.

Warm-Up and Cool-Down Exercises

Every workout should begin with warm-up exercises and end with cool-down exercises. Start your warm-up by doing the flexibility exercises shown here. Spend at least two minutes doing these nine exercises. Then spend another few minutes easing into the main activity of your workout. This portion of your workout increases your heart rate gradually. At the end of your warm-up, you will be ready to begin the vigorous portion of your workout. Your muscles will be flexible, and your heart rate will be at a safe level.

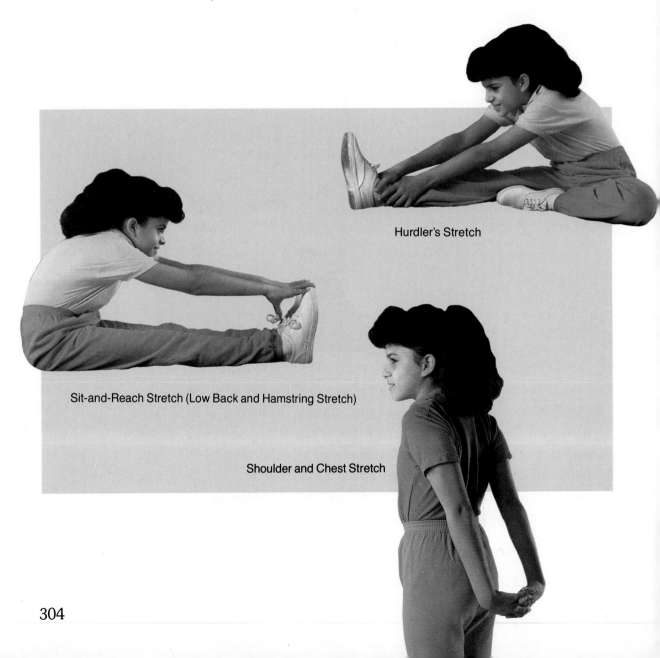

Hurdler's Stretch

Sit-and-Reach Stretch (Low Back and Hamstring Stretch)

Shoulder and Chest Stretch

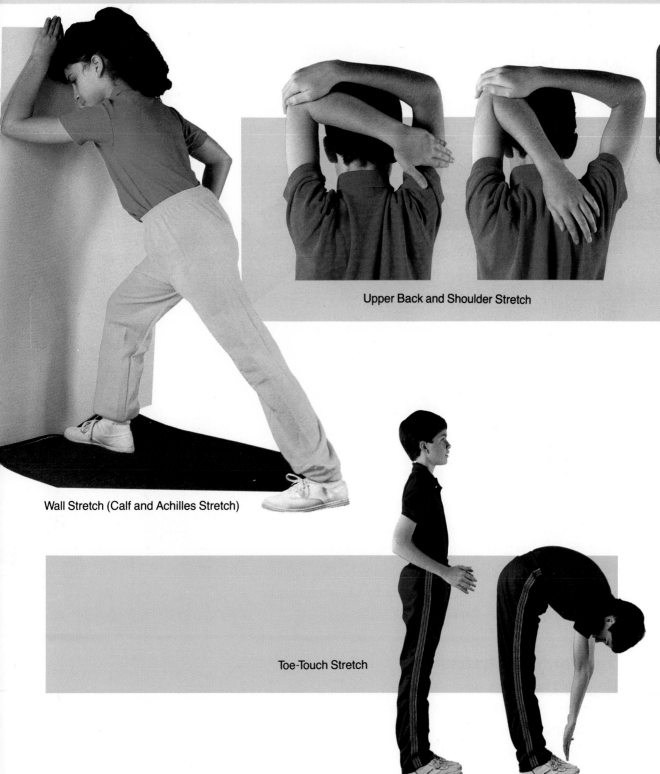

Upper Back and Shoulder Stretch

Wall Stretch (Calf and Achilles Stretch)

Toe-Touch Stretch

305

Thigh Stretch

Butterfly Stretch (Inner Thigh Stretch)

Trunk Twister

At the end of your workout, spend at least five minutes doing cool-down exercises. Do this by simply reversing the sequence of your warm-up. Gradually slow the pace of your activity to slowly decrease your heart rate. Then do a few minutes of flexibility exercises as shown here.

Tips for Safe Stretching

■ Avoid bouncing.

■ Hold each stretch for 15 to 20 seconds.

■ Breathe normally.

■ Stretch to the point at which you feel a slight pull. Do not stretch so hard that you feel pain.

Benefits of Various Sports and Activities

Activity	Health and Fitness Rating			Calories Used per Hour by a Person Weighing:		
	Endurance	Strength	Flexibility	77 lbs. (35 kg)	99 lbs. (45 kg)	110 lbs. (50 kg)
Aerobic dancing	High	Low	High	405	480	515
Archery	Low	Low	Low	195	230	245
Badminton	Medium	Low	Low	215	255	277
Backpacking	Medium	High	Low	375	435	470
Baseball*	Low	Low	Low	175	205	220
Basketball*	High	Medium	Medium	345	405	435
Bicycling						
(moderate)	High	Medium	Low	150	175	190
(vigorous)	High	High	Low	410	480	515
Billiards	Low	Low	Low	105	120	130
Bowling	Low	Low	Low	165	195	210
Canoeing	Low	Medium	Low	390	460	490
Fencing	Medium	Low	Medium	185	220	235
Football*	High	High	Medium	520	610	660
Golf	Low	Low	Low	235	275	295
Gymnastics*	Medium	High	High	165	195	210
Handball	High	Medium	Medium	485	565	610
Hockey	High	Medium	Medium	385	455	485
Jogging (5.5 mph)	High	High	Low	405	480	515
Judo/Karate	Low	Medium	Medium	490	575	620
Jumping rope	High	Medium	Low	865	1015	1090
Racquetball	High	Medium	Medium	340	410	450
Skating						
(ice and roller)	Medium	Medium	Low	215	255	275
Skateboarding	Low	Low	Low	150	175	190
Skiing						
(downhill)	Low	Medium	Low	370	435	465
(cross-country)	High	High	Low	435	510	550
Soccer	High	Medium	Medium	375	435	470
Swimming	High	Medium	High	185	220	235
Table tennis	Low	Low	Low	185	220	235
Tennis	Medium	Medium	Low	265	310	335
Volleyball	Medium	Low	Low	215	255	275
Walking (briskly)	High	Low	Low	165	205	225
Watching TV	Low	Low	Low	50	55	60
Waterskiing	Low	Medium	Low	255	305	335
Weight training	Low	High	Low	235	280	300
Wrestling*	Medium	High	High	490	575	620

*Preparing for these and a few other sports often includes special training that increases cardiovascular fitness, strength, and flexibility. The ratings in this chart are based only on the activity identified. The ratings do not account for any specialized training.

Measurement Conversion Table

REFERENCE

Metric Units	Converting Metric to English	Converting English to Metric
Length		
kilometer (km) = 1,000 meters	1 kilometer = 0.62 mile	1 mile = 1.609 kilometers
meter (m) = 100 centimeters	1 meter = 1.09 yards	1 yard = 0.914 meter
	1 meter = 3.28 feet	1 foot = 0.305 meter
centimeter (cm) = 0.01 meter	1 centimeter = 0.394 inch	1 foot = 30.5 centimeters
millimeter (mm) = 0.001 meter	1 millimeter = 0.039 inch	1 inch = 2.54 centimeters
Mass		
kilogram (kg) = 1,000 grams	1 kilogram = 2.205 pounds	1 pound = 0.454 kilogram
gram (g) = 0.001 kilogram	1 gram = 0.0353 ounce	1 ounce = 28.35 grams
Volume		
kiloliter (kl) = 1,000 liters	1 kiloliter = 264.17 gallons	1 gallon = 3.785 liters
liter (l) = 1,000 milliliters	1 liter = 1.06 quarts	1 quart = 0.946 liter
milliliter (ml) = 0.001 liter	1 milliliter = 0.034 fluidounce	1 pint = 0.47 liter
		1 fluidounce = 29.57 milliliters

Temperature Conversion Scale

The left side of the thermometer is marked off in degrees Fahrenheit (F). To read the corresponding temperature in degrees Celsius (C), look at the right side of the thermometer. For example, 50 degrees Fahrenheit is the same temperature as 10 degrees Celsius. You may also use the formulas below to make conversions.

Conversion of Fahrenheit to Celsius:

degrees Celsius =
    5/9 (degrees Fahrenheit − 32)

Conversion of Celsius to Fahrenheit:

degrees Fahrenheit =
    9/5 degrees Celsius + 32

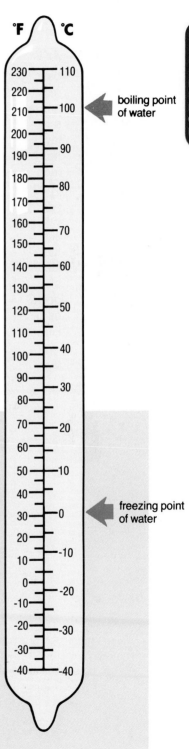

°F   °C

boiling point of water

freezing point of water

Glossary

PRONUNCIATION KEY

Sound	As In	Phonetic Respelling	Sound	As In	Phonetic Respelling
a	bat	(BAT)	ow	out	(OWT)
ah	lock	(LAHK)	oy	foil	(FOYL)
	argue	(AHR gyoo)	s	cell	(SEHL)
ai	rare	(RAIR)		sit	(SIHT)
aw	law	(LAW)	sh	sheep	(SHEEP)
awr	horn	(HAWRN)	th	thin	(THIHN)
ay	face	(FAYS)	u	pull	(PUL)
ch	chapel	(CHAP uhl)	uh	medal	(MEHD uhl)
ee	eat	(EET)		talent	(TAL uhnt)
	feet	(FEET)		pencil	(PEHN suhl)
	ski	(SKEE)		onion	(UHN yuhn)
eh	test	(TEHST)		playful	(PLAY fuhl)
eye	idea	(eye DEE uh)		dull	(DUHL)
ih	bit	(BIHT)	uhr	paper	(PAY puhr)
ihng	going	(GOH ihng)	ur	fern	(FURN)
k	card	(KAHRD)	y	ripe	(RYP)
	kite	(KYT)	y	yes	(YEHS)
oh	over	(OH vuhr)	z	bags	(BAGZ)
oo	pool	(POOL)	zh	treasure	(TREHZH uhr)

A

accident (AK suhd uhnt), unexpected event.   (**232**)

accident prevention (AK suhd uhnt • prih VEHN chuhn), keeping accidents from happening.   (**237**)

acute (uh KYOOT), present for a short time, usually less than a month.   (**155**)

advertising (AD vuhr tyz ihng), process of giving people information that encourages them to buy things.   (**87**)

aerobic exercise (air OH bihk • EHK suhr syz), activity that causes deep breathing and a fast heart rate for at least 20 minutes.   (**132**)

agency (AY juhn see), group of government workers who are responsible for one kind of service.   (**265**)

AIDS (AYDZ), acquired immunodeficiency syndrome; caused by HIV, a virus that attacks blood cells and harms the body's ability to defend itself against other infections.   (**157**)

air pollution (AIR • puh LOO shuhn), dirt and other harmful matter in the air.   (**274**)

alcohol (AL kuh hawl), drug found in drinks such as beer, wine, and whiskey. (**207**)

alcoholic (al kuh HAWL ihk), person who has a drinking disorder. (**210**)

alcoholism (AL kuh haw lihz uhm), drinking disorder. (**210**)

allergy (AL uhr jee), noncommunicable disorder in which a person has a bad reaction to a certain substance. (**170**)

alveoli (al VEE uh ly), tiny air sacs in the lungs. (**43**)

antibodies (ANT ih bahd eez), chemicals in the body that help fight disease. (**164**)

artery (AHRT uh ree), blood vessel that carries blood away from the heart. (**46**)

asbestos (as BEHS tuhs), type of building material that is dangerous to people when small bits of it are in the air. (**274**)

athlete's foot (ATH leets • FUT), fungal infection of the skin between the toes. (**159**)

B

bacteria (bak TIHR ee uh), very small, single-cell microbes, each of which is called a bacterium. (**158**)

balanced diet (BAL uhnst·DY uht), healthful amounts of foods from all five basic food groups; gives the body the nutrients it needs to stay healthy. (**106**)

ball-and-socket joint (bawl • uhn • SAHK uht • JOYNT), joint, such as a shoulder joint, that lets one bone move in many directions. (**36**)

basic research (BAY sihk • rih SURCH), studies done in laboratories to discover scientific principles. (**173**)

bicuspid (by KUHS puhd), tooth with two points for grinding and crushing food. (**66**)

blood (BLUHD), liquid that carries nutrients and oxygen to the cells of the body. (**44**)

blood vessel (BLUHD • VEHS uhl), long, thin tube through which blood flows in the body. (**46**)

body system (BAHD ee • SIHS tuhm), group of organs that work together to do a certain job in the body. (**30**)

bonding (BAHND ihng), method of using liquid plastic to repair a tooth. (**74**)

booster (BOO stuhr), vaccine that is given again to make a person's immunity to a disease stronger. (**166**)

bowel movement (BOW uhl • MOOV muhnt), process of moving wastes out of the body. **(41)**

brain (BRAYN), main organ of the body's nervous system. **(48)**

C

caffeine (ka FEEN), natural drug found in coffee and most cola drinks. **(187)**

calculus (KAL kyuh luhs), hard, yellow material that collects on teeth. **(69)**

cancer (KAN suhr), noncommunicable disease caused by cells growing out of control. **(169)**

capillary (KAP uh lehr ee), tiny blood vessel that connects an artery to a vein. **(46)**

carbohydrate (kahr boh HY drayt), nutrient in foods such as fruits, vegetables, breads, and cereals; should be the body's main source of energy. **(99)**

carbon dioxide (KAHR buhn • dy AHK syd), gas that the cells of the body make but cannot use. **(39)**

carbon monoxide (KAHR buhn • muh NAHK syd), poisonous gas from the burning of some materials, such as the tobacco in cigarettes. **(214)**

cavity (KAV uht ee), hole that forms in a tooth due to decay. **(69)**

cell (SEHL), smallest working part of the human body and of other living things. **(28)**

chemotherapy (kee moh THEHR uh pee), cancer treatment in which the patient is given special drugs to fight cancer cells. **(172)**

chronic (KRAHN ihk), continuing for a long time, usually more than a month. **(155)**

clinic (KLIHN ihk), place where people receive medical services. **(270)**

clinical research (KLIHN ih kuhl • rih SURCH), study of better ways to treat patients. **(173)**

cocaine (koh KAYN), illegal drug that dangerously speeds up the working of the body. **(193)**

commercials (kuh MUR shuhlz), forms of advertising on television and radio. **(87)**

communicable disease (kuh MYOO nih kuh buhl • dihz EEZ), illness that can be spread to a person from someone else or from something. **(154)**

R E F E R E N C E

community (kuh MYOO nuht ee), group of people who live in the same area. (**264**)

consequence (KAHN suh kwehns), what happens as a result of a behavior. (**197**)

controlled substance (kuhn TROHLD • SUHB stuhns), drug that is illegal to produce, possess, sell, or use in any amount. (**193**)

cool-down (KOOL down), activity done to allow the body to gradually return to normal after hard exercise. (**135**)

crosswalk (KRAW swawk), marked place where people can cross a street safely. (**248**)

crown (KROWN), top part of a tooth; can be seen above the gum. (**66**)

cuspid (KUHS puhd), tooth that has one point and tears food. (**66**)

decay (dih KAY), to rot. (**68**)

dental floss (DEHNT uhl • FLAWS), strong thread used for cleaning between teeth. (**71**)

dental hygienist (DEHNT uhl • HY jeen uhst), person who cleans people's teeth and tells people how to care for their teeth. (**73**)

dentin (DEHNT uhn), thick layer under the enamel of a tooth. (**66**)

diet (DY uht), combination of foods that a person eats each day. (**104**)

digestive juices (dy JEHS tihv • JOOS uhz), liquids in the body's digestive system that help digest foods. (**39**)

disease (dihz EEZ), breakdown in the way the body works. (**152**)

disorder (dihs AWRD uhr), noncommunicable health problem that may appear at birth or later in life. (**168**)

drug (DRUHG), any substance, other than food and water, that causes changes in the body. (**180**)

drug abuse (DRUHG • uh BYOOS), use of any harmful or illegal drug or use of medicine in the wrong way. (**191**)

drug abuser (DRUHG • uh BYOOZ uhr), person who uses harmful or illegal drugs or uses medicines in an unhealthful manner. (**191**)

drug dependence (DRUHG • dih PEHN duhns), condition in which a person needs a drug in order to feel all right. (**191**)

E

ear canal (IHR • kuh NAL), ear tube through which sound passes to cause the eardrum to vibrate. (**80**)

eardrum (IHR druhm), thin piece of flexible tissue that separates the outer ear from the middle ear. (**80**)

earwax (IHR waks), substance made by the ear to help trap dust that gets inside the ear canal. (**80**)

emergency (ih MUR juhn see), situation in which help is needed right away, as in a serious accident. (**232**)

emotion (ih MOH shuhn), feeling. (**6**)

emphysema (ehm fuh ZEE muh), noncommunicable disease that makes breathing difficult. (**216**)

enamel (ihn AM uhl), thin, hard outer layer of a tooth. (**66**)

endurance (ihn DUR uhns), ability to be active a long time without getting too tired to continue. (**131**)

energy (EHN uhr jee), ability the body has to do things. (**29**)

environment (ihn VY ruhn muhnt), everything in and around people. (**272**)

esophagus (ih SAHF uh guhs), tube made of muscle that squeezes food down into the stomach. (**41**)

exercise (EHK suhr syz), any activity that makes the body work hard. (**124**)

F

farsighted (FAHR syt uhd), unable to see nearby things clearly. (**76**)

fat (FAT), nutrient that gives the body the greatest amount of energy. (**99**)

fever (FEE vuhr), body temperature that is higher than normal. (**158**)

fiber (FY buhr), substance in some plants that helps keep the body's digestive system healthy. (**102**)

first aid (FURST • AYD), emergency care given to an injured or ill person. (**234**)

flexible (FLEHK suh buhl), able to move the joints of the body easily and without tightness or pain. (**133**)

fluoride (FLUR yd), substance often put in toothpaste and drinking water to help tooth enamel stay hard. (**72**)

fungi (FUHN jy), tiny plantlike organisms, some of which cause disease; fungus is the word for just one. (**159**)

REFERENCE

G

glare (GLAIR), uncomfortably bright light.   (**78**)

gum (GUHM), pink tissue around teeth.   (**66**)

H

hazard (HAZ uhrd), condition that is not safe.   (**237**)

health consumer (HEHLTH • kuhn SOO muhr), someone who buys things to help in taking care of his or her body.   (**84**)

healthful (HEHLTH fuhl), good for a person's health.   (**10**)

hearing loss (HIHR ihng • LAWS), condition that keeps a person from hearing the sounds he or she should hear.   (**80**)

heart (HAHRT), hollow organ that pumps blood and keeps it moving through the body at all times.   (**46**)

heart murmur (HAHRT • MUR muhr), sound not usually made by a healthy heart.   (**169**)

heartbeat (HAHRT beet), each squeeze of the heart followed by a rest.   (**46**)

hinge joint (HIHNJ • JOYNT), joint, such as a knee joint, that lets a bone swing back and forth like a door on a hinge.   (**36**)

hospital (HAHS piht uhl), place where people receive health care they cannot get at home.   (**270**)

I

illegal (ihl EE guhl), against the law.   (**190**)

immovable joint (ihm OO vuh buhl • JOYNT), joint in which the bones fit too tightly together to move.   (**36**)

immunity (ihm YOO nuht ee), ability of the body to defend itself from a certain disease.   (**163**)

incisor (ihn SY zuhr), tooth with a sharp, straight edge that cuts food.   (**65**)

infection (ihn FEHK shuhn), growth of disease microbes inside the body.   (**156**)

ingredients (ihn GREED ee uhnts), materials used to make a food product.   (**112**)

injection (ihn JEHK shuhn), method of giving a person a vaccine or other medicine by inserting it through the skin with a needle; also called a shot.   (**165**)

J

joint (JOYNT), place where two bones meet.   (**34**)

L

land pollution (LAND • puh LOO shuhn), wastes, such as garbage and litter, that make the environment unhealthful and ugly. (**274**)

landfill (LAND fihl), place where solid wastes from a community are buried. (**280**)

large intestine (LAHRJ • ihn TEHS tuhn), hollow tube in which wastes are stored until they leave the body. (**41**)

lung (LUHNG), one of the two large, spongy respiratory organs inside the chest. (**43**)

lung cancer (LUHNG • KAN suhr), disease in which cancer cells grow in the lungs and produce harmful lumps in the lungs. (**216**)

M

marijuana (mair uh WAHN uh), illegal drug that is made from a certain plant and is usually smoked. (**192**)

medicine (MEHD uh suhn), drug that is used to treat or cure a health problem. (**180**)

microbe (MY krohb), living thing so small it can be seen only with a microscope. (**156**)

mineral (MIHN uh ruhl), nutrient that does not give energy but is used by the body for growth and to do work. (**101**)

molar (MOH luhr), wide tooth in the back of the mouth; crunches and grinds food. (**66**)

muscle (MUHS uhl), tissue that is attached to body parts and makes them move. (**36**)

muscle strength (MUHS uhl • STREHNGTH), ability of the body to apply force with its muscles. (**129**)

N

nearsighted (NIHR syt uhd), unable to see faraway things clearly. (**75**)

need (NEED), something that a person must meet or satisfy to be healthy. (**10**)

nerve (NURV), bundle of nerve cells that carry messages to and from the brain. (**48**)

nerve cells (NURV • SEHLZ), special cells that make up the nervous system of the body. (**48**)

nicotine (NIHK uh teen), drug in all tobacco products; makes the heart beat faster and makes the blood vessels smaller. (**214**)

REFERENCE

911, special telephone number for emergencies.   **(233)**

noise pollution (NOYZ • puh LOO shuhn), loud sounds in the environment; can harm people's hearing and health.   **(277)**

noncommunicable disease (nahn kuh MYOO nih kuh buhl • dihz EEZ), illness that cannot be spread from person to person.   **(154)**

nutrients (NOO tree uhnts), the healthful parts of food.   **(39)**

nutrition (nu TRIHSH uhn), how the body uses food.   **(112)**

O

oral cancer (OHR uhl • KAN suhr), noncommunicable disease caused by harmful cells growing in the mouth; often caused by use of smokeless tobacco.   **(216)**

organ (AWR guhn), group of tissues that work together in the body.   **(30)**

OTC medicine (OH tee see • MEHD uh suhn), medicine that can be bought without a prescription in pharmacies and in most food stores.   **(182)**

oxygen (AHK sih juhn), gas, in the air, that is needed by the cells of the body.   **(39)**

P

pedestrian (puh DEHS tree uhn), person who is walking to get from one place to another.   **(247)**

peer pressure (PIHR • PREHSH uhr), influence on a person by a group of people of about the same age.   **(209)**

permanent tooth (PUR muh nuhnt • TOOTH), adult tooth.   **(65)**

personality (puhrs uhn AL uht ee), combination of ways that a person thinks, acts, and feels; makes a person different from every other person.   **(7)**

pharmacist (FAHR muh suhst), person trained to prepare medicines.   **(182)**

physical fitness (FIHZ ih kuhl • FIHT nuhs), condition in which the body works the best that it can.   **(125)**

pinkeye (PIHNGK eye), eye infection caused by bacteria.   **(160)**

plaque (PLAK), mixture of food and germs that forms a clear, sticky film on teeth.   **(69)**

platelets (PLAYT luhts), tiny cell parts that help slow bleeding and form a scab when a person gets cut.   **(46)**

pollution (puh LOO shuhn), unhealthful matter, or material, in the environment.   **(273)**

REFERENCE

posture (PAHS chuhr), how a person holds his or her body.   (**130**)

prescription (prih SKRIHP shuhn), order from a physician for a certain medicine.   (**181**)

prevent (prih VEHNT), to keep something from happening.   (**154**)

primary tooth (PRY mehr ee • TOOTH), one of the set of first teeth a person has as a baby; a baby tooth.   (**64**)

problem drinker (PRAHB luhm • DRIHNG kuhr), person who has a habit of drinking or a drinking disorder.   (**210**)

protein (PROH teen), nutrient that the body uses for the growth and repair of cells.   (**99**)

public safety (PUHB lihk • SAYF tee), community protection.   (**267**)

pulp (PUHLP), soft tissue in the middle of a tooth; contains nerves and blood vessels.   (**67**)

pulse (PUHLS), the push of blood through the blood vessels of the body with each heartbeat.   (**127**)

R

recycle (ree SY kuhl), to use again.   (**281**)

red blood cell (REHD • BLUHD • SEHL), tiny, round cell that carries oxygen to and carbon dioxide from the cells of the body.   (**46**)

relax (rih LAKS), to become calm.   (**136**)

resin (REHZ uhn), sticky liquid plastic used to repair teeth.   (**74**)

resistance (rih ZIHS tuhns), ability of the body to fight disease microbes by itself.   (**166**)

resource (REE sohrs), something people use in meeting their needs.   (**272**)

ringworm (RIHNG wuhrm), skin infection caused by a fungus.   (**159**)

R.N. (AHR • EHN), registered nurse.   (**90**)

root (ROOT), the part of a tooth that is in the jawbone and is covered by pink gum.   (**66**)

S

safety measure (SAYF tee • MEHZH uhr), something that is done to keep safe.   (**238**)

sanitary (SAN uh tehr ee), clean.   (**266**)

self-concept (sehlf KAHN sehpt), how a person thinks about himself or herself.   (**3**)

self-esteem (sehl fuh STEEM), good feeling a person has about himself or herself. **(8)**

sense organ (SEHNS • AWR guhn), organ that senses, or makes a person aware of, certain information about the world. **(50)**

sensory nerves (SEHNS uh ree • NURVZ), nerves that carry messages from the body's sense organs to the brain. **(50)**

serving (SUR vihng), for one food, the amount someone would be likely to eat during a meal. **(107)**

side effect (SYD • ih FEHKT), unwanted or unneeded change in the body, caused by medicine. **(184)**

sidestream smoke (SYD streem • SMOHK), tobacco smoke that is breathed in by a person other than the smoker. **(217)**

skeleton (SKEHL uht uhn), all the bones in the body. **(34)**

small intestine (SMAWL • ihn TEHS tuhn), hollow tube in which most digestion takes place. **(41)**

smokeless tobacco (SMOH kluhs • tuh BAK oh), tobacco that is used by putting it directly into the mouth. **(213)**

solid waste (SAHL uhd • WAYST), garbage and litter. **(274)**

special (SPEHSH uhl), different from everyone or everything else. **(2)**

spinal cord (SPYN uhl • KAWRD), large group of nerves in the center of the spine. **(48)**

spine (SPYN), stack of bones that protects the spinal cord; also called the backbone. **(48)**

stomach (STUHM uhk), organ that squeezes and mashes food during digestion. **(41)**

strength (STREHNGTH), something a person does well. **(7)**

stress (STREHS), emotion that can make a person feel tense, as if the person were about to run or fight. **(142)**

sunscreen (SUHN skreen), substance that blocks the sun's harmful rays and protects the skin against sunburn. **(244)**

symptom (SIHMP tuhm), sign or feeling of a disease. **(153)**

T

tar (TAHR), sticky, dark brown substance formed by the particles in tobacco smoke. **(214)**

thrush (THRUHSH), fungus infection in the mouth. **(159)**

tissue (TIHSH oo), group of one kind of cells working in the body together. **(29)**

trachea (TRAY kee uh), tube that lets air go from the nose and mouth into the chest; also called the windpipe. **(43)**

trait (TRAYT), something about a person that shows what he or she is like. **(3)**

treatment (TREET muhnt), care given a person who has a disease. **(153)**

tumor (TOO muhr), harmful lump that may grow in the body and may be made of cancer cells. **(216)**

V

vaccine (vak SEEN), substance that helps the body form immunity to a communicable disease. **(165)**

vein (VAYN), blood vessel that carries blood back to the heart. **(46)**

vibration (vy BRAY shuhn), back-and-forth motion. **(79)**

viruses (VY ruhs uhz), smallest kind of disease microbes. **(157)**

vision (VIHZH uhn), ability to see. **(75)**

vitamin (VYT uh muhn), nutrient that does not give energy but helps cause a specific reaction in the body. **(100)**

volunteer (vahl uhn TIHR), person who offers to do something without being paid. **(270)**

W

warm-up (WAWR muhp), activity done to start harder exercise slowly. **(133)**

waste (WAYST), material that the body cannot digest or use. **(41)**

water pollution (WAWT uhr • puh LOO shuhn), harmful matter in oceans, lakes, rivers, and streams. **(273)**

water treatment plant (WAWT uhr • TREET muhnt • PLANT), place in the community where water is made safe for people to use. **(278)**

weakness (WEEK nuhs), something a person does not do well. **(7)**

wellness (WEHL nuhs), high level of health. **(3)**

white blood cell (HWYT • BLUHD • SEHL), blood cell that helps the body fight certain kinds of illness by attacking germs in the blood. **(46)**

wound (WOOND), break or cut in the skin. **(234)**

INDEX

Index

REFERENCE

REFERENCE

CREDITS

Harcourt Brace & Company Photographs

KEY: (t) top, (b) bottom, (l) left, (r) right, (c) center.

vi(b), Maria Paraskevas; vii(t), Maria Paraskevas; (b), Jerry White; viii(t), Joy Glenn; (b), Annette Stahl; ix(t), Rob Downey; (b), Rob Downey; x(t), Rob Downey; (b), Charlie Burton; xi(b), Annette Stahl; xii(t), Jerry White; (b), Annette Stahl; xiii(c), Michael Sullivan; (bl), John Blasdel & Bob Barrett; (bc), Dale Higgins; (br), Brent Jones xiv(t), Richard Haynes; (c), Jerry White; xv(l), Jeff Blanton; (r), Jeff Blanton; (bl), Maria Paraskevas; (br), Richard Haynes; xvi–1(background), Annette Stahl; (br), Rob Downey; 2(t), Maria Paraskevas; (b), Maria Paraskevas; 3, Maria Paraskevas; 4, Richard Haynes; 5, Maria Paraskevas; 6, Maria Paraskevas; 7(l), Maria Paraskevas; (r), Maria Paraskevas; 10, Maria Paraskevas; 13(t), Maria Paraskevas; (c), Maria Paraskevas; (b), Maria Paraskevas; 16, Richard Haynes; 17(t), Maria Paraskevas; (b), Maria Paraskevas; 18, Maria Paraskevas; 20, Brent Jones; 21, Brent Jones; 26–27(background), Annette Stahl; 28(t), Maria Paraskevas; 33, Maria Paraskevas; 35, Greg Leary; 36, Maria Paraskevas; 37, Greg Leary; 39, Eric Camden; 40, Earl Kogler; 42, Greg Leary; 45, Greg Leary; 49, Greg Leary; 51, Maria Paraskevas; 53(l), Maria Paraskevas; (r), Maria Paraskevas; 54, Maria Paraskevas; 55, Jerry White; 57, Dale Higgins; 62–63(background), Annette Stahl; (bl), David Phillips; 65(l), Jerry White; (r), Jerry White; 66, Jerry White; 71(tr), David Phillips; (tl), Maria Paraskevas; 72(l), Annette Stahl; (r), Annette Stahl; 73(l), Maria Paraskevas; 76(t), Maria Paraskevas; (c), Maria Paraskevas; (b), Maria Paraskevas; 77, Maria Paraskevas; 81, Maria Paraskevas; 83, Maria Paraskevas; 90, Michael Sullivan; 91, Michael Sullivan; 96–97(t), Maria Paraskevas; (b), Jerry White; 98(t), Beverly Brosius; (b), Beverly Brosius; 99, Jerry White; 101, Jerry White; 103(l), Jerry White; (c), Earl Kogler; (r), Earl Kogler; 104, Maria Paraskevas; 105 (t), Jerry White; (c), Jerry White; (b), Jerry White; 106, Jerry White; 108, Richard Haynes; 109, Jerry White; 110, Jerry White; 111, Earl Kogler; 112(l), Jerry White; (r), Jerry White; 114(t), Charlie Burton; (b), Earl Kogler; 115, Earl Kogler; 116, Earl Kogler; 117, Earl Kogler; 121, Earl Kogler; 122–123(background), Annette Stahl; 124(t), Richard Haynes; (b), Joy Glenn; 125(tl), Joy Glenn; 126, Dale Higgins; (inset), Dale Higgins; 128(l), Maria Paraskevas; (r), David Phillips; 129, Maria Paraskevas; 130(tl), Joy Glenn; (tr), Joy Glenn; (bl), Joy Glenn; (br), Joy Glenn; 131(l), David Phillips; (r), David Phillips; 132, Maria Paraskevas; 134(tl), Maria Paraskevas; (tr), Maria Paraskevas; (bl), Maria Paraskevas; (br), Maria Paraskevas; 135(l), Joy Glenn; (r), Joy Glenn; 136, Joy Glenn; 139, Jerry White; 141, Richard Haynes; 142(l), Richard Haynes; (r), Richard Haynes; 144, Wendy Neefus; 145, Sidney Brown; 150–151(background), Wiley & Flynn; (t), Annette Stahl; 152, Maria Paraskevas; 153, Maria Paraskevas; 154(l), Earl Kogler; (c), Earl Kogler; (r), Earl Kogler; 155 Rob Downey; 156(r), Earl Kogler; 161(t), Annette Stahl; (c), Annette Stahl; (b), Annette Stahl; 162(l), Annette Stahl; 163, Charlie Burton; 166, Earl Kogler; 170, Earl Kogler; 171(tl), Jerry White; (tr), Jerry White; 172, David Doyle; 173, David Doyle; 178–179(background), Wiley & Flynn; (t), Earl Kogler; (r), Charlie Burton; 180(l), Charlie Burton; (r), Charlie Burton; 181(tl), Charlie Burton; (r), Charlie Burton; (b), Charlie Burton; 182, Charlie Burton; 183, David Phillips; 184, Annette Stahl; 185, Annette Stahl; 187, Rob Downey; 188, Annette Stahl; 189, Rob Downey; 191, Jerry White; 196(c), Rob Downey; (b), Rob Downey; 198, John Blasdel & Bob Barrett; 199, John Blasdel & Bob Barrett; 203, Earl Kogler; 206, Rob Downey; 209(t), Eric Camden; (b), Maria Paraskevas; 210, Earl Kogler; 213(l), Rob Downey; (r), Earl Kogler; 215, Joy Glenn; 217(l), Rob Downey; (r), Annette Stahl; 218, Jerry White; 219, Annette Stahl; 221, Rob Downey; 222, Rob Downey; 230(background), Annette Stahl; (tl), Rob Downey; (bl), David Phillips; (br), Joy Glenn; 231, Maria Paraskevas; 232, Rob Downey; 233(r), Maria Paraskevas; 234, Earl Kogler; 235(l), Charlie Burton; (r), Charlie Burton; 236, Rob Downey; 237(l), Earl Kogler; 238(l), Earl Kogler; (r) Earl Kogler; 239, David Phillips; 240(t), Earl Kogler; (c), Earl Kogler; (b), Earl Kogler; 242(l), Earl Kogler; (r), Earl Kogler; 244(l), Charlie Burton; (r), Charlie Burton; 247(l), Charlie Burton; (r), Charlie Burton; 249, Jerry White; 250, Maria Paraskevas; 251, Rob Downey; 254, Rob Downey; 255(l), Rob Downey; (r), Rob Downey; 256, David Brownell; 257, David Brownell; 261, David Phillips; 262–263(background), Jerry White; 264, Jerry White; 265, Maria Paraskevas; 266, Jerry White; 268, Jerry White; 269(l), David Phillips; 272, Jerry White; 279, David Doyle; 282, Charlie Burton; 283, Charlie Burton; 293–301, Terry Sinclair; 302, Maria Paraskevas; 303–307, Terry Sinclair.

All Other Photographs

ii–iii(background), Thomas Braise/The Stock Market; (inset), Chris Jones/The Stock Market; vi(t), John Coletti/Stock, Boston; xi(t), Peter A. Simon/Phototake; xiii(t), Houston Police Department; xiv(b), Art Tilley/After Image; xvi–1(tl), Henley & Savage/The Stock Market; (tr), Janeart Ltd./The Image Bank; (bl), Jeffry W. Myers/The Stock Market; 8(l), John Coletti/ Stock, Boston; (r), Gabe Palmer/Mug Shots/After Image; 11, Art Tilley/After Image; 12, James Casey/Nawrocki Stock Photo; 15, Gardon/Reflexion/H. Armstrong Roberts, Inc.; 25, The Granger Collection; 26–27(l), Jeff Perkell/The Stock Market; (c), Manfred Kage/Peter Arnold, Inc.; (r), Howard Soshurek/The Stock Market; 28(b), Biophoto Associates/Photo Researchers; 29(l), Runk/Schoenberger/Grant Heilman Photography; (r), Runk/Schoenberger/Grant Heilman Photography; 30, Phil Degginger/Bruce Coleman, Inc.; 61, Justitz/Zefa/H. Armstrong Roberts; 62–63(tl), David Bentley/Nawrocki Stock Photo; (tr), Gabe Palmer/The Stock Market; (br), Kalish/DiMaggio/The Stock Market; 64(l), Camilla Smith/Rainbow; (c), Michael Skott/The Image Bank; (r), Michael Philip Manheim/The Stock Shop; 68, F. Faulconer, DDS/Tom Stack & Assoc.; 70(t), Dr. R. Gottsegen/Peter Arnold, Inc.; (bl), Stanley L. Gibbs/Peter Arnold, Inc.; (br), Dr. R. Gottsegen/Peter Arnold, Inc.; 71(br), Stanley L. Gibbs/Peter Arnold, Inc.; (bl), Stanley L. Gibbs/Peter Arnold, Inc.; 72(r), D. C. Lowe/Medichrome/The Stock Shop; 74(l), F. Faulconer, DDS/Tom Stack & Assoc.; (r), F. Faulconer, DDS/Tom Stack & Assoc.; 79, Bob Daemmrich/The Image Works; 80, David Bentley/Nawrocki Stock Photo; 96–97(background), Ralph B. Pleasant/After Image; (l), Gabe Palmer/Palmer/Kane/The Stock Market; (r), John P. Endress/The Stock Market; 102, D. Cavagnaro/DRK Photo; 122–123(tl), Roy Morsch/The Stock Market; (tr), E.R. Degginger/Bruce Coleman, Inc.; (bl), Jon Brenneis/FPG; (br), Rothwell/After Image; 124(tr), Elyse Lewin/The Image Bank; (b), Focus On Sports; 133, Shostal Assoc.; 137, Tom Stack/Tom Stack & Assoc.; 140, David Madison; 143, Bill Ross/West Light; 150–151(c), Manfred Kage/Peter Arnold, Inc.; (b), Biomedical Communications/Bruce Coleman, Inc.; 156(l), David M. Phillips/Visuals Unlimited; 157(l), CNRI/SPL/Photo Researchers; (c), CNRI/SPL/Photo Researchers; (r), CNRI/SPL Photo Researchers; 158(t), David M. Phillips/Visuals Unlimited; (b), George T. Wilder/Visuals Unlimited; 159(t), Manfred Kage/Peter Arnold, Inc.; (b), Biophoto Associates/Photo Researchers; 160, Martin M. Rotker/Taurus Photos; 162(r), Hans Pfletschinger/Peter Arnold, Inc.; 164, Marcel Besis/SPL/Photo Researchers; 169, Stock Imagery; 171(b), George H. Harrison/Grant Heilman Photography; 177(l), C. Johnson/Gamma-Liaison; (r), Lawton/Gamma-Liaison; 178–179(l), Bob Daemmrich/Stock, Boston; (b), Becky Danley/Highland Hospital of Rochester; 186, Larry Gatz/The Image Bank; 193(l), M. P. Fogden/Bruce Coleman, Inc.; (r), W. H. Hodge/Peter Arnold, Inc.; 194(t), David M. Doody/Tom Stack & Assoc.; (b), S. Ferry/Gamma-Liaison; 196(t), Bob Daemmrich/Stock, Boston; 204–205(background), Sheila Terry/SPL/Photo Researchers; (l), Robert J. Bennett/FPG; (r), Martin M. Rotker/Taurus Photos; 208(l), SIU/Photo Researchers; (r) Dianora Niccolini/Medichrome/The Stock Shop; 211, Pressman/International Stock Photo; 212, Vito Palmisano/Nawrocki Stock Photo; 214(l), O. Auerbach/Visuals Unlimited; (r), Stock Imagery; 224, courtesy, Houston Police Department; 225, courtesy, Houston Police Department; 230(tr), J. Sylvester/FPG; 233(l), Amy Ellis; 237(r), Roger Dollarhide/Monkmeyer Press; 245, Phil Degginger/Click/Chicago; 246(t), Susan McCartney/Photo Researchers; (b), Suzanne L. Murphy/After Image; 262–263(tl), Michael S. Renner/Bruce Coleman, Inc.; (tr), Kevin Galvin/Bruce Coleman, Inc.; (bl), Michael Gallagher/Bruce Coleman, Inc.; (br), Jan Titus/Nawrocki Stock Photo; 267(t), Tom McCarthy/Gamma-Liaison; (b), Donald C. Wetter/The Stock Shop; 269(r), Barry Runk/Grant Heilman Photography; 270, Ed Simpson/After Image; 272(t), Nancy Hill/FPG; (b), M. Thonig/H. Armstrong Roberts; 274, Kent & Donna Dannen/Photo Researchers; 275, Bruce Coleman, Inc.; 276, Comstock; 277(t), Andras Dancs/After Image; (b), Kevin Galvin/Bruce Coleman, Inc.; 278, Werner H. Miller/Peter Arnold, Inc.; 280, Larry Lefever/Grant Heilman Photography; 281, Jim Whitmer/Nawrocki Stock Photo; 284, courtesy, Charlotte Fire Department; 285, courtesy, Charlotte Fire Department; 290–291, Peter A. Simon/Phototake.

ILLUSTRATIONS: Lynn Adams, 299; Leon Bishop, 44, 47, 158, 165, 207, 215; Len Ebert, 88; Howard Friedman, 46; C. W. Hoffman, 31, 35, 37, 40, 42, 45, 49, 51, 66; Laurie Marks, 87, 243, 249, 252, 253; Francesca Moore, 235; Marlies Merk Najaka, 101; Michael O'Reilly, 9, 85, 98, 99, 105, 113, 128, 139, 237, 240, 279; Harriet Phillips, 34, 38, 67, 69, 75, 76, 79, 168; Joel Snyder, 14, 84, 86, 188, 195; Mary Williams, 309.